PENGUIN B

DIAL M FOR MURDOCH

'Reads like a thriller – a gripping and indispensable first account . . .
like a cross between *The Insider* and *All the President's Men*'
Peter Jukes, *Daily Beast*

'Has the moral force and anger of a prosecutorial summing-up of
the case against Mr Murdoch' *Economist*

'*Dial M* is our best-to-date account of the snoopers, bully-boys,
bully-girls and pseudo-hacks succed lavishly by Newscorp onto anyone
whose alleged turpitude might somehow advance its ambitions . . .
The book to sink an empire?' Bruce Page, openDemocracy

'As Watson and Hickman clinically demonstrate, [the Murdochs]
behaved like mafia dons, in the sure knowledge that no-one
would reveal the extent of their criminality . . . Reading like an
upmarket thriller, *Dial M for Murdoch* describes in lucid, compelling and
often shocking detail why public trust in the media, politicians and
the police has reached an all-time low' Alan Taylor, *Herald*

'A well-written and, at turns, devastating book about a very dark media
and political scandal' Joy lo Dico, *Independent on Sunday*

'The only cogent book available on the most important media story
since the birth of newspapers' Neville Thurlbeck, *New Statesman*

'Rarely do a book and its author so perfectly align with real-time events'
Julie Bosman, *New York Times*

'A clear, fluent narrative of the hacking scandal and the attendant
side-scandals and cover-ups, from a decade ago to the present day'
Brian Cathcart, *Independent*

'Besides detailing the extent to which a cover-up has taken place,
Dial M for Murdoch tells how the British establishment backed away
from tackling the media moguls even after it knew that wrongdoing
was rampant' Mark Hennessy, *Irish Times*

'The book covers the countless strands of the hacking story with
admirable gusto and thoroughness. A masterful summary of the scandal
so far. The attention to detail is exemplary' Lloyd Evans, *Spectator*

'Almost all the events described in *Dial M for Murdoch* have been well-documented in daily news coverage in Britain. The book's value is in pulling them together into a single narrative. The impact is powerful: we come away with a clear picture of the sordid relationship that existed between the Murdoch press, the police and senior politicians' *Washington Post*

'Watson and Hickman ... do particularly well in tracing the complex evolution of James Murdoch's many defences of his own behaviour. Given the large number of criminal trials in the offing, it would be injudicious to speculate about who knew what when, but *Dial M for Murdoch* makes it clear that lots of people knew a great deal, and knew it from early on. Anyone who claims otherwise is unfamiliar with the way that businesses work, or a liar' *London Review of Books*

'In twenty-two fast-paced and pithy chapters based on highly detailed research, *Dial M* draws together the fragmented pieces of 'the worst scandal in British public life in decades' to fit the jigsaw together ... The result is a highly readable and entertaining piece of journalism which charts the scandal from its early origins ... Should the book ever get past Wendi Deng onto her husband's bedside table in their Mayfair apartment, he may find it hard to put down' Athalie Matthews, *Inforrm (The International Forum for Responsible Media Blog)*

ABOUT THE AUTHORS

Tom Watson is the MP for West Bromwich East. He campaigns against unlawful media practices and led the questioning of Rupert and James Murdoch when they appeared before Parliament in July 2011. He is the deputy chair of the Labour Party.

Martin Hickman has worked for the *Independent* since 2001, and has driven the paper's coverage of the phone hacking scandal. He was named Journalist of the Year by the Foreign Press Association in 2009.

TOM WATSON
and
MARTIN HICKMAN

Dial M for Murdoch

*News Corporation and the
Corruption of Britain*

PENGUIN BOOKS

PENGUIN BOOKS

Published by the Penguin Group
Penguin Books Ltd, 80 Strand, London WC2R ORL, England
Penguin Group (USA) Inc., 375 Hudson Street, New York, New York 10014, USA
Penguin Group (Canada), 90 Eglinton Avenue East, Suite 700, Toronto, Ontario, Canada M4P 2Y3
(a division of Pearson Penguin Canada Inc.)
Penguin Ireland, 25 St Stephen's Green, Dublin 2, Ireland (a division of Penguin Books Ltd)
Penguin Group (Australia), 707 Collins Street, Melbourne, Victoria 3008, Australia
(a division of Pearson Australia Group Pty Ltd)
Penguin Books India Pvt Ltd, 11 Community Centre, Panchsheel Park, New Delhi – 110 017, India
Penguin Group (NZ), 67 Apollo Drive, Rosedale, Auckland 0632, New Zealand
(a division of Pearson New Zealand Ltd)
Penguin Books (South Africa) (Pty) Ltd, Block D, Rosebank Office Park,
181 Jan Smuts Avenue, Parktown North, Gauteng 2193, South Africa

Penguin Books Ltd, Registered Offices: 80 Strand, London WC2R ORL, England

www.penguin.com

First published by Allen Lane 2012
Published with new material in Penguin Books 2012
003

Copyright © Tom Watson and Martin Hickman, 2012

The moral right of the authors has been asserted

Set in 9.25/12.5pt Sabon LT Std
Typeset by Jouve (UK), Milton Keynes
Printed in Great Britain by Clays Ltd, St Ives plc

A CIP catalogue record for this book is available from the British Library

ISBN: 978-0-241-96104-9

www.greenpenguin.co.uk

ALWAYS LEARNING   **PEARSON**

For
Saoirse and Malachy
and
Rachel, Kate and Finlay

Really what Rupert Murdoch managed to do was break the civil compact of this country through achieving a degree of control over the essential institutions of a free society: the press, the police and the politicians.

I've been one who has never accepted any of this 'gate' stuff and all the parallels – that are usually made by the Murdoch press – to some sex scandal . . . but this is for real. And the parallels are remarkable.

– Carl Bernstein, asked how the hacking scandal
compares to Watergate, 29 September 2011

Contents

List of Illustrations

SECTION ONE

SECTION TWO

THE COTSWOLD TRIANGLE

Dramatis Personae

NEWS CORPORATION

Rupert Murdoch, chairman and chief executive
James Murdoch, chief executive, News Corp Asia and Europe;
    chairman, BSkyB
Les Hinton, chief executive, News International

News of the World
Rebekah Brooks (née Wade), editor
    (Later editor of the *Sun* and chief executive, News International)
Andy Coulson, editor
    (Later, communications director, Conservative Party)
Colin Myler, editor
Tom Crone, legal director
Neville Thurlbeck, chief reporter
Clive Goodman, royal editor

METROPOLITAN POLICE

Sir Paul Stephenson, Commissioner
Andy Hayman, Assistant Commissioner
John Yates, Assistant Commissioner
Sue Akers, Deputy Assistant Commissioner

PRIVATE DETECTIVES

Steve Whittamore
Glenn Mulcaire
Jonathan Rees

LAWYERS

Mark Lewis
Charlotte Harris
Mark Thomson

POLITICIANS

John Prescott
Tom Watson
Chris Bryant

LITIGANTS

Gordon Taylor
Max Clifford
Sienna Miller
Steve Coogan
Hugh Grant
Max Mosley
Charlotte Church

JOURNALISTS

Guardian
Nick Davies
Amelia Hill

New York Times
Don van Natta Jr
Jo Becker
Graham Bowley

BBC
Glenn Campbell

Independent
Martin Hickman
Cahal Milmo

Preface

This book tries to explain how a particular global media company works: how it came to exert a poisonous, secretive influence on public life in Britain, how it used its huge power to bully, intimidate and to cover up, and how its exposure has changed the way we look at our politicians, our police service and our press. Some political 'friends' have tried to portray the hacking and bribery which has exposed the workings of News Corporation as part of the price you pay for good tabloid journalism. They're wrong. Of course, tabloids sometimes get out of hand, but this is not (at least, not much) a story of harmless mischief, of reporters in false moustaches and rollicking exposés of hypocrites. It is not just the famous and wealthy who have been damaged, but ordinary decent people who happened to be in the wrong place at the wrong time.

The legendary Fleet Street names whose reputations have been tarnished could almost (but not quite) be considered tiny pawns. This is a power game played out in the boardrooms and dining salons of the elite, and every political party, mine included, has had an inner circle of people on the Murdoch invitation list. Ultimately this scandal is about the failure of politicians to act in the interests of the powerless rather than themselves. As the book shows, I hope beyond any doubt, prime ministers, ministers, Parliament, the police, the justice system and the 'free' press became collectively defective when it came to investigating the activities of News Corp. Now that Murdoch's corrupt grip on our national institutions is loosening, and thanks to Lord Justice Leveson's public inquiry into this affair, these individuals and public bodies are belatedly starting to clean up their acts.

I know from personal experience what it's like to be attacked by Rupert Murdoch's organization. In the book, I give a first-hand account of some of the worst moments – though they were infinitely less bad, of course, than others have suffered. Sometimes, now, I can laugh at my former situation: a well-connected ex-minister in parliament, altering his route home at night, fearful of someone who might be in pursuit. But the affair has taken its toll: the failure of my marriage, the loss of friends and intense stress over many years. Even though the mechanisms of intimidation have now been exposed, I still obsessively memorize the number plates of unfamiliar vehicles parked outside my house. That's what it does to you when you're at the receiving end of the Murdoch fear-machine – the threats, bullying, covert surveillance, hacking, aggressive reporting and personal abuse make you permanently wary.

That was the state I was in – suspicious and paranoid – when Martin Hickman called me in October 2010, for the first time in ten years. I was distrustful of most reporters and at a low ebb, but Martin was an old friend: we had known each other well at Hull University, where he'd set up a newspaper and I'd become president of the Students' Union. At that stage, a trusted journalist seeking to investigate a media cover-up was rare. Regularly from then on, we would meet quietly at the Fire Station bar next to Waterloo station in South London, often for black coffee and breakfast before work, or occasionally late at night over a beer. Whilst the commuters tapped into their laptops and the revellers partied, we would sit in the corner, away from prying MPs and journalists, talking about developments as they happened.

Of course, I wasn't working in isolation. Many individuals, most notably the *Guardian*'s Nick Davies, the BBC's Glenn Campbell and lawyers Mark Lewis and Charlotte Harris, played critical parts in unravelling this complex scandal. Even so, in the early days, it was a lonely pursuit. We became close in the face of opposition from Murdoch's UK executives, the Metropolitan Police, the Crown Prosecution Service, the Press Complaints Commission and many of my fellow politicians. We were all helped by the brave whistleblowers who summoned the courage to share key information with us. Though still too frightened to go public, they know who they are, and believe me, they are heroes.

Because I was involved, I come into the book myself from time to time, as Martin does occasionally too. But though the story is inevitably coloured by personal experiences, we didn't want to over-emphasize our roles, and for that reason it is written in the third person: I am not 'me' or 'Tom' but 'Tom Watson'; similarly Martin is 'Martin Hickman'.

Martin is calm and cautious. I am not. I hope our contrasting characters have created an accurate and informative account, albeit one which leaves you in no doubt as to what we think of the events and organization we are writing about. Many of the events are public knowledge, but they have become so in fits and starts and the connections between them have not been made. We believe that seeing the story whole, as it is presented here for the first time, allows the character of the organization to emerge unmistakably.

Please tell us what *you* think. We're on Twitter at @tom_watson and @Martin_hickman.

This story is not yet over, but it extends deeper into the past than some may realize. For most, it really began when a newspaper story about the hacking of a missing girl's phone prompted a national wail of outrage so loud it was heard in the lofty world of Rupert Murdoch, and the mighty proprietor had to account for his actions to representatives of the people for the first time. So this is where our story begins – in the middle of those tumultuous days.

Tom Watson
April 2012

I

The Wrong Headlines

They caught us with dirty hands
  – Rupert Murdoch, 19 July 2011

On a clear summer's day in July 2011, a black chauffeur-driven Range Rover weaved its way through the streets of London towards the House of Commons. As it stopped at a red light diagonally opposite Big Ben, photographers crowded round the rear window and snapped its eighty-year-old passenger; he offered up a weak smile. Rupert Murdoch was three hours early for his first appointment with British democracy.

For decades, the media proprietor had operated from the shadows. A fortnight before he had been about to receive approval for his long-planned takeover of Britain's biggest television network, Sky – despite evidence of rampant law-breaking in his newspapers. The government had been secretly assisting his executives with the £7bn bid, giving them inside information and encouragement – all without the public's knowledge. The takeover would have handed Murdoch full control of 80 per cent of pay TV revenues to Murdoch, in addition to the 40 per cent of national paper sales.

But on 4 July, days before the go-ahead could be given, a damning fact emerged: Murdoch's *News of the World* had hacked into the mobile phone messages of a missing thirteen-year-old girl. Over coming days the public learned that his newspaper journalists had also targeted the parents of murdered children, soldiers' widows and survivors of terrorist bombings. Gutter journalism had sunk into the

sewer and Murdoch had been hauled before a parliamentary committee to do something uniquely humiliating: explain himself. Questions
abounded.

One was how the Australian-born tycoon had come to exert such a
grip on Britain's public life that his newspaper group had been able
to cover up its misbehaviour for years. Emboldened by powerful
connections, News International's executives had destroyed evidence, run smear campaigns, lied to Parliament and threatened and
intimidated journalists, lawyers and politicians. Despite their efforts,
campaigners had slowly uncovered the truth about the 'dark arts' of
newsgathering inside the organization's headquarters in Wapping,
east London.

While publicly defending law and order, Murdoch's journalists had
been illegally hacking into the mobile phone messages of princes, pop
stars, TV presenters, Hollywood actors, Premiership footballers and
cabinet ministers and their employees, friends and families. Through
a network of corrupt police officers and public officials, they also
obtained private phone numbers, emails, vehicle registrations, and
tax, income, employment and medical records. Crucially, their targets
were not just the wealthy and famous: if misfortune called, the grieving and even the dead could be swept into their sights.

As the facts tumbled inconveniently into the public domain, Murdoch had tried to manoeuvre himself out of trouble, but such was the
howl of outrage that it ruined the careers of several of his closest
executives, wiped $10 billion from the value of his US holding com-
pany, News Corporation, and placed it at the centre of an FBI
investigation into its treatment of the victims of the 9/11 terrorist
attacks. Britain's political leaders, for so long servile, rose up together
against Murdoch and opposed the Sky takeover. The Prime Minister,
David Cameron, launched a judicial inquiry into the broken ethics of
the press.

In all his years in business, these were the heaviest blows to rain
down upon Rupert Murdoch. Yet in the first, extraordinary days of
July 2011, increasingly remote from the country which had largely
funded his worldwide expansion, he had not realized the seriousness
of his situation. While the story dominated radio and TV bulletins, he

had stayed in the US and tried to shrug off the fuss, as he had done in the past whenever touched by controversy, which was often. When he had belatedly arrived in London on 10 July, he had smiled for the cameras. As if to underline his position in an elite space above democracy, he had initially refused an invitation to appear before a parliamentary committee which had investigated the connections between his executives and the politicians and police. The MPs on the Culture, Media and Sport Committee of the House of Commons then did something unimaginable only a fortnight before: they formally summoned Murdoch and his son and heir-apparent, James, to appear before them. Theoretically Murdoch could have been jailed if he had disobeyed the summons, but its true significance was that Parliament had asserted its will against a figure it had never dared before to challenge. In an instant, Murdoch's four-decade spell over British public life was broken.

On the morning of 19 July, the public queued round the block for seats at the inquisition of the Murdochs in a modern annexe to the House of Commons. Rupert Murdoch arrived at Portcullis House looking pale and diminished on the white upholstery of his four-wheel drive. After four days of preparation, the Murdochs planned to minimize the bad publicity by reading out a public apology, but the MPs forbade it and James's eyes flashed with anger. As he blustered, Rupert touched his arm and said: 'I would just like to say one sentence . . .' and his lips uncurled a headline: 'This is the most humble day of my life.'

The humility only went so far. The Murdochs insisted they had not known about the criminality at the *News of the World* and blamed staff. They stressed what a small part of their global business the *News of the World* was. 'My company has 52,000 employees,' Rupert explained. 'I have led it for fifty-seven years and I have made my share of mistakes. I have lived in many countries, employed thousands of honest and hard-working journalists, owned nearly 200 newspapers.'

So who, wondered the committee member Jim Sheridan, did he blame for the tabloid's excesses and the loss of the Sky bid? Rupert's reply was clear – the *News of the World*'s behaviour had been exaggerated by competitors: 'They caught us with dirty hands and they built the hysteria around it.'

As the three-hour session drew to a close, one of the nine Parliamentarians, Tom Watson, had a question. During his two years delving into the murk of Murdoch's business, the MP for West Bromwich East had whispered conversations with contacts who spoke of collusion between Murdoch's news-gatherers and the security services and London's police force, and at one stage he had melodramatically (but not entirely unreasonably) feared for his life. He wanted to know about an incriminating document about an extraordinarily large payment to a hacking victim, whose silence was bought. 'James – sorry, if I may call you James, to differentiate,' Watson said. 'When you signed off the Taylor payment, did you see or were you made aware of the "For Neville" email, the transcript of the hacked voicemail messages?' James looked straight at Watson and replied: 'No, I was not aware of that at the time.' The future of the dynasty would hang on the truthfulness of those ten words.

Rupert Murdoch had entered his ninth decade running a global media empire like no other. Every day, one billion people digested his newspapers, magazines, books, TV shows and feature films. In Britain, News Corp, of which Murdoch was largest shareholder, chairman and chief executive, owned a 39 per cent stake in Sky's owner BSkyB, the *Sun*, *News of the World*, *Times* and *Sunday Times*; in Australia 70 per cent of the newspaper market and the only national title, *The Australian*; and in the US, the *Wall Street Journal*, 20th Century Fox studio and Fox TV. Murdoch was, as the title of a recent biography put it, *The Man Who Owns the News*.[1]

A questing, restless – some would say, tyrannical – tycoon, he had built all this from a single newspaper inherited from his domineering father in 1952, *The News* in Adelaide. The young proprietor had expanded first throughout Australia in the 1950s and 60s, then Britain in the 70s and 80s, then the United States, where he took citizenship in 1985 and completed his company's transformation from a print-dominated business into a multi-media conglomerate.

He owed his rise to ferocious hard work, constantly jetting round the world, berating his executives and doing deals, a shrewd grasp of the possibilities of new technology, and the ethics of an alley cat.

From the start of his career, in Australia, he ruthlessly identified and published what sold and his newspapers luridly reported sex, celebrity, crime, scandal and sport – ideally, all together – with brasher and bolder headlines than rivals. One early biographer, Thomas Kiernan, summed up Murdochian journalism:

> The exaggerated story filled with invented quotes; the rewriting of cryptic, laconic news-service copy into lavishly sensationalized yarns; the eye-shattering, usually ungrammatical, irrelevant and gratuitously blood-curdling headline ('Leper Rapes Virgin, Gives Birth to Monster Baby' read a typical early front page) ... all wrapped in cheap, smudgy tabloid form and promoted with the apocalyptic fervour and energy of Bible Belt evangelism.[2]

In 1991, Richard Belfield, Christopher Hird and Sharon Kelly wrote in *Murdoch: The Great Escape*: 'For the last 40 years, UFOs have landed in the pages of Murdoch's papers, Hollywood and TV stars have unfolded the secrets of their diets, and city streets have been terrorised by the type of people who do not read a respectable family newspaper, like the one Rupert Murdoch has just sold them.'[3] His tabloid sensitivity implanted itself in most of his ventures: at the *Sun*, he promoted the naked page three girl and declined to sack its editor Kelvin Mackenzie despite the printing of false stories such as the infamous front-page falsely claiming that football fans had pickpocketed the dead during the 1989 Hillsborough Disaster; at the *Sunday Times* he published the fraudulent 'Hitler Diaries'.

As soon as he took over a newspaper Murdoch persistently broke his promises. After buying the *News of the World* in 1969 he swiftly eased out its chairman Sir William Carr despite promising to keep him; at the *Sun* he abandoned his assurance that he would maintain its support of Labour when it backed the Conservatives in 1979; and at *The Times* and the *Sunday Times* he broke all his guarantees of editorial independence in his first year of ownership in 1981. Harry Evans, *The Times*'s respected erstwhile editor, recalled:

He put his point of view very simply to the home editor of *The Times*, Fred Emery, when he summoned him from holiday on 4 March to his office shortly before asking for my resignation: 'I give instructions to my editors all round the world, why shouldn't I in London?' He was reminded of his undertakings to the Secretary of State. 'They're not worth the paper they're written on,' Murdoch replied.[4]

Murdoch was adroit at courting and cajoling politicians, but he also used his newspapers to advance his own political views. He started with a bust of Lenin in his room at Oxford University, but soon espoused the hard-right-wing views common among the super-rich: supportive of strong leadership, low taxation and light regulation and hostile to trade unions, the European Union and global-warming science. His newspapers strengthened his power by being politically promiscuous, periodically switching support from waning parties to challengers who, encumbered by gratitude, might advance his political and commercial agenda, particularly by granting him favours in the heavily regulated TV industry.

During the 1980s, he championed the Conservative leader Margaret Thatcher, whose government approved his purchase of the *Times* titles, ordered the police to assist his fight against the print unions at Wapping (where he installed industry-changing new technology – an achievement which transformed the finances of newspapers), and exempted his Luxembourg-based Sky satellite business from foreign ownership rules.

In the 1990s, disenchanted with Thatcher's pro-European and unpopular successor John Major, Murdoch began wooing Labour's youthful leader Tony Blair, who reciprocated. Determined to end Labour's electoral drubbings, in 1995 Blair made a transcontinental pilgrimage to Hayman Island off Australia, where he addressed News Corp executives and held talks with Murdoch himself. In his book *Where Power Lies*, the former Labour spin doctor Lance Price wrote: 'A deal had been done, although with nothing in writing. If Murdoch were left to pursue his business interests in peace he would give Labour a fair wind.'[5] According to the diaries of Piers Morgan, the former *News of the World* editor, Blair told him: 'Piers, I had to court him ... It is better to be riding the tiger's back than let it rip your throat out. Look what Murdoch did to Kinnock.'*[6]

Murdoch's newspapers endorsed Tony Blair at three general elections, and Blair scrapped or softened attempts to limit the proprietor's power. In 1996 Blair's Labour Party opposed plans to impose tougher cross-media ownership rules, in 1998 rejected calls for a ban on the predatory pricing of newspapers and lobbied the Italian Prime Minister Romano Prodi over a TV network Murdoch was interested in acquiring – and frequently gave interviews and important announcements to his papers, such as the date of the 2001 general election.

As Murdoch travelled the world overseeing his business interests, his editors became his powerbrokers in his absence. He became particularly enamoured of one of them, Rebekah Wade. Educated at a state school in Warrington in England's industrial north, her father a tugboat worker, Wade turned up at the *News of the World* as a 21-year-old red-haired secretary in 1989. One of the paper's reporters recalled that her 'charisma' matched her ambition. 'She was very tactile, touching you on the arm, looking straight into your eyes as though there was no one more important in the room. From the way she acted, you would think she wanted to sleep with you [but] she was way too up the scale for that.'[7]

By 2000, Wade was editor of the *News of the World* and, three years later, editor of the *Sun*. She enjoyed Murdoch's full support, despite admitting to a parliamentary committee that his newspapers had bribed police.† She was very friendly with senior politicians, notably

---

* During the 1992 general election campaign, the *Sun* campaigned vigorously against Labour leader Neil Kinnock. On polling day its front page superimposed his head on a lightbulb with the warning: 'If Kinnock wins today will the last person to leave Britain please turn out the lights.' How far such attacks (or endorsements) actually affect the behaviour of voters is uncertain, but newspapers set the news agenda all the time, and politicians fear them.

† On 1 March 2003, giving evidence to a media inquiry by the House of Commons Culture, Media and Sport Committee, Wade painted a picture of a responsible newsgathering operation. But a glimpse of the truth slipped from her lips when Chris Bryant, a committee member, asked her whether News International paid police for information. In a Commons tearoom a fellow backbencher, Kevin Brennan, had told Bryant that after losing his wallet at a London restaurant, the *News of the World* had run an innuendo-laden piece about an MP losing money late at night in Soho, a red-light

Blair, and during his ten years at 10 Downing Street, those who crossed Blair often saw themselves attacked by her papers.

By 2006, Tom Watson had grown disenchanted with Blair. As a defence minister in Blair's government, Watson's nightly papers contained details of the soldiers killed in Iraq and Afghanistan, but it was trivialities which convinced him that the Prime Minister had lost touch: reports that Blair had billed the Labour Party for his wife Cherie's haircuts during the 2005 general election, and that he had ordered the redecoration of his quarters in the nuclear bunker at public expense.

On Thursday 31 August 2006, during the summer recess, Watson was pushed into outright rebellion when he learned that Blair had given an interview – to the next day's *Times* – in which he refused to timetable his departure. Infuriated, the backbencher Chris Bryant drafted a letter urging Blair to say when he would go. The letter was signed by twenty-four Labour MPs, including seven ministerial aides and Watson – who resigned on 6 September. In an angry statement, Blair (who later that week announced he would step down the following year) called Watson 'disloyal, discourteous and wrong'. A few miles east of Downing Street, in another centre of power, the editor's office of the *Sun*, Wade was irritated. On 7 September, the *Sun* denounced Watson as the ringleader of the 'plotting gang of weasels' and complained he had 'shamefully' walked out of his job. At the Labour Party conference the following month, the *Sun*'s political editor George Pascoe-Watson told Watson: 'My editor will pursue you for the rest of your life. She will never forgive you for what you did to her Tony.'

Wade was true to her word when, in April 2009, Watson – made a Cabinet Office minister by Blair's successor, Gordon Brown – was erroneously linked to a smear exercise against leading Conservatives

---

district. To the surprise of the committee members, Wade replied: 'We have paid the police for information in the past.' In his diaries, the editor of the *Daily Mirror*, Piers Morgan, remarked: 'Rebekah excelled herself by virtually admitting she's been illegally paying police for information. I called her to thank her for dropping the tabloid baton. She said: "That's why I should never be seen or heard in public."'[8]

(at the time Murdoch's papers were undergoing another periodic political shift, this time back towards the Conservatives). In an email to a former Labour colleague, Brown's special adviser Damian McBride had regurgitated rumours that the Tory leader David Cameron had an embarrassing medical condition and that his close ally George Osborne had taken drugs with a prostitute – which he suggested could be circulated on a new left-wing website, Red Rag. The right-wing 'Guido Fawkes' blogger, Paul Staines, somehow obtained McBride's emails, and passed the story to Murdoch's *News of the World* and *Sunday Times*. McBride resigned, but one of the emails had mentioned Watson in passing and the political blogger Iain Dale falsely claimed the minister had been involved. Watson issued a denial, but the *Mail on Sunday* ran the story on 12 April. As Watson and his wife Siobhan travelled to Cornwall, where his brother-in-law was about to undergo a double organ transplant, neighbours at his constituency home chased off three men who had scaled a 6ft gate to rifle through paperwork in his garage.

On 14 April, the *Sun*'s knives came out. Its columnist Fergus Shanahan wrote:

> There is another unsavoury creature lurking in the shadows who should join McBride on the dole – and he's not a civil servant like McBride but a minister appointed by Brown. Treacherous Tom Watson – a tub of lard who is known without affection at Westminster as 'Two Dinners' Tommy – is suspected of being in this up to his bloated and bulging neck.

Under the headline 'Mad Dog was trained to maul', the *Sun*'s political writer Trevor Kavanagh attacked 'hatchet man Tom Watson' and the paper demanded Watson's sacking, saying his employment was 'a stain on the Prime Minister's judgement and the government's credibility'. Wade also texted someone personally close to Brown urging him to fire the minister. George Pascoe-Watson later told Brown's spokesman Michael Dugher that Wade had forced him to write 'bollocks' stories about Watson. The Prime Minister refused to dismiss Watson but, stung by the coverage, he asked whether he had registered the Red Rag website.

As he lay in bed in the Ship Inn in Perranporth on 15 April, Watson's mind was abuzz and he constantly replayed events. He had hired a researcher on a temporary contract for three months, who had been a blogger. What if she had set up Red Rag without his knowledge? At 3 a.m., in a frantic, whispered conversation, he asked if she had been responsible. She had not. Shortly before dawn, Watson bought the papers. His picture was at the top of another, front-page story in the *Sun* about pressure building on Gordon Brown. That day *The Times* had mocked up McBride, Watson and four other Brown supporters as characters from the gangster movie *Reservoir Dogs*. As Watson walked along the beach, he was in tears.

The following morning, Siôn Simon remembers taking a call from Watson:

> At first I thought something really cataclysmic had happened, like someone had died or got arrested. He's been one of my closest friends for a long time, and I've never heard him sound like that before or since. He was literally raving. Struggling to choke back tears most of the time, his voice was broken and distorted, and he was just talking crazy. Usually the most hard-headed hyper-rationalist you'll come across, he was just saying ridiculous things: 'I'm going to resign, today or tomorrow; I'm completely innocent of everything they're saying. It's all just lies and bile, but I'm going to resign anyway, just to show them.'
>
> I told him that it would have no impact, that in any other circumstances, he wouldn't even be thinking like that . . . He held it together and didn't resign. We talked it all through again a few days later, and he was saying: 'Yes, yes I know. Yes, you're right. Yes I know. I know.' But he didn't sound like he really knew anything any more.[9]

At the next reshuffle, in June 2009, Watson returned to the backbenches. He had had enough; his marriage was under strain and most political commentators thought he was a Brownite thug. By coincidence, five weeks later, he found himself investigating a scandal rooted in Rupert Murdoch's sprawling empire.

2

Wapping's News Factory

Our motto is the truth
— News of the World, 1 October 1843

The *News of the World* started with a moral purpose. Founded in 1843 as a digest of news for 'respectable tradesmen', its first edition proclaimed: 'Our motto is the truth; our practice is the fearless advocacy of the truth.' Circulation rose steadily from a few thousand at launch to 4 million by 1939. By the 1950s, with sales at an all-time high of 8.5 million, the paper was chiefly known for its salacious and enthusiastic chronicling of fallen women, adulterous vicars and deviant scoutmasters.

Under Rupert Murdoch's ownership from 1969, the 'carnal business' moved slowly forward to the front pages. Indeed Murdoch brashly affirmed his faith in sex and sensationalism in his first months by buying the memoirs of the Profumo scandal call-girl Christine Keeler, saying: 'People can sneer as much as they like, but I'll take the 150,000 extra copies we're going to sell.'[1] By the late 1990s, the *News of the Screws*, as it became known, was serving a weekly diet of sizzling, lust-filled romps, 'kiss and tells' and perversion to 10 million readers.

Exhorted by Murdoch to smash the rival *People* and *Sunday Mirror*, the *NoW*'s management aggressively fostered an ultra-competitive atmosphere. Reporter was set against reporter and executive against executive. Two competing teams of journalists – the news desk and the features desk – connived and backstabbed to land the front-page story, the 'splash'. Fearful about the consequences of carrying out their orders, reporters sometimes illictly taped the briefings they received from news editors.[2] Management regularly totted up the numbers of bylines, and reporters who failed to live up to expectations were summarily dismissed, sometimes on a whim. Among the most feared managers were two long-serving news editors, Greg Miskiw and Alex Marunchak, both of Ukranian descent. Miskiw and Marunchak were known to be particularly hard-nosed in their pursuit of stories. On the side, they ran an import–export business selling vodka.

In his memoirs, *Hack*, Graham Johnson, a reporter on the paper in the late 1990s, recalled the gut-wrenching, all-pervasive fear inside 'Fortress Wapping' in London's Docklands:

> Security guards [were] on permanent lockdown. Red signs in the corridor warned of threats and attacks because of 'the business we are in'. Like the Death Star, the atmosphere was drenched in fear and repression. Dread so powerful at times, so tangible, that it weighed down on the bodies of reporters like the atmospheric pressure under the ocean, often crushing them.[3]

Some staff drank to cope and the atmosphere was sleazy; one senior Wapping executive remarked that after walking through the *News of the World*'s newsroom he 'felt like taking a shower'.[4] Sharon Marshall gave what she said was a frank account of the alcohol-fuelled shenanigans at the paper in *Tabloid Girl: A True Story*, straplined 'Sex. Scandal. Celebrities. All in a Day's Work'. Published in 2010, the book purported to be an amalgam of newspaper newsrooms, but was often a thinly disguised account of the *NoW*, where Marshall worked as a reporter between 2002 and 2004 (between 1998 and 2002 she was at the *People*). Marshall's tabloid days were a blast of infiltrated 'vice dens', exaggerated kiss and tells, marathon drinking sessions and fiddled expenses. The drinking was 'harsh': often a 9 a.m. whisky in the pub as the executives departed for the morning news conference, followed by a bottle of wine at lunch, followed by more drinking with contacts in the afternoon, 'slipping casually into an evening's absolute bender'.

My career was kick-started with booze and it carried on that way for the ten years I worked on tabloids.' It was expected and, in times of need when you'd overdone it, your colleagues would rally round to help. We had a small glass box – about four foot square – next to the newsdesk, with soundproofed walls. It contained an armchair and a TV. If someone was so supremely drunk they could no longer be relied on to stay conscious at their desk, or ran the risk of disrobing and hurling obscenities at the editor at a moment's notice, we'd throw them into the chair, stick on a DVD of some footage from an under-cover job and lock the door . . .

Addressing the question of whether reporters fabricated stories, Marshall wrote: 'Yes. Sometimes the quotes were written before we ever left the office. Before we knew who we were interviewing.' Asked to write an article that 'sounded' as if it had been written by the glam-our model Jordan, she went home, drank two bottles of white wine and fabricated 1,000 words.

Graham Johnson, who was sacked for conspiring to fake a picture of the mythical Beast of Bodmin (and later recanted and became an investigative journalist at the *Sunday Mirror*) saw many of his 'stunts-up' printed in the pages of the *News of the World*. One suggested that Ecstasy sellers had targeted the drug at football fans during the Euro 96 football championships in England, as well as selling fake tickets. Johnson wrote in *Hack*:

> Best made up quote? 'Menacing McManus, a 40-year-old Glaswe-gian, selling his vile wares in Liverpool and Manchester, gloated: "Business is good. Football and Drugs. What more can you ask for? The E's are bang on at 5 pound each. What about £90 a sheet for the trips?"' Evil Roy McManus was of course as real as Mary Poppins.

Another of his fake stories, billed as a special investigation, began: 'Car sprayer Paul Humphreys looks like a harmless grease monkey in overalls and baseball cap – but he shamelessly deals in putting con-victed killer drivers back on the road with fake licences.'

Exaggeration was also used in the *NoW*'s sex stories, usually by juicing up kiss and tells, but also when reporting visits to 'vice dens'.

A special investigations team set up to satisfy the prurience of the saucy seaside postcard-buying British public, winkled out unusual sexual habits across the UK by infiltrating swingers' and sado-masochists' parties. Typically the investigators would obtain sufficient evidence to 'make their excuses and leave', but in 1998, one crime correspondent, Neville Thurlbeck, failed to follow that tradition when visiting a naturists' guesthouse in Dorset. Suspicious at his voyeuristic demands, the guesthouse's owners, Sue and Bob Firth, had secretly videoed him watching them having sex and recorded him masturbating. Thurlbeck naturally made no mention of his own behaviour in his report, 'The Guesthouse Where All Rooms Come with En-Suite Pervert', which included demonstrably false embellishments such as that the Firths had 'insisted on putting on a sex show', and that their home had a 'plunge pool', when it had a regular-sized bath. In retaliation, the Firths posted the pictures to the *NoW* with a request for £250,000 for lost earnings and distress, prompting the paper to hit back with another story: 'The Nudists, Our Naked Reporter and £¼m Hush Money', in which Thurlbeck quoted his uncle as saying: 'If you want to catch a rat, be prepared to jump into the sewer.' An investigation by the Press Complaints Commission and the paper's management cleared Thurlbeck of wrongdoing and he kept his job. The Firths were not paid off.

According to executives, Murdoch was a constant invisible presence demanding ever greater performance – pressure which was passed, brutally, down the chain. His combative management style was felt most keenly by tabloid editors, but also by the editors of his quality papers. Andrew Neil, editor of the *Sunday Times* between 1983 and 1994, likened his position as editor to that of 'a courtier at the court of the Sun King – rewarded with money and status by a grateful King as long as you serve his purpose, dismissed outright or demoted to a remote corner of the empire when you have ceased to please him or outlived your usefulness'.[5] Although Murdoch sometimes left Neil alone for weeks, he regularly made menacing calls peppered with expletives. Neil wrote that since nobody was sure 'when the next autocratic intervention will take place (or on what subject), they live in fear of it and try to second-guess what he would want, even in the most unimportant of matters'. Murdoch did not necessarily expect to see his views reflected in the next edition of the *Sunday Times*, 'but', Neil recalled, 'he had a quiet, remorseless, sometimes threatening way of laying down the parameters within which you were expected to operate ... stray too far too often from his general outlook and you will be looking for a new job'.[6]

From the mid-1990s, Murdoch preferred to appoint inexperienced young journalists – whose outlook had been shaped by him and who would for ever be grateful to him – as editors of his tabloid titles. In their late twenties and early thirties, these journalists were pitched into a lucrative, adrenaline-charged whirl, the backseat of chauffeur-driven limousines and – to their surprise – the dining chairs of Downing Street. In 1994 the first was Piers Morgan, whom Murdoch plucked, aged twenty-eight, from the *Sun*'s celebrity gossip column to edit the *News of the World*, then the highest-selling newspaper in the English-speaking world.

The proprietor would regularly enthuse, berate and gossip with his young protégé. In *The Insider*, Morgan described one of their many conversations. On 1 April 1995, Morgan had obtained a picture of the gangster Ronnie Kray in his coffin. Murdoch roared: 'What? You're splashing on a dead body?' 'Erm, yes, Mr Murdoch,' Morgan replied. Murdoch paused, then said: 'Look, it's not my job to edit the papers, but one thing I can tell you is that stiffs don't sell papers.' Instead, Morgan ran a picture of Earl Spencer's wife Victoria at an alcohol and bulimia clinic, earning him a rebuke from the PCC [Press Complaints Commission] and soon after from Murdoch, who publicly criticized his 'young' editor. On 22 May, after delivering the slapdown, Murdoch called again. Morgan realized there was no point complaining because 'he just wants to hear precisely how you intend to smash the opposition into oblivion'. 'I'm sorry about all that press complaining thingamajig,' Murdoch explained. 'We had to deal with it the way we did or they'd all have been banging on about a privacy law again and we don't need that right now. Anyway, it's done now. How are you going to sell me more papers?'[7]

Under Morgan, the paper bribed staff on the *Sunday Mirror*

and the *People* to obtain their newslists and stole other papers' exclusives – including those of other News Corp titles.[8] On 15 October 1994, he sent his new features editor, Rebekah Wade, to hide in a toilet so she could run back to the *News of the World* from Wapping's printworks with a copy of the *Sunday Times*'s serialization of Jonathan Dimbleby's new book on Prince Charles. On another occasion he laughed at a letter from the *Mail on Sunday* warning him not to lift a copyrighted interview being published that night with the rugby player Will Carling and his wife Julia. Morgan consulted Tom Crone, the *News of the World*'s veteran lawyer ('superbright, fearless and cunning'). He wrote:

> To save time I just shouted to our lawyer across the room: 'Hey Tom, how many fingers will this cost if we nick it all?' Tom flicked five fingers at me: £50,000 maximum damages. Well worth a front page and two spreads inside. We got the *Mail* at about 7 p.m. and set about excavating every word ... At about 9 p.m. we got another fax from the *Mail* legal team, issuing dire warnings about our 'flagrant breach of copyright' ... We laughed again.[9]

Paul McMullan, deputy features editor between 1994 and 2001, happily swindled the source of a story about the actor Robert de Niro sharing a bubblebath with two women. Because she had not insisted on a formal contract McMullan did not pay her the £10,000 he had promised; 'as I recall, I got a 750 quid bonus for ripping off the source of the story'.[10] On another occasion, McMullan was asked to find the woman in France who, supposedly, had taken John Major's virginity: 'We found her but couldn't get the picture of her with her new boyfriend. I think the cleaner was in so I blagged my way in and pinched it off the mantelpiece. Rebekah said: "No, put it back, we're not allowed to nick stuff", but Piers said: "Well done."'[11]

After her stint as Morgan's deputy in the mid-1990s, Rebekah Wade's mega-watt charm and ruthlessness were recognized by Rupert Murdoch. Her *modus operandi*, explained one former executive, was 'to solve your problem'.[12] She became friends with Elisabeth Murdoch and learned to sail – because the Murdochs sailed. In May,

Murdoch gave Wade her biggest break: the editorship of the *News of the World*. She was thirty-two.

She immediately set about repaying Murdoch's confidence by launching a campaign against paedophiles. 'For Sarah', named after Sarah Payne, an eight-year-old abducted in West Sussex, demanded parents be able to access police records to identify local paedophiles. Under the headline 'NAMED SHAMED' and the subheading: 'Everyone in Britain has a child sex offender living within one mile of their home ...' on 23 July, the *NoW* published forty-nine pictures of paedophiles and announced its intention in coming weeks to publish the identities of all of the UK's 110,000 child sex offenders. The campaign provoked a wave of reprisals, most notably in Portsmouth, where more than 100 vigilantes marched through the streets and rioted outside the home of a local taxi driver. Another child sex offender identified by the paper, James White, a father of five, committed suicide after a mob surrounded his home in Oldham, Greater Manchester. While his case may not have elicited public sympathy, there were several instances of mistaken identity, such as in Portsmouth, where four innocent families were forced out of their homes, and in Plymouth, where a family had to flee after the father was mis-identified as a paedophile. Police, probation officers and children's charities warned the campaign would push offenders underground and, amid official unease, Wade called a halt to it after two weeks, saying the government had agreed to back her demands. The Home Office minister Paul Boateng contradicted that – but Wade had raised her profile and put on 95,000 sales.

Wade's style with her staff could be dictatorial and, sometimes, abusive. For her amusement, in 2001, for instance, she instructed a reporter, Charles Begley, to change his name to Harry Potter and dress up as the fictional wizard at news conferences. A few hours after the September 11 attacks on the Twin Towers, Begley was rebuked for not wearing his robes and being 'in character'.* In January 2003, following

---

* Begley went home and later rang in sick with stress. After a couple of days to-ing and fro-ing with executives, Greg Miskiw came on the line at Begley's home. Begley taped and transcribed the conversation, as reported in the *Daily Telegraph*:

'I don't think I can make a final decision on my future right now,' Begley told Miskiw.

the drive-by shooting of two teenagers in Birmingham, her news editor, Greg Miskiw, sent the investigations editor, Mazher Mahmood, to show how easy it was to buy a gun. When Mahmood arrived in a car park to buy two handguns, he was mugged by a machete-wielding gang for the £1,500 he had obtained from petty cash. He reported the incident to Miskiw. 'Greg asked me if I was all right and, as soon as I'd shakily said "Yes, I think, I'm okay," continued: "OK, don't worry about the money, but you have got to get me a gun for this week. The editor really wants the story." '[13]

Mahmood became the paper's 'Fake Sheikh', a bogus Arab prince who would spend tens of thousands of pounds hiring helicopters, Rolls-Royces, five-star penthouse suites and first-class flights to gull minor celebrities, sportsmen and royals into committing indiscretions, often an offer to sell him cocaine.

Despite its tawdry reputation, the *News of the World* considered itself to be a serious paper, a moral force for good, and cultivated contacts in high places. Senior journalists schmoozed leading politicians, many of whom were persuaded to write columns for a fee several times their MP's salary, such as the former Conservative leader William Hague, recruited as a columnist in 2003 for around £200,000 a year. Executives were also friendly with others in power. Among the paper's more exalted police contacts was Sir John Stevens, the Commissioner of the Metropolitan Police, with whom Rebekah

---

'I'm not forcing you into a decision,' Miskiw said. 'I'm telling you something that will benefit you.'

'I'm so wound up about this.'

'Charles, Charles, Charles, let me tell you something. This is not a business for prima donnas. You know that and I know that.'

'I'm disillusioned,' Begley said.

'I've told you that this isn't going to be held against you. Charles, you should think very seriously about coming in on Tuesday.'

'Well, to be frank Greg, as far as my future at News International is concerned, I haven't toed the line for the editor's pet project. I didn't prance around while the World Trade Center was being bombed for her personal amusement. I can't just stroll in.'

'Why not?' Greg urged him. 'Charles, this is what we do – we go out and destroy other people's lives.'

Wade dined three times at the Ivy between August 2002 and December 2004 – the last after she had admitted to Parliament that News International bribed police. After he left the force in 2005, Sir John wrote for the *News of the World*, receiving up to £7,000 a column, and his autobiography, *Not for the Faint-hearted*, was serialized by both the *NoW* and *The Times*. Other senior Metropolitan Police officers such as Andy Hayman and John Yates were also friendly with the paper's staff.

There was also co-operation at a lower level: Mazher Mahmood, for instance, worked closely with Scotland Yard,* which often nabbed the criminals he had exposed after publication, so that his stories would not be foiled by the law of contempt of court, which forbids prejudicial media reporting after the making of arrests. In 2000, Neville Thurlbeck even stood trial for corrupting a detective constable on the National Criminal Intelligence Service, the liaison body between Scotland Yard and the security service MI5. Richard Farmer had allowed Thurlbeck to see criminal records which enabled him to write thirty-six stories, including one about an obscene act by a Labour MP; in return he passed tips about criminals to Farmer. But there was no hard evidence of payment and a judge at Luton Crown Court, Justice McKinnon, acquitted both men.

After promoting Rebekah Wade to the *Sun* in January 2003, Rupert Murdoch made her 32-year-old deputy, Andy Coulson, editor of the *News of the World*. The bespectacled Coulson did not look like a stereotypical tabloid hack: he was neat, calm and polite, but with hard edges. Educated at a comprehensive school in Wickford, Essex, Coulson, too, had shone on the *Sun*'s showbusiness column. He had an instinctive feel for what made tabloids edgy and fun. He sent a reporter to find the 'family' of a whale stranded in the Thames and suspended a veteran reporter in a perspex box in the newsroom for twenty-four hours to emulate a stunt by the illusionist David Blaine.

* In this book, Scotland Yard is used synonymously for the Metropolitan Police; similarly, Fleet Street stands, somewhat anachronistically, for the national newspaper industry, and Wapping for News International.

He also poached executives from other papers, most notably the editor of the rival *People*, Neil 'Wolfman' Wallis, a grinning chancer with a gift for innovation, whom he made deputy editor. A legend in tabloid newsrooms, the 52-year-old Wallis had acquired his 'Wolfman' tag on account of his pinched facial features and his theory that the Yorkshire Ripper struck only during full moons. His false story that Elton John had visited a rent boy led to the *Sun* paying record libel damages of £1 million in 1988. In 2004, a year after he joined the *NoW*, Wallis headhunted two of his protégés at the *People*, the news editors Ian Edmondson and James Weatherup.

With these new signings, the *NoW* led the tabloid pack in 2004, breaking a string of circulation-boosting stories, such as the kiss and tell on David Beckham ('Beckham's Secret Affair'), for which Beckham's personal assistant Rebecca Loos was paid £300,000, and 'Blunkett's Affair with a Married Woman', which prompted the resignation of the Home Secretary, David Blunkett. The title's targets tended to accept their humiliation, but occasionally they fought back. In October 2004, the paper's allegations about the sex life of the founder of the Scottish Socialist Party, Tommy Sheridan, prompted the start of an epic legal battle.

At the time, however, Sheridan's case against News International was merely an irritation during an otherwise glorious period for its best-selling title. On a Tuesday night in March 2005, Coulson's *NoW* won Newspaper of the Year at the British Press Awards. The judges said it had shown vitality and originality and, in the Beckham and Blunkett exposés, had broken 'important stories with far-reaching consequences'. In keeping with the heady atmosphere in newspapers, the ceremony at the Hilton Hotel in London's Park Lane was a raucous affair; journalists booed and jeered awards for rivals. As the *Sun* accepted the Cudlipp Award for Popular Journalism, the Live Aid founder Sir Bob Geldof stormed the stage, swore and remarked that a visit to the lavatory had confirmed that rock stars 'have bigger knobs than journalists'. Jeremy Clarkson, the motoring writer and TV presenter who at the previous year's awards had punched Piers Morgan (by now editing the *Daily Mirror*), renewed the feud onstage, announcing: 'Piers Morgan, you are an arsehole.'

'Even by its normal debased standards it was a remarkable event,' noted the *Independent*'s media commentator, Stephen Glover.[14] The *New York Times* said the awards less resembled a mutually respectful celebration of British newspapers than a football match attended by 'a club of misanthropic inebriates'. Quality papers were upset by the *News of the World*'s triumph and, soon after, ten non-Murdoch national newspapers agreed to boycott the awards. In a rare interview with the *Evening Standard*, Coulson shrugged off criticism, pointing out that his paper was not all about sex. He had a simple answer to those questioning his paper's conduct: 'If we'd done anything wrong, there's a pretty well-established set of Press Complaints Commission rules, and there's the law. We know the law, we know the PCC code, and we work within it.'[15]

Media pundits wondered how the *News of the World* obtained its agenda-setting stories. A *News of the World* 'source' explained the mystery to the journalist Tim Luckhurst for an article in the *Independent*, saying that while luck played a part, 'it's mainly down to good old-fashioned journalism and a reputation for paying well for good news, pictures and information'.[16]

But that was a lie; the *News of the World* was conducting its own secret affair. As well as outspending rivals by opening its large cheque-book for celebrity kiss and tells, it was short-circuiting traditional journalism by illegal means. One technique in particular transformed the newsroom: phone hacking. Listening to other people's mobile phone messages was a trick discovered by tabloid showbusiness reporters in the late 1990s. A reporter phoned a mobile number and, if the line was engaged, the call went through to a voicemail inbox: inboxes also had their own number, and, if that was known, it could be rung directly. Either way, once the inbox had been accessed, the voicemails could be unlocked by inputting a personal identification number, or PIN code. Usually the manufacturer's default code worked because people tended not to set their own code, but if PINs had been changed, private investigators could obtain them from bent phone company employees. Eavesdropping on the trivia of people's lives message by message divulged political intrigue, extramarital affairs and other secrets.

Another technique was 'blagging' confidential records, or paying corrupt police, tax or other officials for private data. At the *News of the World*, a sports reporter, Matt Driscoll, stumbled across the practice after receiving a tip that Sir Alex Ferguson, the manager of Manchester United, had a health problem. He went about the story the old way, calling his contacts; it was clear it might be true.

> But then I couldn't get any further forward on it because I hit a brick wall in terms of getting anyone to go on record ... and in the end I had to go to my sports desk and say: 'I really don't think I can get any further forward with this.' And then my sports editor said: 'Leave it with me. We'll see what we can come up with.'

Later that day his sports editor said: 'You're absolutely right. The story is true. I have his medical records with me at the moment.'

Driscoll said: 'I was told that sometimes you'd get a situation where if an investigator sent a fax to a GP or a hospital saying: "I'm his specialist, I need these details," it was incredible how many times they would just get sent straight back.'[17]

The *NoW* also used 'leverage': offering to soften or suppress especially embarrassing information in exchange for exclusive quotes, or, better, continuing cooperation and a steady supply of new stories. At best 'leverage' was the paper earning a favour from someone in a position of power; at worst it was a form of blackmail. In Sir Alex's case, the paper offered to keep his health problem a secret and, Driscoll said, 'because of that, he then started cooperating with the paper ... a few months later he gave us some stories.'*

Driscoll concluded:

> It seemed to me that any method that could stand a story up was fair game. It was also clear that there was massive pressure from the top to break stories. It was largely accepted that this pressure came from the proprietors and editors on the basis that big, sensational stories sell papers and therefore make more money.[18]

---

* In 2011, when Driscoll made his comments, Sir Alex declined to respond to them.

Celebrities were put under covert surveillance. During the Blair years, the *NoW*, in common with its rivals, had become obsessed with the private lives of actors and pop stars. At the time publicists were tightening access to big stars, who tended to say something interesting only when they had a product to promote; other interviews became bland. (As a result, according to *Heat*'s editor Mark Frith, readers developed a taste for stories that were 'fast, pacy and unapproved' and paparazzi shots which would have fetched £5,000 in 2000 made £100,000 in 2005.)

Recalling a sense of siege from the mid-1990s onwards, the actor Hugh Grant said: 'I used to sue a lot and the libel lawyers would say: "By the way you should be careful of this or that" and "Do you realize that the *News of the World* have a white van that sits outside people's houses?"'[19] After his arrest for lewd behaviour in Los Angeles in 1995 there was a 'fishy event' when his flat in London was broken into:

> It was quite a violent break-in, they smashed the front door down, and nothing was taken; the only thing that happened was that the details of what the inside of my flat looked like and a few personal details appeared in the papers in the subsequent days. It became clearer and clearer in the mid to late 1990s, to me and whoever else was in the public eye, that if you had a burglary, or you got mugged or your car was broken into, you had to think really hard about whether you were going to call the police – because the first person that came round was always a pap or a journalist, not a policeman.[20]

Grant developed 'permanent paranoia' and had his car and phone checked for listening devices:

> When I would say this to people, normal people, they would slightly roll their eyes and think 'fame's gone to his head', especially when I started to say: 'You don't know how powerful they are, they've corrupted the police, and they've corrupted the government, successive governments, they're completely in their pockets.'[21]

Trickery was another (legal) tactic. The comedian Steve Coogan recalled how he had been lulled into a false sense that he could trust the *News of the World* in 2002 when a showbusiness reporter, Rav Singh, alerted him that a kiss and tell girl would shortly call him (with the paper's then deputy editor, Coulson, listening in to the conversation) in an attempt to extract intimate details from him. The call duly took place, Coogan 'deadpanned' the questions and the story was not published.

In April 2004, Singh phoned again. Coogan said:

> He wanted to 'negotiate' about an article that was to be printed the next day about a relationship I had had. Singh said that if I were to admit certain parts of the story the paper would omit other details that I felt would be embarrassing to my family. I trusted him, partly as a result of the earlier tip-off, so I had a conversation with him on what I thought was a confidential basis. Afterwards, Coulson, by then the editor of the *News of the World*, called my publicist and told him they had recorded the whole phone conversation and would publish all the details including those they had agreed not to. The promises had been a sham to get me on the phone and get more details in my own words. I was in a vulnerable state at that time in any event and they knew it and used my vulnerability to their advantage.[22]

The paper bullied staff who failed to embrace its culture. Matt Driscoll, the sports reporter, became a marked man when he failed to stand up a tip from Andy Coulson that Arsenal would play in purple shirts during their last season at Highbury. Arsenal told Driscoll the story was not true, but a few months later it was in the *Sun*. Driscoll recalled: 'I got a phone call from my sports editor at the time saying: "We're dead. Coulson's going to go absolutely crazy over this and will want to know why we got this wrong and why this appeared in the *Sun*."'[23] After being disciplined for failing to tape an interview with a footballer (using the traditional technique of taking a shorthand note instead), Driscoll wrote to Coulson saying he would take the warning but still did not feel he had done anything wrong. On 11 November 2005, Coulson replied: 'In my view your actions on this matter merited dismissal.'[24]

In 2005, another long-standing reporter, Sean Hoare, fell foul of

Coulson, his old friend and colleague. As a showbusiness reporter on the *Sun*'s 'Bizarre' column in the late 1990s, Hoare had lived a rock and roll lifestyle with pop stars, but when he became addicted to drink and drugs and struggled at work, he was sacked.

The *News of the World* was vicious, but Driscoll and Hoare knew secrets about its workings that would one day haunt Andy Coulson.

3
The Dark Arts

Oliver Twist to the press's Fagin
           – private investigator Steve Whittamore on his
           relationship with newspapers, 21 September 2010

Fleet Street was never innocent. Newspapers had always paid dodgy characters for tips and exclusives, and dispatched sweet-talking reporters to extract quotes from the doorsteps of the grieving or guilty. Reporters, particularly on tabloid titles, bullied, harried, tricked, embellished and distorted. But most of the investigative work was done traditionally. To trace individuals, reporters flicked through phone books, checked the electoral roll and companies register and phoned friends, neighbours and colleagues. These methods were legal but time-consuming, and fallible. By the late 1990s, reporters began outsourcing checks to private investigators who could instantly, if illegally, access the growing volume of information stored on computer databases. Private detectives had contacts inside the police, vehicle and tax offices – and blaggers who could extract health records from GPs' receptionists and phone numbers from phone companies.

One of the first signs to the outside world of the existence of this network of PIs emerged not in London, the citadel of Britain's national media, but in rural Devon. In 2001 David Welsh, a former nightclub owner who wanted to develop an outdoor swimming pool in Plymouth, complained to the police that he was being blackmailed about his criminal record. In January 2002, Devon and Cornwall Police launched Operation Re-proof into the sale of confidential data and discovered that a serving detective constable in Exeter, Philip Diss, had been covertly checking criminal records on the Police National Computer and passing them to his former boss, a retired police inspector called Alan Stidwill, who ran a private investigations agency, SAS Investigations, in the seaside town of Exmouth. As they began to unravel Stidwill's connections, in autumn 2002, Devon and Cornwall asked the government body which polices confidential databases for an officer to accompany its detectives on a raid of another firm of private investigators, in case it found any data protection breaches in addition to those of the Police National Computer. Alec Owens, senior investigating officer at the Information Commissioner's Office (ICO), accompanied the raid on Data Research Ltd in Surrey in November 2002. As he wandered around the agency's office, Owens, a former police detective inspector, saw a sheaf of car registration numbers on a desk, picked them up and contacted the Driver and Vehicle Licensing Agency (DVLA). The DVLA revealed that the numbers had been searched by a now deceased manager at a regional branch, and, after his death in March 2002, by a junior employee. In the diary of the dead manager, the DVLA found one number marked 'Protected', which Owens knew from his time in Special Branch was either an unmarked undercover police vehicle or the car of a senior police officer. That particular check had been ordered by another private detective, who turned out to be one of the most important figures in the phone hacking scandal: Steve Whittamore.

While Devon and Cornwall carried on its inquiry, the ICO began Operation Motorman, an investigation into Whittamore. On 8 March 2003 – two years before Andy Coulson stepped on stage at the Hilton Hotel – Owens and four other ICO investigators raided Whittamore's house in Orchard Grove, New Milton, a market town on the edge of the New Forest in Hampshire. 'We went there not knowing what the hell we would find,' Owens said later.[1] They found that from an office in the three-bed bungalow, Whittamore was supplying a thriving black market in illegal data. He was furnishing journalists with a vast array of ex-directory numbers, car registration numbers, health records and criminal records, on targets ranging from the actress Elizabeth Hurley to Kevin and Nicola Wells, whose daughter Holly was murdered at Soham, Cambridgeshire, in 2002.

Whittamore had been obtaining the information from a network of corrupt officials and blaggers. They included a civilian worker at Tooting police station in London who invented reasons for checking criminal records on the National Police Computer; DVLA workers who sold names and number plates; and a Hell's Angel who blagged ex-directory and Friends & Family numbers from British Telecom. Whittamore's best customers were Britain's top-selling national newspapers and women's magazines. The *Daily Mail*, *People*, *Daily Mirror*, *Mail on Sunday* and *News of the World* had placed the most orders, and the journalists requesting searches included the *News of the World*'s Greg Miskiw and Rebekah Wade.

Unfortunately for his Fleet Street customers, Whittamore had kept detailed notes of his work. Each request was recorded with a code – 'XD' for an ex-directory number, 'CRO' for a criminal records check and 'Veh Reg' for tracing the owner of a number plate: all of which broke the law on data protection, fraud or bribery, depending on the method used.

It was a lucrative trade. Whittamore's company, JJ Services Ltd, charged £75 to find the address of the owner of a phone, £150 to £500 for a DVLA check and £750 for mobile phone records. Between 2001 and 2003 he had received 17,489 orders – and billed £1.8 million. Owens recalled: 'He was living the high life. He had just come back from a fortnight in Goa. There was an extensive wine cellar in his garage.'[2]

Despite facing a jail term, Whittamore would not snitch on his paymasters. Owens said: 'Whittamore made it very [clear] that whilst he would admit to his own wrongdoing, under no circumstances would he say anything which would incriminate any member of the press. I was undecided as to whether this was because he feared the press or whether he anticipated some financial recompense in return for his silence.'[3]

Whittamore's records showed clear breaches of Section 55 of the Data Protection Act which made it an offence to obtain, disclose or procure the disclosure of personal information 'knowingly or recklessly'. The offence was punishable by a fine of up to £5,000 in the magistrates' court and an unlimited fine in the Crown Court. In the Information Commissioner's Office in Wilmslow, Cheshire, Owens and his fellow investigators started working through the material with a view to prosecuting the journalists who had commissioned Whittamore. What happened next is still a matter of controversy. According to Owens in 2011, a week after the raid:

> An informal meeting was arranged with Richard Thomas, the Commissioner, and Francis Aldhouse, Deputy Commissioner and Head of Operations, to update them. It was at this meeting that I was able, by using examples of the paperwork seized, to show ICO were in a position to prove that a paper chain existed right through from identified journalists working for named newspaper groups requesting information be obtained from a private detective who in turn used corrupt sources or 'blaggers' to obtain such information. We could also prove by way of the seized bills for payment and numbered invoices for payments settled by the newspaper groups exactly how much money had been paid for each transaction and by and to whom it had been paid. Where the information involved such requests as Criminal Record Checks, VRM details, ex-directory numbers, conversions and family and friends without any claim of 'public interest' we were in a position to prosecute everyone in the chain from the 'blagger' right up to the journalists and possibly even the newspaper groups.
>
> It was at this point Francis Aldhouse with a shocked look on his face said: 'We can't take the press on, they are too big for us.' Richard Thomas did not respond, he merely looked straight ahead appearing to be somewhat bemused by the course of action I was recommending. For my own part I remember thinking 'It's our job to take them or indeed anyone else on, that's what we are paid to do. If we do not do it then who does?' At this point Richard Thomas thanked me for updating him and at the same time congratulated me and the team for a job well done.[4]

Owens and his investigators started to prepare twenty-five to thirty prosecution cases, but within weeks 'were informed that we were not to make contact with any of the newspapers identified and we were not to speak to, let alone interview any journalists. Despite our protests we were told that this was the decision of Richard Thomas and that he would deal with the press involvement by way of the Press Complaints Commission. We were now instructed to restrict our investigation solely to the bottom of the pyramid, those involved with correctly supplying information or "blagging" information.'

On 4 November 2003, Richard Thomas wrote to the new chairman of the Press Complaints Commission, Sir Christopher Meyer, indicating that the matter could be dealt with by rewriting the PCC's code of practice on data protection, rather than by prosecuting journalists. He told Meyer:

> I am considering whether to take action under the Data Protection Act against individual journalists and/or newspapers. My provisional conclusion, however, is that it would be appropriate first to give the Press Complaints Commission and its Code Committee the prior opportunity to deal with the issue in a way which would put an end to these unacceptable practices across the media as a whole ... Following your review of any such material, I anticipate that this would at least lead to revision of the code. The approach I have in mind ... could provide a more satisfactory outcome than legal proceedings.[5]

While the ICO waited (in vain) for action from the PCC, Owens and his colleagues interviewed around seventy 'victims' of Whittamore, including Hugh Grant, the singer Charlotte Church and the TV presenter Chris Tarrant. In February 2004, it handed over all evidence to the ICO's Legal Department.

In the meantime, the Metropolitan Police, alerted by Devon and Cornwall Police to the sale of criminal records by the civilian police worker Paul Marshall, had begun its own investigation into data theft, Operation Glade. In August 2003, police arrested Marshall and found he had stolen a truncheon, handcuffs and other equipment for sex games with his partner. At a court hearing for the thefts, a judge gave Marshall – who was dying – a conditional discharge.

The leniency of that punishment hindered Whittamore's subsequent prosecution. On 15 April 2005, prosecutors at Blackfriars Crown Court – quoting from articles in the *Sunday Mirror*, *Mail on Sunday* and the *News of the World* – said Whittamore had provided journalists with 'very personal and confidential details' about high-profile figures such as *EastEnders* stars Jessie Wallace and Clifton Tomlinson, and Bob Crow, the general secretary of the Rail, Maritime and Transport

Union. Whittamore and a fellow private detective, John Boyall, pleaded guilty to breaching the Data Protection Act, while Paul Marshall and Alan King, a recently retired police detective, pleaded guilty to conspiracy to commit misconduct in public office. But because Marshall had been given a conditional discharge for the more serious offence of theft, Judge John Samuels QC felt unable to give him and his fellow conspirators a higher sentence for the lesser data offence. The four men received two-year conditional discharges and walked triumphantly out of court. None of the 305 journalists who had requested information from Whittamore had been put in the dock.

Nor would they. The Information Commissioner dropped its prosecution of Steve Whittamore, Taff Jones, the Hell's Angel in Sussex who had been blagging phone numbers, another private detective, John Gunning, who denied any wrongdoing, and the surviving corrupt DVLA worker, who has not been named. Referring to the disappointing outcome at Blackfriars Crown Court, Richard Thomas later justified the decision to Lord Leveson*: 'We were subsequently advised by external counsel that the leniency of the sentence meant that it would not be in the public interest to continue or pursue parallel and further prosecutions.' Alec Owens said: 'I was disappointed and somewhat disillusioned with senior management because I felt as though they were burying their heads in the sand. It was like being on an ostrich farm.'[6] He believed the ICO was 'frightened' of the press.[7] In 2010, Whittamore would complain about the failure to call the newspapers to account. 'I suppose you could view it as my Oliver Twist to the press's Fagin,' he said. 'Requests were asked of me by people whom I viewed as really being above reproach. They were huge corporations.'[8]

During its three-year investigation, Devon and Cornwall Police

---

* The Leveson Inquiry into the Culture, Practices and Ethics of the Press was set up by the government in July 2011. Presided over by Lord Justice Leveson, an Appeal Court judge, its assessors were: Sir David Bell, non-executive director of the *Economist* and former chairman of the *Financial Times*; Shami Chakrabarti, director of Liberty; Lord Currie, founding chairman of the media regulator Ofcom; Elinor Goodman, former Channel 4 political editor; George Jones, former political editor of the *Daily Telegraph*; and Sir Paul Scott-Lee, former Chief Constable of the West Midlands.

had separately pieced together its own networks of PIs. The retired police inspector in Exmouth, Alan Stidwill, had been supplying criminal records checks on Labour politicians to another private detective, Glen Lawson. In a raid on Lawson's firm in Newcastle upon Tyne, Abbey Investigations, in February 2003, Devon and Cornwall found that in late 2000 he had supplied checks of the criminal records of Gordon Brown, then Chancellor of the Exchequer, his ally Nick Brown, the Agriculture Minister, and another Labour MP, Martin Salter, to a national newspaper. The newspaper has never been named but, in 2000 and 2001, News International was siding with Tony Blair in his frequent rows with Gordon Brown, and Rebekah Wade's *News of the World* had placed Salter on a 'naming and shaming' list for criticizing the 'For Sarah' campaign.

In all, Devon and Cornwall had investigated thirty-seven people but to avoid over-complicating the prosecution just six others were charged: Philip Diss; Alan Stidwill; a serving CID officer; a council investigations officer who could access the computer system at the Department for Work and Pensions; and two others. But at Gloucester Crown Court in March 2006, Judge Paul Darlow threw out the case, saying it was 'not a proportionate use of valuable resources to prosecute these matters'. Stidwill, the retired policeman who ran SAS Investigations, said: 'It's been a dreadful waste of taxpayers' money.' Devon and Cornwall's investigation, like that of the ICO, and arguably that of the Metropolitan Police's Operation Glade, had ended in failure. The trade in illegal newsgathering techniques flourished.

A former Devon and Cornwall detective was quoted in the *Western Morning News* in July 2011 as saying: 'Between 2002 and 2006, Devon and Cornwall Police were right at the heart of what we now know was going on at the *News of the World*. It was a very thorough and professional investigation. The question is why it was kicked out of the courts and why, particularly, the Metropolitan Police didn't follow up on it.'

For the moment, the 'dark arts' had stayed hidden – but that was about to change.

In November 2005, courtiers at Clarence House, Prince Charles's official residence in London, became alarmed when they read stories about his sons, Princes William and Harry, in the *News of the World*. These were not the usual royal stories about the death of Princess Diana, Prince Charles meddling in politics, or whether his wife, Camilla, would become queen. They were tittle-tattle. The first appeared on page 32 on 6 November, at the top of the 'Blackadder' gossip column ('Your snake in the grass of the rich and powerful'). The six paragraph story began: 'Royal action man Prince William has had to postpone a mountain rescue course – after being crocked by a ten-year-old during football training.' The Prince, it explained, had pulled a tendon in his knee after a kickabout and was having physiotherapy near Highgrove, Prince Charles's country home in Gloucestershire.

On the Richter scale of royal revelations, this was barely a tremor, but it caused a shock because courtiers were mystified how it had appeared. The following Sunday, Blackadder reported that Prince William had borrowed some television equipment from a journalist: 'If ITN do a stock take on their portable editing suites this week, they might notice they're one down. That's because their pin-up political editor Tom Bradby has lent it to close pal Prince William so he can edit together all his gap year videos and DVDs into one very posh home movie.' Neither William nor Tom Bradby had leaked the story, which had been known about only by themselves and two people 'incredibly close' to the prince. Bradby explained to William and his brother Harry that during his time as a royal correspondent, redtop reporters sometimes hacked voicemail messages. Later, Bradby recalled: 'They felt – rightly, as it turned out – that the tabloids were invading every aspect of their lives and the question who might be betraying them and how was a preoccupation, bordering on an obsession. So I told them what I thought was going on and suggested it might be a good idea to talk to the police.'[9] St James's Palace called in the Metropolitan Police's Anti-Terrorist Branch, responsible for royal security, and on 21 December began one of the most controversial inquiries in Scotland Yard's 183-year history, Operation Caryatid.

4
First Heads Roll

Undoubtedly the newspaper business is a tough business
– John Kelsey-Fry QC, Old Bailey, 26 January 2007

For Scotland Yard, the investigation could not have come at a worse time. Six months before, on 7 July 2005, Islamic extremists had detonated four bombs on London's transport system, killing fifty-two people and injuring 700 – the first suicide bombings in Britain – and the Met's Counter-Terrorist Branch had drafted in hundreds of officers from other forces to investigate the attacks.

Still, the suspected interception of royal voicemails was a concern, since anyone accessing them might have knowledge of the movements of members of the royal family. Six officers in the counter-terrorism unit SO13 began Operation Caryatid in secrecy and advised members of the royal household to continue leaving messages for each other and not to let their friends or relatives know that they suspected that, somewhere, the *News of the World* was listening.

They did not have far to look for a suspect: the 'Blackadder' column was written by Clive Goodman. In the late 1990s, Goodman had been one of the *News of the World*'s stars, landing 'splash' after 'splash' about the troubles of Charles and Diana, and her death. As royal editor, he had cultivated a network of informants and some of their rarefied airs, wearing Savile Row suits, tweeds and occasionally a fob chain and monocle. But he was now forty-eight, St James's Palace had rooted out leaks by staff and his pre-eminence on the royal beat was being challenged by a young reporter, Ryan Sabey. Under the dynamic regime of Andy Coulson, Goodman turned to a trick to find stories without leaving his home or his office: phone hacking. He was nicknamed 'the eternal flame' because, it was said, he never went out.

Inside New Scotland Yard, the office block headquartering the Met, SO13 kept a check on Blackadder's stories and the phone numbers calling the Royal Household's voicemails. By the end of January, SO13 had established from Vodafone that nine 'rogue numbers' were calling the inboxes of two royal aides: Princes William and Harry's private secretary, Jamie Lowther-Pinkerton, and Helen Asprey, their personal secretary. The princes' phones were being accessed too. One of the 'rogue numbers' was that of Goodman's home in Putney, southwest London.

While the detectives slowly uncovered more victims, Goodman continued reporting the minutiae of the princes' lives. In April 2006, one of his stories was based on a phone call made by Prince William to Prince Harry. Headlined 'Fury After He Ogled Lapdancer's Boobs', it read:

> Shame-faced Prince Harry has been given a furious dressing-down by Chelsy Davy over his late-night antics in a lapdancing bar. His loyal girlfriend discovered how strippers perched on the edge of his chair as he partied with a string of naked dancers and ogled their boobs. Yesterday the repentant prince took an ear-bashing call as news broke.
>
> 'It's Chelsy. How could you? I see you had a lovely time without me. But I miss you so much, you big ginger, and I want you to know I love you,' said a hysterical voice.
>
> Luckily the caller was joker brother, Prince William. He thought the whole episode was hilarious and decided to take the mickey by putting on a high-pitched South African accent like Chelsy's.[1]

Police had identified 'five or six potential victims', but continuing Caryatid prolonged the security risk. At the same time, Detective Superintendent Philip Williams, leading the operation, was concerned that it was taking resources away from counter-terrorism and that 'the media might seek to criticize the [Met] and SO13 for the use of anti-terrorist resources against what, albeit [with] far wider security implications of the voicemail networks, appears to be a non-terrorist motivated intrusion on the privacy of a member of the royal family where non-terrorist-related criminal offences have been committed'.[2]

In April, SO13* held a case conference with the Crown Prosecution Service to discuss what charges might be laid against Goodman. The CPS advised that one reading of one of three relevant laws, the Regulation of Investigatory Powers Act, suggested that the eavesdropping was only a crime if a message had not been heard before it was intercepted – but added that that interpretation was 'untested'. In essence, the provisional advice from the CPS was that if someone had already listened to a message, someone else – such as a reporter – hacking into that message would not be committing an offence. This was an odd interpretation of the law and would become important, because the police would later claim that it significantly limited their investigation.

While SO13 continued monitoring Goodman's calls, Scotland Yard was keen, as always, to maintain its good relationship with the press – and in particular the country's biggest newspaper group, News International. One of the officers friendliest with journalists was Andy Hayman, the Assistant Commissioner in charge of counter-terrorism. Hayman – who had enterprisingly combined his early career in uniform in Essex with running a mobile disco – was also the Association of Chief Police Officers' 'media lead', a duty he carried out with enthusiasm. He was in close touch with the *News of the World*'s crime reporter, Lucy Panton – herself married to a serving Scotland Yard officer – and with its editors. On 25 April, in the middle of Operation Caryatid, he and Scotland Yard's Director of Public Affairs, Dick Fedorcio, dined at the Soho House private members' club in central London with Andy Coulson and his deputy Neil 'Wolfman' Wallis – the executives running the newspaper his officers were investigating.

By early May, officers on Operation Caryatid had made another discovery. The phone company O2 alerted Scotland Yard to some 'suspicious activity': a man posing as a member of staff was calling its

---

* By April, SO13 had been merged with another unit to form SO15. For continuity, we will continue to refer to it as SO13.

operatives and asking them to reset the PINs of Helen Asprey and another royal aide, Paddy Harverson, Prince Charles's communications secretary, to the default numbers. O2's recordings of the calls showed that 'John Jenkin from credit control' had the current password which allowed him to change the PINs, even though it was itself changed regularly – suggesting he was, somehow, receiving inside information from O2. Tracking back through the phone system, detectives discovered the calls had originated from phone lines registered to a 'Paul Williams' at the Kimpton industrial estate in Sutton, south London. They also soon discovered that 'Paul Williams' was an alias of a former part-time footballer with AFC Wimbledon, Glenn Mulcaire. In 1998 Mulcaire had been taken on by News International as a 'researcher'. By 2006, NI was paying his company, Nine Consultancy UK Ltd, £104,988 a year, ostensibly for performing electoral roll and other legal checks. Mulcaire was also receiving £500 cash a week from Clive Goodman, who listed him on his expenses as 'Alexander' – a confidential royal source. The detectives soon realized that Mulcaire was not a legitimate researcher nor a legitimate royal source, but a hacker whose specialist skill was blagging phone companies into switching PINs back to the manufacturer's default.

By monitoring Mulcaire's phone lines, officers realized he was also accessing the voicemails of the publicist Max Clifford, who had spectacularly fallen out with the *News of the World* the previous year. Clifford's pitch was that he could keep stories out of the papers as well as put them in; but Andy Coulson had ignored his pleas not to run a story in 2005 about the cocaine habit of one of his clients, the singer Kerry Katona.

While the police secretly tracked Goodman and Mulcaire's calls, the Information Commissioner's Office gave the first public hint of the illegal data trade behind many newspaper stories. On 13 May 2006, it published a report to Parliament, 'What Price Privacy? The Unlawful Trade in Confidential Personal Information', which revealed that confidential data was being bought by loan firms, local authorities and criminals intent on witness or juror intimidation, and mentioned a 'major case' where a private detective had supplied private information to '305 named journalists working for a range of newspapers'. Though it did not name Steve Whittamore, the report outlined the type of records found in his house, published his tariff of charges and mentioned Rebekah Wade's comments to Parliament about paying police for information, explaining that the disappointing outcome of the case at Blackfriars Crown Court had frustrated its own attempts to seek justice. It did not mention that in March 2003, three years previously, it had ample evidence to prosecute journalists and had chosen not to do so, instead lobbying the Press Complaints Commission. Nor did it state the total number of requests (17,489), nor name any of the newspapers or media groups which had made the requests. But in the absence of any prosecutions of journalists by his own office and any action by the PCC, the Information Commissioner, Richard Thomas, used the report to launch a campaign for a two-year custodial sentence for breaches of Section 55 of the Data Protection Act. In November 2011, Alec Owens, the ICO's frustrated investigator, complained:

> I felt it was no coincidence that this report was not published until May 2006, only a few weeks before the Mulcaire scandal broke. It is my belief that when ICO became aware that the Metropolitan Police were conducting yet another investigation involving more wrongdoing by the press, they decided to pre-empt and deflect any criticism which was bound to be directed towards them in relation to their lack of action against the press in Operation Motorman. All the evidence published in this report had been gathered and had been available since March 2003 ... why did it take over three years to prepare it, and [then] not publish it until thirteen months after the prosecution against Whittamore had concluded?[3]

News International was not greatly concerned by the ICO's report. On 16 May 2006, three days after its publication, Andy Coulson walked on to the stage at Claridge's hotel in London to accept the Sunday Newspaper of the Year Award for the third year running. The judges at the London Press Club described the *News of the World* as the paper they would least like to be without, 'an incredible sledgehammer of a production'. On Sunday 21 May, the paper headlined its triumph: 'We're Crowned Triple Champs', stressing: 'No other paper has ever achieved this hat-trick.'

With the applause of his peers ringing in his ears, Coulson set about victimizing Matt Driscoll. After a complaint from Charlton Football Club in March 2006 about a small story (which turned out to be true), the sportswriter faced a trumped-up disciplinary hearing. In July 2006, Coulson emailed his deputy, Neil Wallis, saying he wanted Driscoll 'out as quickly and cheaply as possible'.[4] That month, Driscoll went on sick leave, suffering from severe depression. Despite knowing that his doctor had advised that he should distance himself from work, the paper bombarded him with daily phone calls and sent multiple recorded letters to his home. News International then stopped his pay.

By now Scotland Yard had become aware that the *News of the World* was hacking not just the princes and their aides but a growing number of high-profile figures. Mindful of the seriousness of the terrorist threat – and perhaps also its relationship with Rupert Murdoch's papers – the force decided to limit the scope of its investigation. A Crown Prosecution Service note dated 14 July 2006 stated 'the police have requested initial advice about the data produced and whether the case as it stands could be ring-fenced to ensure that extraneous matters will not be dragged into the prosecution area'. By 25 July, the CPS had agreed privately with the police that the case should be 'deliberately limited' to 'less sensitive' witnesses. A senior Crown Prosecution Service lawyer wrote: 'It was recognized early in this case that the investigation was likely to reveal a vast array of offending behaviour. However the CPS and the police concluded that aspects of the investigation could be focused on a discrete area of offending relating to JLP and HA [the royal aides] and the suspects Goodman and Mulcaire.'[5] For a long time the Crown Prosecution Service and Scotland Yard excluded the existence of this strategy from their public announcements and their subsequent testimony to Parliament.

With their horizons sufficiently narrowed and with ample call data and matching newspaper stories, the police finally struck. Clive Goodman's career as one of Britain's most senior journalists came to a noisy end at 6 a.m. on 8 August 2006 when officers burst into the house he shared with his wife and eighteen-month-old daughter in Putney, arrested him and took him to a police station while they searched his home, where they found an important internal memo in a chest of drawers in his bedroom.

Later that morning, four officers executed a search warrant at the *News of the World* in Wapping with the intention of seizing material from Goodman's desk and financial records. In the absence of the *NoW*'s holidaying lawyer Tom Crone, the company called Julian Pike, a partner at News International's solicitors, Farrer & Co (ironically, also the Queen's lawyers), and asked him 'to assist' the search. The four officers met with a hostile reception but managed to retrieve some documents from Goodman's desk, as Detective Chief Inspector Keith Surtees later explained:

> My officers were confronted with photographers, who were sum-
> moned from other parts of News International, and they were taking
> photographs of the officers. A number of night or news editors chal-
> lenged the officers around the illegality of their entry into News
> International. They were asked to go to a conference room until law-
> yers could arrive to challenge the illegality of [the warrant], and it
> was described to me as a tense stand-off by the officer leading that
> search. The officer tried to get our forensic management team, our
> search officers into the building. They were refused entry, they were
> left outside. Our officers were effectively surrounded and photo-
> graphed and not assisted in any way, shape or form. That search was
> curtailed. Some items were taken. The search did not go to the extent
> I wanted it to.[6]

The officer leading the search, Detective Inspector Pearce, feared that the *News of the World*'s staff 'may offer some form of violence against the small police team in the building', though none occurred – because the police soon left. They did not return because, as Detective Chief Inspector Surtees explained, the 'moment had been lost with regard to the information we sought'.[7] Details of this obstruction and intimidation of the police by News International were made public only six years later.

At the same time as they arrested Goodman, detectives raided the home and offices of Glenn Mulcaire, from which they took away an extensive array of paperwork, CD-roms, audio cassettes and white-boards recording PIN numbers, security codes and bank details of his targets. Mulcaire and Goodman stayed silent in their interviews. The day they were released on bail, 9 August, the Counter-Terrorism Branch arrested twenty-five people for a conspiracy to blow up nine transatlantic airliners: resources were again under strain.

Detective Chief Inspector Surtees ordered a team of Special Branch officers to work round the clock drawing up a list of potential victims from Mulcaire's notes. He had scrawled down thousands of names, phone numbers and PIN codes onto 11,000 pieces of A4 paper. Cru-cially, in the top left-hand corner of each page, Mulcaire had written the names of twenty-eight different journalists who had commis-sioned him, such as 'Clive'.

Just as the Information Commissioner's Office had at the home of Fleet Street's data thief Steve Whittamore two years before, the police had stumbled on an industrial intrusion into the private lives of newsworthy individuals. In all, the Special Branch officers inputted the names of 418 'potential victims' into a computer spreadsheet. Here was evidence that Mulcaire, at least, had targeted not just the princes and their aides and a few others but hundreds upon hun-dreds of high-profile figures. Among them were two serving cabinet ministers, the Deputy Prime Minister, John Prescott (whose Chief of Staff, Joan Hammell, was in the notes), the Culture Minister, Tessa Jowell, who had responsibility for media policy, the former Home Secretary David Blunkett, whose affair had been one of the NoW's award-winning splashes two years earlier, the Conservative front-bencher Boris Johnson, the Respect Party leader, George Galloway, and Sir Ian Blair, the current Commissioner of the Metropolitan Police. Among the many names in the notes were two other senior police officers: Assistant Commissioner John Yates and his fellow Assistant Commissioner Andy Hayman (who was overseeing the investigation).

Despite the size of the haul and clear evidence of the involvement of other journalists, detectives made only a cursory attempt to identify wrongdoers other than Goodman and Mulcaire. According to Crown Prosecution Service records, they also kept prosecutors in the dark. At a case conference on 21 August, Detective Superintendent Philip Williams told the CPS that there were potentially around only 180 victims. (He later told the Leveson Inquiry this was meant only as 'an indicative number'.) The CPS said later: 'We enquired whether there was any evidence connecting Mulcaire to other *News of the World* journalists. Again we were told that there was not, and we never saw any such evidence.'[8]

On 7 September, Scotland Yard made a half-hearted attempt to identify other wrongdoers, writing to News International asking for its notes and files on Mulcaire and the records of phone calls made to him. Burton Copeland, a law firm contracted by News International to 'assist' the police, replied on 14 September that its client could find only one document (which has not been made public) and refused to hand over the phone records, ostensibly to protect 'sources'. Under the 1984 Police and Criminal Evidence Act, officers could only obtain a search warrant for 'journalistic premises' if the company was not cooperating. The police decided that News International was not cooperating, but it still did not request a search warrant.

Then the police did something strange. Someone inside Scotland Yard – it is not known who – approached Rebekah Wade, by now editing the *Sun*, and gave her details of the operation. The rationale for this seems to have been that Wade was herself in Mulcaire's notes. She was thus potentially a victim of the *News of the World*'s news-gathering operation. An internal email sent by Tom Crone, the *News of the World*'s lawyer, to its editor, Andy Coulson, captured the briefing:

From: Tom Crone
Sent: 15 September 2006 10.34
To: Andy Coulson
Subject: Strictly private and confidential

Andy,

Here's [what] Rebekah told me about info relayed to her by cops:

1. They are confident they have Clive [Goodman, former royal editor] and GM [Mulcaire] bang to rights on the Palace intercepts;

2. [on Mulcaire's] . . . accesses to voicemails. From these they have a list of 100–110 'victims';

3. The only payment records they found were from News Int, ie the *NoW* retainer and other invoices; they said that over the period they looked at (going way back) there seemed to be over £1m of payments.

4. The recordings and notes demonstrate a pattern of 'victims'. . . replaced by the next one who becomes flavour of the week/month;

5. They are visiting the bigger victims, ie where there are lots of intercepts;

6. Their purpose is to insure that when GM comes up in court the full case against him is there for the court to see (rather than just the present palace charges);

7. All they are asking victims is 'did you give anyone permission to access your voicemail?' and if not 'do you wish to make a formal complaint?'

8. They are confident that . . . they can then charge Glenn Mulcaire in relation to those victims . . . they are keen that the charges should demonstrate the scale of GM's activities . . . so they would feature victims from different areas of public life, politics, showbiz, etc

9. In terms of *NoW*:

   (a) They suggested *News of the World* journalists directly accessing the voicemails (this is what did for Clive).

   (b) But they have got hold of *NoW* back numbers to 2004 and are trying to marry CG accesses to specific stories,

   (c) In one case they seem to have a phrase from a *NoW* story which is identical to the tape or note of GM's access,

(d) They have no recordings of *NoW* people speaking to GM or accessing voicemails,

(e) They do have GM's phone records which show sequences of contacts with *News of the World* before and after accesses . . . obviously they don't have the content of the calls . . . so this is at best circumstantial.

10. They are going to contact RW today to see if she wishes to take it further.[9]

Unsurprisingly, Wade did not wish to submit a formal complaint against her employers. Scotland Yard, which at the time was engaged in seventy live operations, some of which were not being fully staffed for lack of resources, was similarly unenthusiastic about widening the investigation. At the end of September, Deputy Assistant Commissioner Peter Clarke, Andy Hayman's deputy, formally limited the scope of Caryatid to just Goodman and Mulcaire.

Six years later at the Leveson Inquiry, he stood by his decision:

Invasions of privacy are odious, obviously. They can be extraordinarily distressing and at times they can be illegal, but, to put it bluntly, they don't kill you. Terrorists do.[10]

He expressed disappointment, however, at the execution of the police's strategy to inform victims. Officers told thirty-six individuals in the government, military, police and royal household that their phones had been compromised, for reasons of national security. Oddly, they did not contact John Prescott, the Deputy Prime Minister, who was known to have been distrustful of Rupert Murdoch's interference in politics.

Police later said that they understood that the mobile phone companies would alert customers. O2 warned forty straight away but, citing a concern that doing so would prejudice police inquiries, Orange and T-Mobile only notified their forty-five and seventy-one subscribers respectively in July 2011, five years later, while Vodafone waited until January 2012 to contact its forty affected customers. The delay meant those individuals were unaware they could change their PIN codes or sue News International. The overwhelming majority of Mulcaire's victims did not find out that they had been targeted until years later.

Police had found a detailed haul of incriminating evidence indicating that Mulcaire had hacked hundreds of newsworthy targets, but they had misled prosecutors about the number of victims and the involvement of other NoW journalists, failed to inform directly the vast majority of people who were likely to have been eavesdropped on, and rejected other options available to them, such as selecting a wider sample of wrongdoing; pursuing a limited number of heavy users of Mulcaire at the *News of the World*; or farming out the investigation to a less stretched unit.

At Wapping, the overriding emotion was relief. Journalists there had been expecting early morning knocks on the door from the police, but they never came. Faced with the ongoing threat to their reputations from the continuing, albeit limited fallout from Goodman and Mulcaire's arrests, Rupert Murdoch's executives considered how to respond. The first pressing problem was how to minimize the impending prosecution of Clive Goodman. Internal emails at News International in 2006 'revealed quite an active involvement' in the case, according to Lawrence Abramson, a senior lawyer at Harbottle & Co, which later worked for News International: 'They showed [the company] trying to influence the way the prosecution was being conducted or the defence was being conducted.'[11]

Naturally News International did not want its royal editor to suggest that phone hacking was rife at the *News of the World*, nor that he had only been doing what was expected of him. To demonstrate to Goodman that he was still valued, Tom Crone relayed to him Andy Coulson's repeated assurance that he could come back to the *News of the World* once he had served his sentence. News International continued to pay his full salary while he stayed at home, and even called him occasionally for help on royal stories. Glenn Mulcaire, too, continued to receive his salary.

*

While the Crown Prosecution Service finalized the case, News International became belatedly concerned about the campaign by the Information Commissioner, Richard Thomas, to introduce a prison term for data theft. On 24 July 2006, the Department for Constitutional Affairs issued a consultation paper agreeing with the proposal. In an attempt to lobby support, on 27 October Thomas met Les Hinton, the chairman of the Press Complaints Commission's powerful Code Committee, which set its code of practice. Hinton also happened to be one of Rupert Murdoch's most senior employees. Since joining the *News* in Adelaide as a copy boy in 1960, Hinton had worked his way up to become executive chairman of News International, where he had overseen the promotions of Rebekah Wade and Andy Coulson. Although NI was implacably opposed to jail terms for law-breaking journalists, Thomas recalled that the meeting was 'civilized and reasonably constructive' and that Hinton 'talked a lot about the efforts which would be made to tackle misconduct'.[12] Thomas was extremely surprised two days later to see a 'personalized and hostile leading editorial' on him and the ICO in the *Sunday Times* on 29 October 2006:

> Where someone lives, who they are, who their friends and family may be is hardly confidential information. It is common currency that is easily discovered by talking to neighbours, looking at the electoral register or searching the Land Registry, as anyone is entitled to do. To propose imprisonment for reporters – and insurers, solicitors and private investigators – who obtain such deals would be laughable, if it were not so sinister.

A further hostile leader appeared in *The Times* three days later, on 1 November:

> It [the proposal] could all too easily prevent investigative journalists looking at personal data in pursuit of a public-interest story; deter whistleblowers from revealing malpractice; and blow wide open the confidentiality that protects the journalist and his source.

Thomas said: 'At that time, nothing else was appearing in the mainstream press about "What Price Privacy?" to prompt these attacks. The episode raised questions in my mind about proprietorial influence on editorial independence and freedom.'*

At a pleas hearing at the Old Bailey in London in November 2006, the limited nature of the phone hacking prosecution became apparent. Under the Criminal Law Act 1977, Goodman and Mulcaire pleaded guilty to conspiracy to intercept the communications of the royal aides Jamie Lowther-Pinkerton, Helen Asprey and Paddy Harverson. In the eight months before their arrests, they had made 609 calls to the direct dial inboxes of the trio (Goodman making the most, 487). Under the 2000 Regulation of Investigatory Powers Act, Mulcaire also pleaded guilty to hacking the phones of a further five individuals whose inboxes he had called sixty-six times: Max Clifford; Gordon Taylor, chief executive of the Professional Footballers' Association – the footballers' union leader; the sports agent Sky Andrew; the supermodel Elle Macpherson and the Liberal Democrat MP Simon Hughes, who had recently admitted he was bisexual after being confronted by the *Sun* with evidence that he called gay chatlines. All five would have been of interest to the *News of the World*, but probably not to its royal editor – which indicated the involvement of other journalists at the paper.

Even though the charges represented only a fraction of the *NoW*'s true criminality, they were highly embarrassing for News International: one of its senior journalists had been caught illegally snooping on the royal family. As an act of contrition, Coulson wrote

* At the Leveson Inquiry, News International denied that Hinton had required its editors to write the editorials. Under close questioning from its counsel, Rhodri Davies, Thomas appeared to distance himself from his earlier comments. Asked about the supposed proprietorial influence, he told Davies: 'That is absolutely how I saw it at the time. I thought: "Gosh, this is very surprising and strange." Just forty-eight hours or less than that after I'd met the most senior person at News International, here suddenly I'm appearing in a leading article, the lead editorial in the *Sunday Times*, on something which is not part of the public debate at the moment.' He added: 'I've now seen the witness statements from the editor at the time and also from [News International's lawyer] Mr Linklater, and they say categorically they were not directed by Mr Hinton. I have absolutely no reason to challenge or disagree with that. All I've said was at the time to me, and to others around me, it looked strange.'

to Sir Michael Peat, Prince Charles's Private Secretary, apologizing and offering to make a substantial donation to charities of the prince's choosing.

Despite the seriousness of the offences, however, News International still hoped Goodman would be spared jail, and hired John Kelsey-Fry QC, one of the country's most expensive barristers, to represent him. At sentencing on 26 January 2007, Kelsey-Fry painted a sorry picture of the royal editor: 'He was demoted, sidelined, and another younger reporter was appointed to cover the royal family. Undoubtedly the newspaper business is a tough business. It is a ruthless business. It was while under that pressure that he departed from those high standards by which he had lived his entire life.' Seeking to minimize the extent of Goodman's wrongdoing, Kelsey-Fry made plain that his client had not been embroiled in Mulcaire's non-royal hacking, saying very briefly: 'Whoever else may be involved at the *News of the World*, his involvement is so limited.' Kelsey-Fry argued that his client should be spared the 'clang' of the prison gates because of the relative unimportance of the stories, prison overcrowding and his public disgrace. But the judge, Mr Justice Gross, jailed Goodman for four months and Mulcaire for six for the 'grave, inexcusable and illegal invasion of privacy'.

Neither the judge, nor the prosecution, nor the hundreds of victims, nor the wider public had any idea of the scale of the lawbreaking. That knowledge was confined, for the moment, to News International and Scotland Yard.

5
Rogue Defence

Goodman's hacking was aberrational, a rogue exception,
an exceptionally unhappy event in the 163-year history of
the News of the World *involving one journalist*
— Colin Myler, 22 February 2007

If Clive Goodman had been given a suspended sentence or community service, Andy Coulson might have maintained his position, but that was now impossible and his career at Wapping ended with his resignation, at the age of thirty-five, on the afternoon of Goodman's jailing. In a statement to the media, Coulson said that although he had not known about hacking, he 'ultimately' bore responsibility as editor. In a bad-tempered farewell speech to staff, he remarked that the Home Secretary had recently recommended only the most dangerous criminals be imprisoned, to relieve overcrowding, and that only that day a downloader of child pornography had been spared jail.

Wapping carried on paying Goodman's wages as he languished in the maximum security HMP Belmarsh, but that situation was too embarrassing to continue and on 5 February 2007, a week after sentencing, Les Hinton sacked Goodman: the *News of the World* would not, after all, be giving him his old job back. But there was a sweetener – a year's salary, £90,502. 'I recognize this episode followed many unblemished, and frequently distinguished, years of service to the *News of the World*,' Hinton wrote to Goodman. 'In view of this, and in recognition of the pressures on your family, it has been decided that upon your termination you will receive one year's salary. In all

49

the circumstances, we would of course be entitled to make no payment whatever . . .' Goodman was fuming: he believed he had taken the rap and kept his mouth shut, yet he was now being abandoned by his employers.

After firing Goodman, the *News of the World* was faced with fighting off two external inquiries. Shocked by Goodman's behaviour, the Press Complaints Commission had begun an investigation, as had separately the Commons Culture, Media and Sport Committee, which had also been concerned by the ICO's 'What Price Privacy?' report and press harassment of Prince William's girlfriend, Kate Middleton. Under its chairman Sir Christopher Meyer, the PCC decided that because Andy Coulson had 'left the industry', he need not be interviewed, but it wanted to hear from his successor, Colin Myler, an old tabloid hand recruited hastily from Murdoch's *New York Post*. On 22 February Myler explained that Goodman had concealed the identity of his mysterious royal source 'Alexander'; no one else at the paper had known of his hacking and all of the paper's journalists understood the 'necessity of total compliance' with the PCC code of practice. Myler told the PCC: 'Goodman's hacking was aberrational, a rogue exception, an exceptionally unhappy event in the 163-year history of the *News of the World* involving one journalist.' The abandonment of Clive Goodman was complete.

But Goodman was not prepared to sink into ignominy without more cash. On 2 March, despite being jailed for serious professional misconduct, he wrote to News International's director of human resources, Daniel Cloke, giving notice of his intention to request an internal appeal against his dismissal. The letter, concealed by News International for a further four years, left his former employer in no doubt that he could still open his mouth.

Dear Mr Cloke

I refer to Les Hinton's letter of February 5, 2007, informing me of my dismissal for alleged gross misconduct.

The letter identifies the reason for the dismissal as 'recent events'. I take this to mean my plea of guilty to conspiracy to intercept the voicemail messages of three employees of the royal family.

I am appealing against this decision on the following grounds:

I) The decision is perverse in that the actions leading to this criminal charge were carried out with the full knowledge and support of [*]. Payment for Glenn Mulcaire's services was arranged by [*].

II) The decision is inconsistent, because [*] and other members of staff were carrying out the same illegal procedures. The prosecution counsel, the counsel for Glenn Mulcaire, and the Judge at the sentencing hearing agreed that other *News of the World* employees were the clients for Mulcaire's five solo substantive charges. This practice was widely discussed in the daily editorial conference, until explicit reference to it was banned by the Editor. As far as I am aware, no other member of staff has faced disciplinary action, much less dismissal.

III) My conviction and imprisonment cannot be the real reason for my dismissal. The legal manager, Tom Crone, attended virtually every meeting of my legal team and was given full access to the Crown Prosecution Service's evidence files. He, and other staff on the paper, had long advance knowledge that I would plead guilty. Despite this, the paper continued to employ me. Throughout my suspension I was given book serialisations to write and was consulted on several occasions about royal stories they needed to check. The paper continued to employ me for a substantial part of my custodial sentence.

IV) Tom Crone and the Editor promised me on many occasions that I could come back to a job at the newspaper if I did not implicate the paper or any of its staff in my mitigation plea. I did not, and I expect the paper to honour its promise to me.

V) The dismissal is automatically unfair as the company failed to go through the minimum required statutory dismissal procedures.

Yours sincerely
Clive Goodman

cc Stuart Kuttner, Managing Editor, *News of the World*
Les Hinton, Executive Chairman, News International Ltd

In 360 words, Goodman was threatening to explode the company's

---

* Names have been redacted at the request of the Metropolitan Police to avoid prejudicing criminal trials.

defence: he was claiming phone hacking had been carried out routinely, with management's 'full knowledge'.

Four days after the letter was sent, Les Hinton gave evidence to the Commons Culture, Media and Sport Committee into press standards. Hinton had to be careful, since the last time a senior News International executive had appeared before the committee she had admitted that the company bribed police. But the urbane, silver-haired Hinton would never make that mistake. On 6 March 2007, he assured the MPs that phone hacking had been a one-off case, the result of lax controls on payments, which had been exploited by Goodman. The police had carried out 'pretty thorough investigations', with the result that two men had gone to prison, the *News of the World* had paid a substantial sum to charity and the editor had resigned. Hinton looked them in the eye and said: 'I believe absolutely that Andy did not have knowledge of what was going on.'

'There were actually two issues involved in the Goodman case,' he added.

> There had been a contract with Glenn Mulcaire, during which he was carrying out activities which the prosecution and the judge accepted were legitimate investigative work. There was a second situation where Clive had been allowed a pool of cash to pay to a contact in relation to investigations into royal stories. That, the court was told, was where the money came from and the detail of how he was using that money was not known to the editor. That is not unusual for a contact, when you have a trusted reporter – which Clive was . . .

At the end of the session, the committee chairman, John Whittingdale, checked: 'You carried out a full, rigorous internal inquiry, and you are absolutely convinced that Clive Goodman was the only person who knew what was going on?' 'Yes, we have,' Hinton replied, 'and I believe he was the only person, but that investigation, under the new editor, continues.'

A week later, on 14 March, appealing his sacking, Goodman wrote to Daniel Cloke again, asking for a long list of documents to support his case, including emails between himself and several executives and, tellingly, a transcript of Les Hinton's evidence to the MPs.

News International denied Goodman's request for the emails. Instead, Cloke and Jonathan Chapman, the company's legal director, reviewed 2,500 emails between Goodman and the executives, looking for anything which suggested others had known about phone hacking. They found evidence of police corruption, which they ignored since they were civil lawyers engaged in an employment law case, but no 'reasonable evidence' to support his case that management had known about his criminality. They concluded that Goodman had been fairly dismissed. As they pondered what to do with their jailed royal editor, who had already been paid £90,502, the *News of the World* finally took action against another reporter, who had conducted himself legally. On 26 April 2007, the paper sacked Matt Driscoll, still on sick leave with depression. He began an employment tribunal case.

By now News International had another problem: Gordon Taylor, the footballers' union leader whose phone Mulcaire had admitted hacking in court. More particularly, News International was having a problem with Taylor's feisty solicitor, 42-year-old Mark Lewis. By the time he had become head of litigation at the Manchester law firm George Davies, Lewis had overcome a difficult childhood, been the first from his working-class family to go to university and, aged twenty-six, been diagnosed with multiple sclerosis, which disabled his right hand and affected his speech. As he watched the BBC's *Ten O'Clock News* report of Goodman and Mulcaire's jailing in January 2007, Lewis remembered a curious incident a year and a half before. In July 2005, Neville Thurlbeck, by now the *News of the World*'s chief reporter, had turned up on the doorstep of Jo Armstrong, a lawyer at the Manchester-based Professional Footballers' Association, hoping to ask questions about Gordon Taylor's private life. A passer-by had spotted a photographer taking pictures of the pair lunching and had alerted Taylor, who chased after the snapper and discovered he was working for the *News of the World*. Lewis had written to the newspaper on Taylor's behalf denying the story. In its response, the *NoW* explained it had obtained the story through 'proper journalistic inquiry'; Lewis was suspicious of the phrase.

He reasoned that because Mulcaire had admitted intercepting the voicemails of five individuals unconnected to the royal household, those individuals would have a civil claim against News International for breach of privacy – and, given that Goodman was a royal reporter and other victims came from sport, showbusiness and politics, other News International journalists were likely to have been hacking phones too. In early 2007, Lewis wrote to each of the non-royal hacking victims (Max Clifford, Taylor, Sky Andrew, Simon Hughes and Elle Macpherson). Only one, Taylor, wanted to pursue a case; Lewis duly wrote to News International making a civil claim for invasion of privacy.

At that stage, if News International had offered £20,000 damages under a legal manoeuvre known as a Part 36 offer (which puts pressure on a litigant to settle or risk paying the other side's costs if a judge awards a lower amount), Lewis would have advised Taylor to settle, since he had no evidence other than Mulcaire's court admission. That itself was not proof that his communications had been intercepted on behalf of the *News of the World*. But, to his surprise, the *NoW*'s Tom Crone asked if he could visit him in person in Manchester, which he did at the offices of George Davies on 3 May 2007. 'That was their big mistake,' Lewis said later. 'Crone never went outside London. It flagged up they thought they had a really big problem. His starting point was: "We thought this had all gone away, let's settle."'[1] Lewis asked for £200,000 damages. Crone rejected the request, grabbed his coat and left.

News International was now facing trouble on five fronts: the PCC and Culture Committee investigations, which did not know about the use of the dark arts; Clive Goodman and Glenn Mulcaire (who had launched an employment law case against NI), who did; and Gordon Taylor, who suspected but had no proof.

The PCC was easily fooled. On 18 May 2007, the commission – which had not been told of Goodman's letter of 2 March, nor of Gordon Taylor's legal complaint – ruled that while Goodman's behaviour had been appalling, there was 'no evidence' to challenge the *NoW*'s insistence that he was a rogue reporter. Praising the 'numerous examples' of good practice throughout the industry towards data privacy, the watchdog issued six new technical recommendations on covert newsgathering, such as inserting its code of practice into staff contracts and introducing stricter controls on cash payments. With that it let the matter drop.

With one problem gone, News International tried again to silence Clive Goodman. Its legal director Jonathan Chapman asked Lawrence Abramson of law firm Harbottle & Lewis to confirm his and Cloke's decision to reject Goodman's employment appeal. Chapman wrote to Abramson on 9 May: 'Because of the bad publicity that could result from an allegation in an employment tribunal that we had covered up potentially damaging evidence found on our email trawl, I would ask that you or a colleague carry out an independent review of the emails in question and report back to me with any findings of material that could possibly tend to support either of Goodman's contentions.'[2] Abramson and his staff were given electronic access to the same emails Chapman and Cloke had reviewed, though some were strangely blank and others cut off halfway through. Importantly, because Abramson could not access some of them electronically he requested paper copies – which were sent to his office. Abramson agreed with his client: there was no reasonable evidence in the emails to support Goodman's case (again overlooking police corruption, which he was under no professional obligation to report to the police). After some haggling, on 29 May Abramson agreed with Chapman the following response:

Re: Clive Goodman

We have on your instructions reviewed the emails to which you have provided access from the accounts of:

Andy Coulson

Stuart Kuttner

Ian Edmondson

Clive Goodman

Neil Wallis

Jules Stenson*

* Jules Stenson was features editor of the *News of the World*.

I can confirm that we did not find anything in those emails which appeared to us to be reasonable evidence that Clive Goodman's illegal actions were known about and supported by both or either of Andy Coulson, the editor, and Neil Wallis, the Deputy Editor, and/or that Ian Edmondson, the News Editor, and others were carrying out similar illegal procedures.

After completing the exercise, Harbottle & Lewis archived its conclusion, together with the paper copies of the emails, where they lay until they re-emerged with devastating impact four years later. For now, nothing was publicly known about corruption at News International, nor of the attempts to influence the outcome of Goodman's prosecution, nor of his legal action, nor of the ill-treatment of the sports reporter Matt Driscoll. What happened next, though, would dramatically raise the stakes when they resurfaced.

By the spring of 2007, David Cameron, the leader of the Conservative Party, was convinced that he needed to revitalize his press operation. On winning the leadership in December 2005, Cameron had espoused a new more mature politics and, believing that newspaper proprietors were wielding too much power, sought to curb them. Speaking in 2011, Cameron's press chief at the time, George Eustice, said: 'Part of David Cameron's whole prescription of where Blair had gone wrong was that it was all about headlines and endless initiatives and nothing being done, so part of his argument was . . . we're not going to deviate things just to get a headline in a Sunday paper.'[3] Cameron's team decided they would cultivate political reporters rather than their proprietors and would politely decline invitations to address News Corp conferences. Eustice recalled: 'We didn't want to say to them [proprietors]: "We're going to put you in your box." We didn't want it to be like that. We just wanted them to get used to it.'[4]

Cameron had hoped to reposition the Conservatives as a kinder party, more concerned about poverty, public services and the environment. In February 2006 he had made a speech saying that youths who wore hooded tops were misunderstood rather than dangerous (the perception of many voters), and in April of that year had posed on a husky sled on a Norwegian glacier to draw attention to climate change. Despite successfully reshaping attitudes towards his party, the approach alienated some traditional supporters. For one, Rupert Murdoch was particularly unimpressed. In an interview on US television on 20 July 2006, he described Cameron as 'charming', but when asked what he thought of him replied: 'Not much. He's bright. He's quick. He's totally inexperienced.'[5] With Tony Blair having already announced he would not stand for another term, Murdoch said he hoped Gordon Brown would become prime minister a year or two before the next general election to allow a 'match up between Brown and the new Conservative leadership'.[6] In effect, Murdoch had signalled that the support of his newspapers was attainable.

By early 2007, Cameron began to fear his aloofness towards editors and proprietors was damaging his prospects. According to Eustice: 'The media wouldn't say: "We respect what David Cameron is doing," they would react to the game. They would literally say: "Gordon Brown came over for dinner and David Cameron won't speak at our conference, why should we back him?"'[7]

Cameron began looking for a new press secretary. One of his closest political allies, George Osborne, the shadow Chancellor, suggested the newly unemployed Andy Coulson. Osborne had reason to be thankful to Coulson; a year earlier, while still at Wapping, he had taken the sting out of a controversy that could have wrecked Osborne's career. Aged twenty-two, Osborne had known a dominatrix, Natalie Rowe, who was expecting the baby of one of his friends, William Sinclair. In 2005, Rowe (professional name Mistress Pain) had been hawking around a picture of herself with the now rising star of Her Majesty's Loyal Opposition. In the picture, Osborne had his arm around Rowe, and a line of white powder was visible in the background – which she claimed was cocaine.

Rowe had contracted Max Clifford, who sold the story to the *Sunday Mirror*, which published it on 16 October 2005 under the headline: 'Vice Girl: I Snorted Cocaine with Top Tory Boy'. Despite not agreeing a deal with Rowe, the *News of the World* had also somehow obtained the picture and splashed the story. Coulson's version was noticeably gentler on Osborne and included sympathetic quotes from him, such as: 'It was a stark lesson to me at a young age of the destruction which drugs bring to so many people's lives.' Coulson suggested that Osborne had been a young man caught up in a shadowy world, pointing out that he robustly condemned drugs.

Aware that the *News of the World*'s former editor had resigned over phone hacking, Cameron asked Coulson whether there was anything in his past that could embarrass them. Coulson gave the necessary assurances, and on 31 May 2007 was appointed the Conservatives' new director of communications. With his working-class background and media experience, Coulson provided an earthy counter-weight to the upper-class Cameron and Osborne and could 'tabloid proof' policies.

Coulson started reaching out to editors and proprietors and the Conservatives began to roll out policies more appealing to right-wing voters. At the party conference in October 2007, George Osborne announced a plan which would benefit thousands of homeowners in the South-East, to raise the threshold for inheritance tax from £300,000 to £1 million. In his leader's address David Cameron backed a cap on migrants from outside the European Union. The BBC's political reporter Brian Wheeler noted that 'there was none of the New Age rhetoric of last year's "let the sun shine in" speech. He [Cameron] spoke at length about education, calling for a return to traditional standards in the classroom, more discipline and "setting by ability". He set out policies to strengthen the family . . .'[8]

Under Coulson, Cameron quickly adopted the *Sun*'s 'Broken Britain' campaign against social breakdown, employing much tougher rhetoric than he had previously. On 10 January 2008, in a 'time to reclaim our streets' speech in Salford, he said: 'Today, I want to speak about the senseless, barbaric and seemingly remorseless prevalence of violence in our country. A violence that takes our families, torments them with suffering and tears them apart.' Rebekah Wade's *Sun* backed the hard line, on 30 January blazoning Cameron's tough talking on the police on a front page headlined 'Police Cameron Action'.

Political editor George Pascoe-Watson wrote: 'David Cameron yesterday unveiled his plans to mend broken Britain ... and give power back to the police. In an exclusive interview he said officers could be given free rein to stop and search youngsters on the street.'[9]

The frost between David Cameron's Conservatives and Rupert Murdoch's News Corporation was thawing. Just as with Tony Blair's Labour Party, the interests of the two would become interwoven through a series of meetings, personal connections, favourable coverage and policy announcements.

For the moment, though, News International was still confronted with Goodman and Mulcaire's employment cases; the Gordon Taylor legal action; and, more immediately, the parliamentary investigation by the Commons Culture Committee. On 3 July, the Culture Committee published its report. Though more sharply worded than the PCC's complacent findings, it must have been a relief to executives at Wapping. The MPs described Goodman's hacking of the royal household as a serious breach of journalistic ethics but seemingly accepted the company's excuse that it had been the result of lax controls on cash payments. Nonetheless the MPs said it was 'extraordinary' that the Press Complaints Commission had failed to question Andy Coulson, and criticized Fleet Street's 'complacency' towards the Information Commissioner's disclosure of the illegal searches conducted by Steve Whittamore. The committee warned the press that, unless it improved its behaviour, it would undermine its unique ability to regulate itself outside of the law.

In June 2007, Les Hinton settled the employment cases brought by Goodman and Mulcaire, authorizing a payment of £153,000 to Goodman (on top of the £90,000 he had already received) – despite his appeal being dismissed internally and externally – and £80,000 to Mulcaire. Goodman began freelancing at the *Daily Star Sunday*, a paper owned by Murdoch's fellow proprietor Richard Desmond. On being released from prison, Mulcaire was contracted to give security advice to a private security company, Quest, whose chairman, coincidentally, was Sir John Stevens, the former Met Police Commissioner.

Having successfully kept a lid on the phone hacking scandal, Rupert Murdoch consolidated his power. In August, he finally won his battle for the US publisher Dow Jones, giving him control of one of America's grandest papers, the *Wall Street Journal*. Murdoch had at first struggled to overcome the opposition of the owning Bancroft family, who saw themselves as custodians of independent journalism. In May, he had offered a 67 per cent premium to Dow Jones's share price, but the Bancrofts raised the Goodman and Mulcaire prosecution and Murdoch's alleged habit of interfering in the editorial contents of his papers. In a 1,200-word public letter on 14 May, Murdoch swooned over the Bancrofts, praising their 'record of journalistic independence', while attesting to his own virtues:

> Any interference – or even a hint of interference – would break the trust that exists between the paper and its readers, something I am unwilling to countenance . . . I don't apologize for the fact that I've always had strong opinions and strong ideas about newspapers, but I have always respected the independence and integrity of the news organizations with which I am associated.

He paid a top-of-the-market $5.7 billion to take over Dow Jones. Four months after his letter to the Bancrofts, Murdoch ditched any pretence that he did not interfere in his papers when he appeared before a private session of peers on the Lords Communications Committee in New York, on 17 September 2007. An appendix to the committee's report summarized his evidence:

> Mr Murdoch did not disguise the fact that he is hands on both economically and editorially. He says that 'the law' prevents him from instructing the editors of *The Times* and the *Sunday Times*. The independent board is there to make sure he cannot interfere and he never says 'do this or do that' although he often asks 'what are you doing?' He explained that he 'nominates' the editors of these two papers but that the nominations are subject to the approval of the independent board. His first appointment of an editor of *The Times* split the board but was not rejected.
>
> He distinguishes between *The Times* and the *Sunday Times* and

the *Sun* and the *News of the World* (and makes the same distinction between the *New York Post* and the *Wall Street Journal*). For the *Sun* and *News of the World* he explained that he is a 'traditional proprietor'. He exercises editorial control on major issues – like the party to back in a general election or policy on Europe.

In December 2007, Murdoch reshuffled his executives, sending Les Hinton, who had approved the secret payments to Goodman and Mulcaire, to New York to take charge of Dow Jones. He appointed his son James to chief executive of News Corp Europe and Asia, also making him chairman of News International. Promoting James to such a key post was a sign that the 76-year-old tycoon was dealing with a fraught question: his succession. Originally the presumption had been that his eldest son, Lachlan, would take over the chairmanship, but Lachlan had resigned as New's Corps deputy chief operating officer in August 2005, reportedly after a row with Rupert, and moved back to Australia (though he remained a director). Elisabeth, the most independently ambitious of Murdoch's three children by his second wife, Anna Torv, had shunned the family business since 2000, concentrating on growing her TV production company, Shine. She and her husband, Matthew Freud, the PR specialist behind Freud Communications, were powerful figures in London's medialand.

By contrast, James, the youngest son, had been a rebel. At the Horace Mann High School in New York he dyed his hair blond, got a tattoo and had his ears and an eyebrow pierced. Subsequently he dropped out of Harvard to found a hip-hop label, Rawkus, keeping a gun under his table to deal with some of its Uzi-carrying stars. After a succession of business flops, in 2000 James had turned around News Corp's loss-making Asian TV operation, Star, three years later becoming chief executive of Sky, where he increased the number of subscribers and boosted its environmental credentials. James was aggressively bright and impetuous, and conducted business meetings standing up behind his desk. He would soon take centre stage in the phone hacking affair.

While it had been settling the fallout from phone hacking, News International had also been helping to kill off the proposed jail term for data theft. On 13 December 2006 the Information Commissioner, Richard Thomas, had published the six-monthly update on his campaign in a new report, 'What Price Privacy Now?' In the foreword, he wrote: 'Progress has been significant and encouraging.' The report published a league table of Steve Whittamore's customers, naming for the first time his thirty-two newspaper and magazine clients – and the number of journalists ordering searches at each publication. It showed that, at the five most prolific titles, Whittamore had dealt with fifty-eight journalists at the *Daily Mail*, fifty at the *People*, forty-five at the *Daily Mirror*, thirty-three at the *Mail on Sunday* and twenty-three at the *News of the World*. The table put the number of transactions at 3,757 – rather than the 17,489 calculated by Alec Owens.

At the end of 2007, the Ministry of Justice drafted into the Criminal Justice and Immigration Bill a clause providing the option of a jail term for breaches of the Data Protection Act.

But in early 2008, Richard Thomas became aware that several newspaper groups were applying pressure on ministers to scrap the new custodial term, or, as he put it, 'press organizations were engaged in a powerful campaign against the proposal'.[10] On 11 February, the Justice Secretary, Jack Straw, who like most cabinet ministers sought a warm relationship with the press, informed Thomas that the clause was likely to be withdrawn. On 5 March, Thomas met Gordon Brown in Downing Street. Afterwards the Information Commissioner emailed colleagues at the ICO's headquarters in Wilmslow, Cheshire, to report back on a disappointment. While the prime minister considered the trade in personal information to be 'entirely unacceptable' and had been a victim of it personally in the past, 'he is concerned to strike the right balance with protecting freedom of expression, especially in relation to legitimate investigative journalism. Now that some time has been bought, he wants a compromise position to be achieved to minimize media concerns.'[11]

On 3 April, the government dropped Clause 129 containing the custodial option for breaches of the Data Protection Act.* Instead, min-

---

* In a speech to the Society of Editors in Bristol on 10 November 2008, Paul Dacre, editor of the *Daily Mail*, welcomed the end of the 'truly frightening' clause – and disclosed that he, Les Hinton and Murdoch MacLennan, chief executive of the *Daily Telegraph*, had lobbied Brown about it. Dacre said: 'This legislation would have made

isters would be given a reserve power to introduce custodial terms at a later, unspecified date. At the time of writing, this power has not been activated. The press had snuffed out tougher penalties for data theft.

In 2011, Richard Thomas told Lord Leveson: 'Whatever was precisely known about the nature and extent of misconduct across the industry as a whole, it became increasingly clear that the press were able to assert very substantial influence on public policy and the political processes.'

By the spring of 2008, News International had brushed off the Press Complaints Commission and the Commons Culture Committee, paid off both Goodman and Mulcaire and helped stifle stiffer penalties for data theft. A journalist and a private detective had been jailed. Their crimes had exposed the ease with which the security of mobile phones – increasingly widely used over the previous decade – could be breached, but despite a substantial body of evidence, the police had not followed up many leads, the watchdog had been asleep, and the newspaper industry had refrained from embarking on a period of soul-searching. After a brief interval of unemployment, the editor who had resigned had found another, weightier job – as one of the most important and trusted confidants of the next prime minister.

The only outstanding issue was Gordon Taylor.

Britain the only country in the free world to jail journalists and could have had a considerable chilling effect on good journalism. The Prime Minister – I don't think it is breaking any confidences to reveal – was hugely sympathetic to the industry's case.'

6

The Manchester Lawyers

In the light of these facts there is a powerful case that there
is (or was) a culture of illegal information access
— Michael Silverleaf, QC for News
International, 3 June 2008

In his offices in Manchester, Mark Lewis's difficulty was that he still
had no evidence that the *News of the World* had ordered the hacking
of Gordon Taylor's phone. He put together a team to fight the case,
bringing in Charlotte Harris, a media lawyer in George Davies's
sports department, and Jeremy Reed, a barrister at Hogarth Cham-
bers in Lincoln's Inn, London. Together they built an 'inferential' case:
Mulcaire had admitted hacking Taylor's phone; he worked for the
News of the World; therefore the *News of the World* must have
hacked Taylor's phone; therefore it must pay him damages. News
International responded to the case with derision, reserving the right
to have it struck out. Under the legal process of discovery, which com-
pels parties to court actions to disclose relevant information, Lewis
and Harris asked News International for its internal documents about
phone hacking. But, as Harris explained: 'The initial disclosure from
the *News of the World* was almost nothing. It was just a load of articles about the princes and they said they had nothing to disclose.'[1]

Lewis, a cussed individual, did not give up. He demanded Scotland
Yard hand over evidence about the targeting of Taylor from Operation Caryatid. The Metropolitan Police, which had thousands of

pages of Mulcaire's notes and other material, resisted disclosure, but in December 2007 a High Court judge, Nicholas Bragge, ordered its cooperation. At that hearing, according to Lewis, Mark Maberly, a detective sergeant in the Metropolitan Police, told him: 'You're not having everything, but we will give you enough on Taylor to hang them.' (Maberly denies saying this.)

When Taylor's legal team finally received the police evidence in January 2008, Reed phoned Harris at home and said: 'I've got the disclosure in. It's dynamite.' Scotland Yard had handed over three items seized from Mulcaire in August 2006: an audio recording of Mulcaire discussing hacking with an unnamed sports reporter; a contract from February 2005 signed by the NoW's Greg Miskiw promising to pay Mulcaire £7,000 for a story about Taylor; and an email dated 29 June 2005 from a NoW reporter, Ross Hindley, to Mulcaire (at his address shadowmenuk@yahoo.co.uk), titled 'Hello, this is a transcript for Neville'. The 'For Neville' email, as it became known, contained the transcripts of thirty-five voicemail messages, including seventeen left by Taylor on Armstrong's phone and thirteen vice versa. The messages were simply casual exchanges between two colleagues, but they were incriminating because they had clearly been hacked – and had now been disclosed to their victim. On one, Armstrong had told Taylor: 'Thank you for yesterday. You were great.'* At the same time Lewis had obtained from the Information Commissioner News International's requests to Steve Whittamore.

In April, when News International's executives received copies of the police disclosures, they were alarmed. The 'For Neville' email – sent by one *News of the World* journalist with a title referring to another, Neville Thurlbeck – was clear proof that reporters other than Goodman knew about hacking. On 24 May, Tom Crone, the *News of the World*'s lawyer, emailed Colin Myler with the bad news: the email contained a large number of transcripts of voicemails from Taylor's telephone, while the Information Commissioner's material

---

* The incident in July 2005 when Taylor had caught a *News of the World* photographer taking pictures of him and Jo Armstrong now made sense. Lewis explained that Armstrong had been thanking Taylor for delivering the eulogy at her father's funeral.

included a 'list of named *News of the World* journalists and a detailed table of Data Protection Infringements between 2001 and 2003 ...' Crone pointed out: 'A number of those names are still with us and some of them have moved to prominent positions on *NoW* and the *Sun*. Typical infringements are "turning round" car reg, and mobile phone numbers (illegal).'[2] Under the heading 'Where we go', Crone stressed:

> This evidence, particularly the email from the *News of the World*, is fatal to our case. Our position is very perilous. The damning email is genuine and proves we actively made use of a large number of extremely private voicemails from Taylor's telephone in June/July 2005 and that this was pursuant to a February 2005 contract, i.e. a 5/6 month operation. He [Taylor] has no evidence that the *News of the World* continued to act illegally after that but he can prove Mulcaire continued to access his mobile until May 2006 (because Mulcaire pleaded guilty to it). We will be getting guidance from a senior QC next week about our next step.

Mark Lewis told Julian Pike, partner at News International's law firm Farrer & Co, that his client wanted to be 'vindicated [in court] or made rich'. Taylor was effectively demanding a large payment in return for silence, such a big pay-off would have to be approved by News International's new chairman, James Murdoch. On 27 May, Pike recorded Myler's position: 'Spoke to James Murdoch – not any options – wait for silk's view.'

On 3 June, the legal opinion arrived – and it was horrendous. Michael Silverleaf QC said the 'For Neville' email, the Miskiw contract and the requests to Whittamore were 'overwhelming evidence' that a number of News International journalists had broken the law. Silverleaf wrote:

> In the light of these facts there is a powerful case that there is (or was) a culture of illegal information access used at NGN [a News International subsidiary, which owned the *News of the World*] in order to produce stories for publication. Not only does this mean that NGN is virtually certain to be held liable to Mr Taylor, to have this paraded

at a public trial would, I imagine, be extremely damaging to NGN's public reputation.[3]

Silverleaf estimated that if the case went to court a judge could award up to £250,000 damages. That was off the scale for a privacy case. The highest previous privacy payout had been the £14,600 *Hello!* had paid Michael Douglas and Catherine Zeta-Jones in 2000 for publishing unauthorized photographs of their wedding. News International's problem was that Gordon Taylor was furious that he had been illegally targeted and that Hinton had misled Parliament by suggesting that Clive Goodman was a rogue reporter when, Taylor knew, phone hacking had been more widespread.

On 3 June, News International offered Taylor an extraordinary £350,000 plus his costs, a total of about £550,000, in a Part 36 offer – which meant that Taylor could be lumbered with a bill of hundreds of thousands of pounds if he took his case to court. News International probably thought its offer, and the risks of not accepting it, were high enough.

On 6 June, Mark Lewis phoned Julian Pike and demanded a jaw-dropping £1 million damages and £200,000 costs. In his file notes, Pike noted Lewis's explanation of his client's thinking:

Want to show NoW stories – NoW doing this – rife in organization – Palt [Parliament] inquiries told this not happening when it was. I want to speak out on this.

Gordon Taylor and News International were engaged in a high-stakes game of bluff and counter-bluff. If Taylor insisted on humbling the company in court he risked losing hundreds of thousands of pounds; on the other hand, he knew that News International desperately did not want the case to be publicly aired because it would be hugely embarrassing and sink its 'rogue reporter' defence. Other victims of hacking would realize that they too could sue and the costs of those cases would far outweigh the amount he was demanding.

At 2.31 p.m. on Saturday 7 June, in an email neither of them could ever have expected would be made public three years later, Colin Myler informed James Murdoch of developments:

James

Update on the Gordon Taylor (Professional Football Association) case.

Unfortunately it is as bad as we feared.

The note from Julian Pike of Farrer's is extremely telling regarding Taylor's vindictiveness.

It would be helpful if Tom Crone and I could have five minutes with you on Tuesday.

Colin[4]

Myler forwarded Pike's account of his conversation with Mark Lewis the night before. Three minutes after receiving the email chain at 2.34 p.m., Murdoch replied: 'No worries. I am in during the afternoon. If you want to talk before I'll be home tonight after seven and most of the day tomorrow.'[5] He later said he did not 'review the full e-mail chain at the time or afterwards'.

Whether Myler and Murdoch talked that weekend is not known. However, they and Tom Crone met for half an hour at Wapping the following Tuesday 10 June to discuss the case. What happened would be hotly disputed three years later: Crone said that he had taken in the 'For Neville' email and the Silverleaf opinion to show Murdoch – but Murdoch insisted he saw neither. What is indisputable is that James agreed to pay Gordon Taylor even more: £425,000 plus his legal fees of £220,000. Taylor accepted. He had wanted to expose News International's lies but he was prepared to stay silent if paid enough and the balance was tipped at £425,000.

After the wrangling was over, Tom Crone invited Mark Lewis to a conciliatory lunch at El Vino's wine bar in Fleet Street in November 2008. The atmosphere was jovial until Crone settled the bill, at which point Lewis announced that he had two other clients who had been hacked by News International. Crone quickly left the bar.

In early 2009, Lewis's team won further payouts of around £100,000 damages for Jo Armstrong, who had left messages on Gordon Taylor's phone, and another sports lawyer who had dealt with Taylor, John Hewison, a partner at George Davies, who received

£10,000, plus substantial costs. At the insistence of News International, the settlements remained confidential: there was a risk that if the other four non-royal victims found out, they too would start legal actions.

This was a disappointment to Lewis and Harris, who had been hoping that publicity would trigger new claims, which would dismantle what they increasingly suspected was a cover-up. But because the deals were private they received no media coverage. Signing a confidentiality agreement also meant that Taylor could not relay his experience of phone hacking to members of the Professional Footballers' Association, several of whom turned out to be victims too.

Gordon Taylor had not been vindicated in court, but he had been made rich.

While the Taylor settlement had been thrashed out, the *News of the World* had subjected another individual to intrusive reporting. In March 2008, the paper's intrequid chief reporter, Neville Thurlbeck was investigating the private life of motor racing executive Max Mosley, the son of the fascist politician Oswald Mosley. After reading physics at Oxford, Mosley had been called to the bar, but his passion was motor racing and in 1993 he had become president of the world governing body for motor-sport in Paris, the Fédération Internationale de l'Automobile. In his own time, Mosley occasionally participated in sado-masochistic orgies. Although not ashamed of this activity, he was aware that many people would disapprove of it and kept it from his wife, family and colleagues. While the world of S&M usually carefully guarded its secrets, a forthcoming participant at one of Mosley's parties, known as 'Michelle', had mentioned his name to her husband, an MI5 agent, who realized Mosley might make a valuable story and contacted the *News of the World*. Thurlbeck offered 'Michelle' £25,000 and coached her how to record Mosley performing a Sieg Heil salute. The orgy, themed on a correctional camp, duly took place at an apartment in Chelsea on Friday 28 March. After it was over, Mosley and the women had a chat and a cup of tea.

Two days later, the *News of the World*'s front page screamed: 'F1 Boss in Sick Nazi Orgy with Five Hookers', with the strapline 'Son of Hitler-loving fascist in sex shame'. When Mosley showed the paper to his wife she thought her mischievous husband had mocked it up, but it was not a joke. Publication alerted Mosley's wife, his family, his friends, his colleagues at the FIA and tens of millions of people to his sexual behaviour, which he had been lawfully practising in private at private premises. The *NoW* had posted a ninety-second video clip online, where it was watched 1.4 million times.

Mosley, a genial but flinty character, set about getting his revenge. To ensure he was not being eavesdropped by the *News of the World*, he hired the Quest security consultancy, whose operatives stood watch over a walled garden in Chelsea while he met the arranger of the session, 'Woman A', as she was later known in court. Together they worked out he must have been betrayed by 'Michelle'. MI5 sacked her husband after learning he had sold a story to the newspapers.

As Mosley battled to restore his reputation, the *News of the World* sought to gather more material about him for another story the following Sunday. On Wednesday 2 April, Thurlbeck emailed one of the female participants, threatening that unless she and the other women involved agreed to cooperate in a follow-up story, the paper would publish unpixilated pictures of them at the orgy and thus identify them. The women, some of whom had professional jobs, were horrified, but did not give in to the threats.

Tabloids usually bargained that anyone whose sex life had been exposed would not sue because a court case allowed embarrassing details to be reported by all papers and TV stations without fear of legal action. But on Friday 4 April 2008, Mosley sued the *News of the World* for breach of privacy. During the three-week trial in the High Court in July, the *News of the World*'s QC, Mark Warby, subjected Mosley to an extensive cross-examination on his sex life, but he stood firm: he explained that the paper had conflated two scenes, one of an English prison camp and a second where he had happened to speak German, which, he explained, he had done as a favour to one of the women, whose fantasy was to be ordered about in a foreign language. The *News of the World* admitted it had not bothered to translate Mosley's German remarks to check whether they contained Nazi references. 'Michelle' did not turn up to testify for the *NoW* because she was 'feeling unwell'. (The paper had 'renegotiated' her fee down to £12,500 because Mosley had not performed a Sieg Heil.) To the surprise of the *News of the World*, the other dominatrices gave evidence for Mosley.

Delivering judgment on 24 July 2008, Mr Justice Eady described Thurlbeck's testimony as 'erratic and changeable' and remarked that the *News of the World*'s failure to discipline him for sending an email verging on blackmail was 'a remarkable state of affairs'. He ruled there had been no Nazi element to the orgy nor any public interest in the story's publication. On Mosley's use of German, the judge noted: 'It contained a certain amount of explicit sexual language about what the claimant [Mosley] and Woman B were planning to do to those women in the submissive role, but nothing specifically Nazi, and certainly nothing to do with concentration camps.' Eady awarded Mosley £60,000 damages and his costs. However, the court later taxed down* Mosley's costs, meaning that despite winning the case he lost £30,000.

News International's redtops, which had long decried judgments arising from the 1998 Human Rights Act – which enshrined a right to privacy in British law – were furious. The *Sun* described the ruling as a 'dark day for British freedom' and a step towards 'a dangerous European-style privacy law'. The *News of the World* complained that the powerful should not be able to run to the courts to gag papers from publishing 'true' stories, adding: 'This is all about the public's right to know.'

Mosley began suing the *News of the World* in other European countries where the paper had been sold. Just as significantly, from his home in Monaco he started to take an interest in the phone hacking affair. News International had just made an intelligent, tenacious and wealthy enemy.

Meanwhile, David Cameron was making friends – or, more particularly one big friend: Rebekah Wade. Since their school days at Eton,

---

* Courts assess the reasonableness of the victor's costs and sometimes reduce them. In this case, the High Court ruled that News International should pay only £420,000 of Mosley's legal bill, leaving him to find the remaining £90,000.

Cameron had been a pal of Wade's new beau, Charlie 'Looks' Brooks, a racehorse owner and socialite. The couple lived amid the sweet greenery and amber farmhouses of the Cotswolds, a few miles from Cameron's wisteria-clad constituency home in the hamlet of Dean. Cameron and Brooks would play tennis together and go riding, sometimes on a retired police horse called Raisa that Wade had borrowed from the Metropolitan Police after a lunch with the Commissioner, Sir Ian Blair. At 'country suppers', Wade, Brooks, and David and Samantha Cameron discussed politics and other matters of the day. By 2008 and 2009, they were meeting about once a month. Cameron said later:

> We got to know each other because of her role in the media, my role in politics, but we struck up a friendship. The friendship grew, even though at that stage her paper was still supporting Gordon Brown and our friendship got stronger when she married Charlie Brooks, who I've known for some time and who's a neighbour.[6]

So warm was the relationship that Cameron would sign off his frequent text messages to Wade 'LOL', which he thought meant 'Lots of Love'.*

With Rebekah Wade his friend and Andy Coulson leading his media team, Cameron began to reach out to the Murdochs. On 16 August 2008, in a journey redolent of Tony Blair's homage trip to Australia in 1995, he boarded Matthew Freud's Gulfstream jet for Santorini in Greece, where he joined Rupert Murdoch for drinks on his yacht, *Rosehearty*. What Cameron and Murdoch discussed remains a mystery, but from that point their interests began to converge.

Murdoch newspapers had never hidden their dislike of the BBC and Ofcom, respectively Sky's competitor and regulator. The Conservative leader echoed the sentiments. On 3 November 2008, five days after hosting a dinner for James Murdoch and his wife Kathryn, he penned a comment piece for the *Sun* headlined 'Bloated BBC out of

---

* When the extent of the text messaging became clear later, Wade pointed out it usually meant 'Laugh Out Loud' – which is what the country did.

touch with the viewers' protesting at rises in the licence fee.[7] In January 2009, the Conservatives' Culture spokesman Ed Vaizey promised the party would force the BBC to publish the salaries of its highest-paid performers.[8] On 6 July 2009, Cameron announced in a speech that he intended to remove the policy-making powers of Ofcom: 'So with a Conservative government, Ofcom as we know it will cease to exist,' the Conservative leader said.[9] Cameron and Murdoch had got into bed with each other.

Rebekah Wade had been the marriage-broker. In the summer of 2009, she was at the height of her power. Rupert Murdoch had told her that she would shortly become the chief executive of News International, responsible for all its influential newspapers; and in June, her marriage to Charlie Brooks had confirmed her position at the hub of a political and media nexus. Guests at the wedding reception, held on the 284-acre Sarsden estate in Oxfordshire, included Gordon Brown, the Prime Minister, David Cameron, George Osborne, the shadow Chancellor of the Exchequer, Will Lewis, editor of the *Daily Telegraph*, her pop star neighbour Alex James, and the most powerful Murdochs – Rupert and James, and Elisabeth and Matthew Freud, too.

All was going well. Except that a reporter on a rival paper was preparing an explosive story.

7

One Determined Reporter

Very relaxed

    – a spokesman for David Cameron, giving his response
    to Nick Davies's story on Gordon Taylor, July 2009

Nick Davies, a 56-year-old investigative reporter with a swirl of receding white hair, eschewed regular contact with executives at the *Guardian*. His contract stipulated he had to write only twenty-four substantial features a year 'or the equivalent in time and effort' – which meant that unlike the vast majority of journalists he could stay on one story. Working from his home in Lewes, East Sussex, he responded by exploring the hidden sides of British life: poverty, failing schools, drug addiction and child prostitution. Frustrated by the mis-reporting of the Iraq War, in 2007 he wrote a book about falsehood and distortion in the media, *Flat Earth News*, which contained a chapter on Steve Whittamore – and described how Fleet Street news-papers illegally obtained criminal records, car registration details, ex-directory numbers, mobile phone records and bank statements.

Davies then had two strokes of luck which impelled him towards a bigger scandal. The first was that Stuart Kuttner, the *News of the World*'s managing editor, appeared alongside him on BBC Radio 4's *Today* programme in February 2008 and dismissed his newly pub-lished book as 'sour and gloomy'. Kuttner complained: 'If you read Nick's book you get a view of British journalism as a corrupt profes-sion but I think it's the finest in the world. It is admired throughout the world and rightly so. My reporters wouldn't recognize that description at all,' adding that hacking 'happened once' at the *News of the World*. 'The reporter was fired, he went to prison. The editor resigned.' After the programme a *News of the World* insider contacted Davies and told him the scale of illegality at the paper. Davies said: 'I felt it was the sheer, brazen dishonesty of Kuttner that made that person get in touch.'[1]

The second piece of good fortune was that soon afterwards Davies found himself at a social function sitting 'next to somebody very senior from the Met', who casually referred to the fact that Glenn Mulcaire's notes contained 'thousands of names'.[2] By now the notes were in storage at Scotland Yard; that they were opened again owed much to what Davies did next. Throughout 2008 and early 2009, while working on other projects, he scanned back copies of the *News of the World* to identify 'interesting' stories and began contacting their authors. Many former *NoW* journalists willingly spoke to him because of bullying at the paper; and would refer him to others who were similarly aggrieved: 'They would say: "I know such and such hated that boss."' But they wanted to stay anonymous because Rupert Murdoch was so powerful, or because they were freelancing or in PR and were trying to sell stories to News International.[3]

Eventually, Davies gathered enough material. The *Guardian*'s editor, Alan Rusbridger, recalled: 'In early 2009 he came in and closed the door and said: "I've got this amazing story" and he told me about the Gordon Taylor settlement, and it was immediately obvious that this was a story that would cause enormous trouble.'[4] At 5.33 p.m. on 8 July 2009, the *Guardian* website (and the newspaper the following day) published the story: 'Murdoch papers paid £1m to gag phone-hacking victims':

> Rupert Murdoch's News Group Newspapers has paid out more than £1 million to settle legal cases that threatened to reveal evidence of his journalists' repeated involvement in the use of criminal methods to get stories.

It was the single most important story in the phone hacking scandal.* For the first time Davies referred publicly to the 'For Neville'

---

* Davies has never disclosed his 'multiple sources' for the Gordon Taylor story.

email (though he omitted its title) and revealed that Wapping had settled with Taylor for around £400,000 damages plus costs and paid two 'other football figures' [Taylor's two lawyers] £300,000 in damages and costs. Davies quoted a police source as saying News International journalists had hacked into 'thousands' of mobile phones, and suggested that the targets included John Prescott. He also mentioned the *NoW*'s use of Steve Whittamore searches to obtain tax records, social security files, bank statements and itemized phone bills. While many journalists and politicians had been sceptical that Clive Goodman had been the only hacker at the *News of the World*, the proof had been missing. Now it was clear that the *NoW* had paid out a vast sum to secure the silence of a union leader who was likely to have been eavesdropped by other journalists. The Press Complaints Commission, which had fallen for the *News of the World*'s deceit in 2007, launched a new inquiry. From the G8 summit in Italy, Gordon Brown said the story raised serious questions that 'have to be answered'. Prescott urged the Leader of the Opposition to sack Andy Coulson, who had been editing the *News of the World* during the hacking. Geoff Hoon, the Labour former cabinet minister, said: 'It is hard to see how in these circumstances Andy Coulson can continue as David Cameron's communications chief.' However, Cameron's office batted off the demands, telling the *Daily Telegraph* that the Conservative leader was 'very relaxed about the story'. Asked that evening by Bloomberg news wire about the payment to Gordon Taylor, Rupert Murdoch replied: 'If that had happened, I would have known about it.'[5]

Shortly after 9 a.m. the following day, 9 July, the Metropolitan Police's new Commissioner, Sir Paul Stephenson, a Lancastrian former shoe salesman with a reputation for straight talking, announced that he was asking a senior officer to look into the *Guardian*'s allegations. Educated at Marlborough College and a history graduate of King's College London, Assistant Commissioner John Yates was one of a new breed of politically astute senior officers. Like his predecessor in counter-terrorism, Andy Hayman, he regularly dined with journalists, including the *News of the World*'s deputy editor, Neil Wallis, a long-standing friend, with whom he would have regular lunches and dinners that were not declared in the Met's Register of Hospitality on the grounds that they were 'private engagements'. Yates had taken on some high-profile cases, investigating allegations that Labour had sold peerages and that Princess Diana's former butler Paul Burrell had stolen her possessions. Neither had resulted in a conviction, but they established him in the minds of his friends in Fleet Street as a fearless investigator: 'Yates of the Yard'.

That day, too, Keir Starmer, the new Director of Public Prosecutions, launched an 'urgent' examination of the evidence Operation Caryatid had supplied to the Crown Prosecution Service in 2006. The CPS examined the case for a week, but despite the political heat, Yates's review was over in hours. At 11 a.m. he convened a 'gold meeting' in Room 556 of the Victoria Block of Scotland Yard with eight senior staff, including the now-promoted Detective Chief Inspector Philip Williams. The minutes of the meeting gave a curious account of Operation Caryatid:

> Why was there not a more wide-ranging investigation?
>
> There was no evidence to expand the investigation under which if had done, then this would have been an ineffective use of police resources.
>
> Did we alert others?
>
> Yes ... No evidence to support wider phones had been intercepted. Wider people were not informed as there was no evidence to suggest any criminal activities on their phones.
>
> What other journalists were involved?
>
> There was no evidence at that time to implicate the involvement of any other journalists.[6]

The minutes added: 'PW [Detective Chief Superintendent Philip Williams] confirmed that he had no knowledge of John Prescott's phone being intercepted. If he had been subject to interception and evidence supported this then he would have been informed.'[7]

At 5.40 that evening, 'Yates of the Yard' announced that there was nothing new in the story; the Metropolitan Police had been in possession of the 'For Neville' email in 2006 – and its inquiry then had been a success. Yates said: 'Their potential targets may have run into hundreds of people, but our inquiries showed that they only used the tactic against a far smaller number of individuals . . . in the majority of cases there was insufficient evidence to show that tapping had actually been achieved.' Where there was 'clear evidence' of hacking, Yates said, all the individuals concerned had been informed. He concluded: 'I therefore consider that no further investigation is required.'

On 10 July, other papers followed up the *Guardian*'s allegations but focused on Yates's refusal to reopen the inquiry. The *Daily Telegraph* quoted a Conservative Party spokesman as saying: 'Labour have made themselves look stupid by following a story that fell apart within twenty-four hours.'

That afternoon News International, which privately knew the 'For Neville' email was a 'fatal' document, poured scorn on the story. In a statement, the company 'stated with confidence' that there was not and never had been any evidence to suggest that – apart from Goodman's royal hacking and the Taylor case – journalists at the *News of the World* had accessed anyone's voicemails, saying: 'All of these irresponsible and unsubstantiated allegations against the *News of the World* and other News International titles and its journalists are false.' Senior executives knew this to be untrue.

Despite Yates's statement, behind the scenes at Scotland Yard there was some concern that perhaps not all the potential victims had been contacted. At 7.36 p.m. on Friday 10 July (after most newspaper deadlines), Scotland Yard slipped out a statement saying that it would contact anyone where there was 'any suspicion' they had been targeted, adding: 'The process of contacting people is currently underway and we expect this to take some time to complete.' If the original police investigation had indeed been complete, as the Yard claimed, the need to contact new victims was puzzling.

The following day, News International's newspapers launched an offensive against the *Guardian*, starting with *The Times*,* whose then media editor Dan Sabbagh faithfully trotted out the company line:

* At the time, *The Times* was covering up its own newsgathering scandal. A reporter had hacked into the emails of a Lancashire Detective Constable, Richard Horton, to identify him as the anonymous police blogger 'Nightjack'. When Horton launched a legal challenge, *The Times* had misled the High Court by giving the false impression

1. Rupert Murdoch in London in 1969, the year the 38-year-old Australian took over his first British newspaper, the *News of the World*. He dominated Fleet Street for four decades.

2. The 80-year-old tycoon under pressure the day after defending his company's conduct in front of the Commons Culture Committee. Most rival papers' front pages screamed 'Humble pie', but *The Times* came out for its proprietor.

3. Young tabloid editors Piers Morgan, Rebekah Wade and Andy Coulson partying at the home of Elisabeth Murdoch and Matthew Freud in 2004, when the *News of the World* was systematically hacking phones.

4. Flirtatious and charming, at least with the powerful, Wade made sure she was friendly with senior politicians – including Tony Blair, the Labour Prime Minister, who was endorsed by News International papers at three successive general elections.

5. BSkyB's chief executive, James Murdoch, Rupert's son and heir, wooed the new Conservative leader, David Cameron, and his close ally George Osborne, the Shadow Chancellor. In 2007, they enjoyed each other's company at a summit on social responsibility.

6. Tommy Sheridan and his wife Gail celebrate their libel victory over the *News of the World* in 2006, beginning an epic legal struggle between the socialist politician and the Murdochs' British newspaper group.

7. Police found thousands of names and PIN codes in the notes of Glenn Mulcaire. The Crown Prosecution Service charged the private detective with hacking the phones of eight individuals. After his release from prison, News International settled his claim against them for £85,000. He has since remained silent.

8. Clive Goodman, the *News of the World*'s royal editor, was jailed in January 2007 for eavesdropping royal phone calls. He subsequently received settlements totalling £243,000 from News International. Like Mulcaire, has since remained silent.

9. Rupert Murdoch's right-hand man, Les Hinton, authorized the payments to Goodman and Mulcaire in 2007, before leaving the UK to take charge of News Corp's new acquisition, Dow Jones.

10. By splashing the private life of the Formula 1 motor-racing chief Max Mosley over its front page, the *News of the World* made an intelligent, wealthy and tenacious enemy.

11. Gordon Taylor, chief executive of the Professional Footballers' Association, was the first phone-hacking victim to mount a legal challenge to News International. In June 2008 he accepted an out-of-court settlement of £425,000.

12. With her fellow Manchester lawyer Mark Lewis (plate 33), Charlotte Harris took on the *News of the World*. In a failed bid to discredit her, the newspaper placed her under surveillance.

13. From his home in Lewes, East Sussex, the *Guardian*'s Nick Davies was one of the indefatigable individuals who unpicked the 'rogue reporter' defence and humbled Murdoch's $60 billion News Corp.

14. The *News of the World*'s chief reporter, Neville Thurlbeck, for whom the infamous 'for Neville' email was intended.

15. 'Yates of the Yard': John Yates, Assistant Commissioner of the Metropolitan Police, who in 2009 declared his faith in the original police investigation, Operation Caryatid, after a review lasting several hours.

16. John Yates's good friend Neil 'Wolfman' Wallis, deputy editor of the *News of the World*. In 2009, Scotland Yard gave him a job. In 2011 it arrested him.

17. Despite being warned about Andy Coulson's past, the Conservative leader's director of communications was too useful to lose. With the former *News of the World* editor by his side, David Cameron found the 'tabloid touch'.

18. Within months of winning most seats at the May 2010 general election with Murdoch's support, the Conservatives backed News Corp's £7bn takeover bid for Britain's richest TV network, BSkyB.

News International last night criticized 'selective and misleading journalism' by the *Guardian* newspaper and rebutted allegations that reporters on the *News of the World* engaged in widespread hacking into celebrities' mobile phones.

The *News of the World* joined the attack the following day, 12 July, describing the *Guardian*'s reporting as 'inaccurate, selective and purposely misleading'. Both *The Times* and the *News of the World* carried an article by a new columnist who explained that while there had been several hundred names in Mulcaire's notes, only 'perhaps a handful' had actually been hacked. 'Had there been evidence of tampering in the other cases, that would have been investigated, as would the slightest hint that others were involved,' wrote the columnist, who had a special insight into the inquiry. In July 2008, eight months after he had resigned from the Metropolitan Police during an inquiry into his expenses, Andy Hayman, who had overseen Caryatid, had joined News International.* As well as having a former editor next to the Conservative leader, Wapping was now employing a former senior policeman from Scotland Yard.

Some media commentators pointed to the significance of the Taylor story: Andrew Neil, a former editor of the *Sunday Times*, said he was 'shocked' by the allegations of such widespread lawbreaking; others such as the *Independent*'s Stephen Glover condemned the 'hysteria'. On Monday 13 July Glover wrote:

> Mr Davies is a journalist who dislikes much journalism, especially of the tabloid variety. He recently published a book which suggests that the press is wildly dysfunctional. I've never had the pleasure of meeting him, but he seems to me to be a misanthropic, apocalyptic sort of fellow – the sort of journalist who can find a scandal in a jar of tadpoles.

---

that it had obtained the story honestly. *The Times* stayed quiet about the incident for two years, until the truth was dragged out of it in 2012 by the Leveson Inquiry.

* Hayman, who enjoyed champagne dinners with journalists, had racked up £19,000 on his Scotland Yard Amex credit card in two years. He denied he had misused his expenses. In April 2008, an independent report by Gwent's Chief Constable Mike Tongue, overseen by the Independent Police Complaints Commission, cleared him of any misconduct.

On Thursday 16 July, a week after launching his internal inquiry, the Director of Public Prosecutions, Keir Starmer, announced there was no need to reopen the case. After speaking to his predecessor as DPP, Ken Macdonald, and the then Attorney General, Lord Goldsmith, Starmer deemed the original prosecution to have been 'proper and appropriate'. He explained that under the law on phone hacking, the Regulation of Investigatory Powers Act (see p. 36), intercepting a phone communication was illegal only 'in the course of its transmission', and so did not apply when it had been heard by the owner of the phone. Even if there were many names in Mulcaire's notes, they were not necessarily victims. What was striking about this interpretation is that it had not been the one used at Goodman and Mulcaire's trial by the CPS barrister David Perry, who had explicitly stated that RIPA covered saved messages.

Despite the lack of concern from police and prosecutors, the Taylor story prompted Max Clifford to phone George Davies and ask to meet the lawyers who had won his case. The law firm was reluctant to take on another phone hacking case (Taylor had complained about the *Guardian* story) but by then Charlotte Harris had moved to another law firm in Manchester, JMW, and Clifford instructed her to sue.

Another victim, Chris Bryant, now a Foreign Office minister, was also stirred. On 30 November 2003, eight months after the MP had asked Rebekah Wade the tricky question about payments to police, the *News of the World* and the *Mail on Sunday* had published a picture of him in his underpants on the Gaydar website. The following Sunday, the *NoW* reported that Bryant was facing the sack. The *Sunday Times*, in an unusually abusive profile, described the former vicar as a 'pillock' and 'bumptious little berk': 'Short, fair-haired and with his eyes set wide apart, Bryant has used the sanctimonious tones of his former vocation to lecture MPs on morality.' Humiliated, Bryant received hate mail, acquired a stalker and feared his political career was over. He said: 'It's the closest I've ever been to suicidal.'[8] As he read more about the behaviour of the *News of the World*, he remembered that his London flat had been broken into in 2003 and began to fear his phone had been hacked, and perhaps his computer too. After reading Davies's article, he wrote to Scotland Yard asking whether he was in the Mulcaire files. The police took eight months to reply.

The actress Sienna Miller, too, was becoming increasingly convinced that her phone had been hacked. With astonishing accuracy between 2004 and 2006, the *News of the World* had chronicled her life with the Hollywood actor Jude Law, often with punning headlines such as 'How Jude do that?' in August 2005 (about an argument) and 'Jude's not Sien her any more' in July 2006 (about the end of their relationship). During that period calls Miller answered quickly went dead, voicemails she had not listened to appeared in her inbox as 'old', and messages from friends and family never arrived. She changed her mobile phone three times in late 2005 but the stories kept appearing. She began to suspect that she was being betrayed by someone close to her, and started leaving messages for friends with bogus snippets of information which would duly appear in print. She accused her friends and family of betraying her: 'I sat down in a room with my mother, my best friend, my sister, my boyfriend and said: "Someone in this room is lying and selling stories and one of you has got to admit it."'[9] Mark Thomson, Miller's lawyer, wrote to the Met asking whether she featured in Mulcaire's notes. As with Bryant, the letter went unanswered for months.

While the police stonewalled, the MPs on the cross-party Culture Committee decided to look afresh at the *News of the World*. The committee was just concluding another inquiry into the press, prompted by newspapers' repeated libelling of Kate and Gerry McCann, whose three-year-old daughter had gone missing in Portugal. During that inquiry, phone hacking had been so forgotten that the *NoW*'s Colin Myler and Tom Crone were not even asked about it when they gave evidence in May, when the focus had been on the treatment of Max Mosley. (That month, one of Mosley's two sons, Alexander, a long-term drug addict, had died of cocaine intoxication. Alexander had temporarily managed to beat his addiction before the *News of the World*'s exposure of his father's sado-masochism. Mosley believed the story had devastated his son and was a contributory factor in his death.)

Myler and Crone were summoned back to the committee. Its new-est member was Tom Watson. While at the Cabinet Office, Watson had taken the unusual step of suing the *Sun* for smearing him during the Damian McBride affair (see pp.8–10). News International had asked Number 10 aides to pressure Watson into dropping the claim, and he was called by the Attorney General, Baroness Scotland, who advised him it would be 'unwise' to proceed while a minister. Watson did not drop the case, but returned to the backbenches in June and the following month had joined the Culture, Media and Sport Commit-tee, where he hoped to pursue his interest in the digital economy.

On the eve of Myler and Crone's reappearance on 21 July, News International wrote to the committee's chairman, John Whittingdale, demanding Watson be removed from the hearing on the basis that he was still in dispute with the *Sun*, even though it had accepted weeks before that it had defamed him and all that remained was to reach a settlement about the damages and apology. After taking advice from parliamentary lawyers, Whittingdale rejected the request. At the start of the session, Crone repeated the demand, warning Whittingdale: 'If he [Watson] remains we will be making a complaint to the Parliamen-tary Commissioner.' News International never made the complaint but its attempt to eject the MP was a good PR trick: it, rather than the substance of the hearing, became a breaking story on Sky News.

With its demand frustrated, News International now had to sur-vive the session without making any embarrassing admissions. Even without public knowledge that Mulcaire's notes ran to 11,000 pages, that NI's counsel had identified a 'culture of illegal information gath-ering', and that sizeable pay-offs had already been made to Goodman and Mulcaire, the company's story was a mess. Les Hinton had told the committee in March 2007 that Goodman was the only reporter who hacked voicemails; yet it had now emerged that the *News of the World* had secretly paid off another victim who was very unlikely to have been hacked by Goodman.

Myler and Crone's tactics soon emerged: confusion, obfuscation and spectacular feats of memory loss. They could not remember who had done what, nor, they added, could their colleagues. Operation Caryatid had been very thorough, they stressed. Crone said:

The police raided Mulcaire's premises, they raided Goodman's premises, and they raided the *News of the World*'s offices. They seized
every available document; they searched all the computers, all the
files, the emails. Subsequent to the arrests they came to us and made
various requests to us to produce documents. At no stage during their
investigation or our investigation did any evidence arise that the
problem of accessing by our reporters, or complicity of accessing by
our reporters, went beyond the Goodman/Mulcaire situation.[10]

Not much was known, they said, about the 'For Neville' email,
except that it showed the *NoW* had hacked Taylor's phone and thus
the paper had settled. The MPs wanted to know if the Neville was
Neville Thurlbeck, the chief reporter. 'I questioned Neville Thurlbeck
then, and I have spoken to him about the same subject since,' Crone
replied. 'His position is that he has never seen that email, nor had any
knowledge of it.' He explained that Ross Hindley, the journalist who
transcribed the hacked messages, had been unable to remember
whether he had sent the email to Thurlbeck.

Myler and Crone flatly denied any reporter other than Clive Goodman had taken part in phone hacking. When the Conservative MP
Philip Davies challenged that, Myler replied: 'No evidence, Mr Davies, has been produced internally or externally by the police, by any
lawyers, to suggest that what you have said is the truth, is the case.'
Myler failed to point out that Thurlbeck himself – not a lawyer or a
police officer – had alleged the involvement of others (see chapter 21).

The committee was incredulous. Despite the *News of the World*
paying a convicted phone hacker more than £100,000 a year, only
one reporter had apparently colluded with him. Asked whether Mulcaire had been paid £200,000 to stay silent – a report in *Private
Eye* – Myler said: 'I am not aware of any payment that has been
made.' Crone said: 'I had nothing to do with that area, because if there
is any sort of payment or dealings with Mulcaire it is not going to be
in my area.' Pressed by Davies: 'It did not take place?' Crone reluctantly agreed that Mulcaire had been paid something:

> The employment laws as they stand, as I understand it, and I am cer
> tainly no expert in this area, mean that if someone works for you for X

hours a week it does not matter whether he is staff, he is freelance or is on a contract, whatever, he has certain employment rights. Given those employment rights there is a process that has to be followed when that relationship comes to an end. Because of failures, and we can possibly check it out there was a sum of money paid to him. I do not know exactly what it is, but it bears no relation to the figure you have given us.

As senior executives knew, News International had paid Mulcaire £80,000 two years previously (see chapter 5). The Labour MP Paul Farrelly, a former *Observer* journalist, asked whether Goodman, too, had received a pay-off. Initially Crone said he was not 'aware' of one, but later added: 'I have a feeling there may have been a payment of some sort.' (Goodman had received £243,000.)

Tom Watson had barely noticed the jailing of Goodman and Mulcaire in 2007, but he was riled by Crone's attempt to have him thrown out of the hearing. Since returning to the backbenches, he had watched every episode of the American detective TV series *The Wire* and decided to follow the advice of one of its characters, Lester Freamon, to 'follow the money'. He asked if News International's board had authorized the Taylor pay-off. The exchanges give a flavour of the extent to which the company's executives blustered and stalled:

WATSON: A £700,000 payment would be a decision taken at board level. Is that right?

CRONE: I am not aware of that.

WATSON: So the News International board did not agree the payment in any way?

MYLER: What do you mean by the 'board'?

WATSON: Your managing board, the directors of the company.

MYLER: Why would they need to be involved?

WATSON: Because it is a huge amount of money and they have got a responsibility to the proprietor and the shareholders, I assume?

MYLER: Yes, and as I have said, Mr Watson, the sum of money that Mr Taylor first set out to receive was significantly higher than the sum he did receive.

WATSON: I am sorry, I thought that was the easy question. So the board did not know about the payment . . .

CRONE: I do not know. I am sorry. All I do is report to the next stage up.

WATSON: So you could write to us and let us know whether the board took the decision?

CRONE: I could ask the question and give you the answer, yes.

The executives had been unable to say whether News International's board had authorized the payment, but had agreed to find out. Watson changed tack. He asked Crone: 'When did you tell Rupert Murdoch?', to which Crone fired back: 'I did not tell Rupert Murdoch.' Myler then intervened.

MYLER: The sequence of events, Mr Watson, is very simple. Mr Crone advised me, as the editor, what the legal advice was and it was to settle. Myself and Mr Crone then went to see James Murdoch and told him where we were with the situation. Mr Crone then continued with our outside lawyers the negotiation with Mr Taylor. Eventually a settlement was agreed. That was it.

WATSON: So James Murdoch took the ultimate decision?

MYLER: James Murdoch was advised of the situation and agreed with our legal advice that we should settle.

Crone looked unhappy: Myler had just admitted that James Murdoch, a News Corp director and the chief executive's son, had authorized a very large payment to a victim of phone hacking. If James knew that its rogue reporter defence was untrue, neither he nor anyone else at News International had corrected the company's earlier testimony, nor alerted the police to the possibility of more widespread criminality.

In the afternoon, the committee questioned Andy Coulson. David Cameron's director of communications was smooth and assured, insisting that he had neither condoned hacking nor had any 'recollection' of it taking place. During his four-year editorship, he said, his instructions to staff were clear: they were to work within the Press

Complaints Commission code. Alas, he recalled, Clive Goodman had deceived him. 'I have thought long and hard about this,' he told MPs. 'What could I have done to stop this happening? But, if a rogue reporter decides to behave in that fashion I am not sure that there is an awful lot more I could have done.'

Adam Price, a Welsh nationalist MP, asked: 'So far as you were aware the *News of the World*, while you were editor or deputy editor, never paid a serving police officer for information?' 'Not to my knowledge,' Coulson replied. Price checked: 'No journalist on the *News of the World*?' Coulson: 'No.'

Stuart Kuttner, the *NoW*'s former managing editor, appearing alongside Coulson, demanded that Philip Davies withdraw from the hearing for suggesting – falsely, Kuttner insisted – that his departure from the company on 8 July was linked to the Taylor story. Again, Whittingdale rebuffed the request, but it deepened MPs' suspicions that News International was hiding something.

By the close of the session, its executives had wriggled out of trouble by flatly denying anything was wrong. This was difficult to dispute without conflicting evidence, even though their story sounded very dubious. Despite the smokescreen, there were anomalies for the MPs to probe: the company had admitted a Murdoch had authorized the Taylor payment and that Goodman and Mulcaire had been paid off.

With its story faltering in public, News International struck back aggressively in private. Unbeknown to members of the Culture Committee, the *News of the World* ordered a team of journalists to investigate their private lives. As Neville Thurlbeck would later tell Tom Watson, reporters were told to search for any secret lovers or extramarital affairs that could be used as leverage against them. Thurlbeck said:

> All I know is that, when the DCMS [Department of Culture, Media and Sport Select Committee] was formed or rather when it got onto all the hacking stuff, there was an edict came down from the editor and it was find out every single thing you can about every single member: who was gay, who had affairs, anything we can use. Each

reporter was given two members and there were six reporters that went on for around ten days. I don't know who looked at you. It fell by the wayside; I think even Ian Edmondson [the news editor] realized there was something quite horrible about doing this.[11]

Separately, a *News of the World* figure tasked with talking to committee members to glean their question plan informed them that Rebekah Brooks believed Watson and Farrelly were their 'ringleaders'. Watson was privately told by Downing Street insiders that Wapping was using its connections to persuade senior politicians to urge him to hold back. Watson was told that Rupert Murdoch had phoned Tony Blair to ask Gordon Brown to call him off.

Speaking three years later, Alastair Campbell, Tony Blair's former communications director, said:

> I recall Rebekah Wade telling me that so far as she was concerned, with Tom Watson it's personal, and we won't stop till we get him. In July 2009, when the *Guardian* published a story indicating phone hacking was even more widespread than had been thought, I did a number of TV interviews saying this was a story that was not going away, that News International and the police had to grip it and come clean, that David Cameron should reconsider his appointment of Andy Coulson, and that what appeared to be emerging was evidence of systematic criminal activity on a near industrial basis at the *News of the World*. I received a series of what can only be termed threatening text and phone messages from both Rebekah and the office of James Murdoch.[12]

The cover-up was becoming ever more desperate.

8
Intimidating Parliament

I absolutely do not know
        – Les Hinton, 15 September 2009

News International attacked from every direction. At the end of July, its solicitors Farrer & Co wrote to Mark Lewis threatening him with an injunction if he represented any more phone hacking victims, on the grounds that he was privy to sensitive information from earlier cases:

> It goes without saying that our client will object to your involvement in this or any other related case against our client for the reasons set out above. We reserve our client's rights to take injunctive proceedings against you, should you choose to disregard the matters contained in this letter. However, you have an opportunity to correct matters by confirming that you will now accept that you cannot act for any individual wishing to bring a claim against News Group in respect of the voicemail accessing allegations . . .[1]

Lewis paraphrased the letter as saying: 'You know too much, please don't act against us or we will bring the whole weight of the organization down on you.' He said: 'I think it was designed to upset me, but it did not.'[2] In his reply, he threatened to pass the work to another firm, thus informing lawyers about the prevalence of hacking at Wapping. The injunction never materialized.

The *NoW*'s editor, Colin Myler, told the Press Complaints Commission's new investigation that the company's 'internal inquiries' had found no evidence aside from the 'For Neville' email that any staff beyond Goodman had intercepted messages, adding that reports that thousands of phones had been hacked were 'not just unsubstantiated and irresponsible, they were wholly false'.

Separately, Myler indicated to the Culture Committee that News International's patience was wearing thin with its inquiry. In August 2009, he confirmed in writing that payments had been made to settle Goodman and Mulcaire's employment cases, but declined to disclose the amounts on the grounds that they were confidential. He told the MPs: 'We have now answered all the outstanding questions from the committee on 21 July and trust that this now brings to a close our involvement in your committee's proceedings.'

If the business's executives were growing ever more exasperated, it may have been because by now News Corp was planning an audacious deal that would give it unparalleled power in the UK. In the late 1980s, Rupert Murdoch had gambled his fortune on the far-sighted launch of a multi-channel TV network, Sky, but its ruinous costs had forced a merger with its rival British Satellite Broadcasting, to form British Sky Broadcasting, or BSkyB, in which News Corp held a 39 per cent stake. Through adroit marketing, the acquisition of rights to Premier League football and Ashes cricket and the screening of dozens of channels of pornography, BSkyB – still known as Sky – had become a commercial success, with sales of £5.3 billion in the year to June 2009. In mid-2009, News Corp began hatching a plan to secure all of its vast cash-flow for itself: it would launch a takeover for the remaining 61 per cent of shares. James Murdoch said later: 'I remember there was a meeting about it [the takeover] in Los Angeles, in sort of August, but that was sort of where it was starting to come together, thinking: "Would it be possible to do that?".'[3]

A wholly owned Sky could be fully integrated with Sky Italia and Sky Deutschland. More importantly, News International's newspapers could be bundled into TV packages for the network's 10 million subscribers, meaning that News Corp would control not just the country's biggest broadcaster and 40 per cent of national newspapers, but could slowly cripple rival newspapers, giving itself an unassailable dominance over the media. News Corp had the cash to launch the multi-billion-pound takeover, but there was a snag: the takeover would need government approval.

News Corp decided to wait until after the general election, which was looking increasingly likely to be won by David Cameron's Conservatives, who had reversed his earlier chill towards Rupert Murdoch and orientated his party's media policy towards the Murdochs.

For the avoidance of doubt, in August 2009, James Murdoch explicitly set out the dynasty's demands in a lecture to the Edinburgh Television Festival. He identified the BBC as the enemy of free and dynamic programming offered by Sky, protesting: 'The scale and scope of its current activities and future ambitions is chilling.' He complained that the BBC was paying entertainers large salaries out of the reach of rivals and competing unfairly with national papers on the internet. The BBC Trust, the 36-year-old tyro complained, had an 'abysmal record' in restraining the corporation. As to Ofcom – which two months before had ordered Sky to lower its rates for selling sport and films to rival broadcasters – it was placing 'astonishing' burdens on the competition. James concluded: 'There is an inescapable conclusion that we must reach if we are to have a better society. The only reliable, durable, and perpetual guarantor of independence is profit.' The message was clear: the government should hobble the BBC and Ofcom and give commercial broadcasters – such as Sky – a freer run.

David Cameron, who had been advocating just this, soon had his reward. On 10 September he was invited to a meeting with James Murdoch at George, a private members' club in Mayfair. As with other meetings between political leaders and the Murdochs, the public were excluded. Cameron was told that the *Sun* was about to endorse his party; he was being anointed as the next prime minister. The *Sun* would urge its eight million readers to back him. On 21 September, James and his wife hosted a dinner for the Camerons at their house in London.

Away from the dinner tables of Mayfair, MPs on the Culture Committee still suspected that they had been misled by News International and the police. After the summer recess, they asked to hear direct from

Scotland Yard's Assistant Commissioner, John Yates. On 2 September, 'Yates of the Yard' stuck rigidly to his position that Caryatid had been a success. 'As I said previously,' he maintained, 'there is essentially nothing new in the story other than to place in the public domain additional material which had already been considered by both the police investigation into Goodman and Mulcaire and by the CPS and the prosecution team.' Rather ludicrously, he said he could not know the identity of the Neville in the 'For Neville' email because 'It is supposition to suggest Neville Thurlbeck or indeed any other Neville within the *News of the World* or any other Neville in the journalist community.' Even if Thurlbeck had been interviewed by the police, he added, it was '99.9 per cent certain' he would have said nothing, just like Goodman and Mulcaire. 'But there is a series of transcripts of phone conversations,' Paul Farrelly protested. Yates replied: 'Perhaps in 2006 it ought to have been done. I do not know – but in 2009 that is going to take us absolutely nowhere.'

The committee recalled Les Hinton. Like others, Hinton had tried to avoid giving evidence, but the committee agreed to conduct the hearing by live video link from New York, where he was running Dow Jones. On 15 September 2009, Hinton could recall few details of his time at Murdoch's British newspapers, at least about the events which culminated in the jailing of a journalist. On thirty-two occasions he said: 'I don't know,' 'I did not know' or 'I just do not know.' Had Wapping paid Goodman and Mulcaire's legal fees? 'I absolutely do not know,' Hinton replied. 'I do not know whether we did or not. There were certainly some payments made afterwards, but on the matter of legal fees I honestly don't know.'

Hinton, who had been sent Goodman's letter claiming phone hacking had been commonplace, added: 'There was never any evidence delivered to me that suggested that the conduct of Clive Goodman spread beyond him.' As News Corp continued to obfuscate its rottweiler, the *News of the World*, thought it had stumbled on a story which would savage the reputation of one of its sternest critics.

The *News of the World*'s investigations editor, Mazher Mahmood, claimed to have discovered that Tom Watson was having an affair with a female Muslim politician. He relayed this in an email to the news editor, Ian Edmondson headed: 'Labour sex scandal'.

> From: Mazher Mahmood
> To: James Mellor
> CC: Ian Edmondson
>
> Time: 10.05am, 26 September 2009
>
> Tom Watson MP who is a close lackey of Gordon Brown (ex-whip, anti-Blair etc) is shagging a [redacted]. The pair are already in Brighton for the conference and he has been creeping into her hotel. My informant knows her but won't push her any more about where she is staying etc. It will need politics to point out Tom at the conference and then for our biker to follow them. Also if you have someone doing nothing today, can they ring every hotel in Brighton and try to identify where they are staying? They are in separate hotels.[4]

Six minutes later, Edmondson responded 'great story' and: 'Get Derek on the case today.' He added: 'PS. He's v easy to spot. You might want to checks his recent cutts, v interesting!' The cuttings Edmondson was referring to almost certainly included Watson's criticism of News International.[5]

From 28 September until 2 October 2009, in Brighton, at the last Labour Party conference before the general election, the *NoW*'s surveillance expert, Derek Webb, was ordered to follow Watson's every move. From 2003, the paper had paid Webb, a former policeman, to follow people in the public eye in the hope of catching them up to no good. During his eight years with the paper, he had stalked dozens of pop stars, footballers and royals. In 2005, for instance, he had followed Angelina Jolie, Delia Smith and Gordon Ramsay; in 2006, George Michael and the comedian Rik Mayall; and in 2007, the Duke of Westminster. Typically, Webb's work would involve him tailing a target for five days and then noting down where they had gone, who they had met and what they were wearing. At Brighton, though, amid tight security inside the conference centre, he had difficulty tracking down Watson. (Ironically, on the first night, 28 September, Webb would have been more successful had he phoned the *News of the World*'s political editor, Ian Kirby, who had spent the night drinking with Watson in the bar of the Grand Hotel, where they sang songs round the piano until the early hours.) The surveillance was kept secret for two years.

Politically, News International was about to intervene at Brighton. On the evening of 29 September, hours after Gordon Brown made his rallying conference speech, the *Sun* publicly announced it was switching its support to the Conservatives. In a front page headed 'Labour's Lost It', the paper wrote:

> Twelve years ago, Britain was crying out for change from a divided, exhausted government. Today we are there again.
>
> In 1997, 'New Labour', shorn of its destructive hard-left doctrines and with an energetic and charismatic leader, seemed the answer. Tony Blair said things could only get better, and few doubted him. But did they get better? Well, you could point to investment in schools and shorter hospital waiting lists and say yes, some things did – a little.
>
> But the real story of the Labour years is one of under-achievement, rank failure and a vast expansion of wasteful government interference in everyone's lives.

In his hotel suite that night with his allies Peter Mandelson, Ed Miliband, Ed Balls and Tom Watson (still oblivious he was being followed), Gordon Brown was shocked at the brutality: Britain's best-selling daily paper was sabotaging his last conference before polling day. Over the coming months, he was harried and goaded by the *Sun*, in the same way it had mocked John Major before backing Tony Blair in 1997. On 9 November, the *Sun*'s front page screamed 'Bloody Shameless', denouncing the half-blind prime minister's alleged mis-spelling of the name of a soldier killed in Afghanistan in a letter to his mother. The *Sun* covertly taped Brown's subsequent phone call of apology to the woman.

Behind the scenes at the Conservative conference in Manchester the following week, Rebekah Brooks fulsomely expressed the deepening ties between News International and David Cameron. At 4.45 p.m. on 7 October, the eve of his speech, she texted Cameron: 'I am so rooting for you, not just as a personal friend but because professionally we are in this together. Speech of your life? Yes he Cam!'[6]

On Friday 9 October, the *Sun*'s front page lauded the speech:

> David Cameron shows he has the strength to get battered Britain back on its feet as he makes a power-packed speech at the Tory conference yesterday.
>
> He declared the Conservatives ready and able to rescue the nation from financial and social chaos.

Within ten days, the Conservatives launched another attack on the BBC. In an interview with the *Financial Times* on 19 October, Jeremy Hunt, the shadow Culture Secretary, said the corporation was 'out of touch' and crushed competition (such as Sky). He promised the Conservatives would abolish the BBC's governing body, the BBC Trust – criticized by James Murdoch in his MacTaggart lecture in Edinburgh.[7]

On 9 November, the Press Complaints Commission gave further comfort to News International. Now being chaired by Baroness Buscombe, a 55-year-old former Conservative frontbencher from Oxfordshire, the PCC reported the results of its second investigation into the *News of the World* – and humiliated itself by again exonerating the paper. Showing little scepticism or insight, it accepted the police's and News International's explanations about the extent of illegality at Wapping, despite the 'For Neville' email, the Taylor settlement and the pay-offs to Goodman and Mulcaire. Its report stated:

> The PCC has seen no new evidence to suggest that the practice of phone message tapping was undertaken by others beyond Goodman and Mulcaire, or evidence that the *News of the World* knew about Goodman and Mulcaire's activities. It follows that there is nothing to suggest that the PCC was materially misled during its 2007 inquiry.
>
> Indeed, having reviewed the matter, the Commission could not help but conclude that the *Guardian*'s stories did not quite live up to

the dramatic billing they were initially given. Perhaps this was because the sources could not be tested; or because Nick Davies was unable to shed further light on the suggestions of a broader conspiracy at the newspaper; or because there was significant evidence to the contrary from the police; or because so much of the information was old and had already appeared in the public domain (or a combination of these factors).

The verdict was a hammer blow to the *Guardian*; not only had the watchdog dismissed its front-page exclusive, it was effectively accusing it of sensationalism. Alan Rusbridger resigned from the PCC's Code Committee in disgust.

Despite News International's public vindication, it was privately making efforts to bury its past. Four months after its settlement to Gordon Taylor became public, in November 2009 it developed plans for the mass deletion of emails. Under the heading 'Opportunity', one of the aims of the new policy was 'to eliminate in a consistent manner across NI (subject to compliance with legal and regulatory requirements) emails that could be unhelpful in the context of future litigation in which an NI company is a defendant'.[8]

Aware of the potential embarrassment that might ensue, to both itself and Andy Coulson, it fought Matt Driscoll's employment claim every inch of the way – as he explained later:

> Ignoring the medical warnings as to the possible effect on my health, they chose to fight me for two years. They insisted, despite my health situation, on forcing me into a two-week tribunal. Having hired one of the country's top employment barristers they called no fewer than ten witnesses ... they remained relentless toward me. Three times they appealed against my successful claim for unfair dismissal. Though each appeal was thrown out, the ordeal cost me my health, my career, my life savings and £150,000 in legal costs.[9]

News International still lost the case. On 23 November, an employment tribunal in east London ordered it to pay Driscoll £792,736 for what it called a campaign of bullying. The tribunal said that it had been orchestrated by Coulson, stating: 'The original source of the hostility towards the claimant was Mr Coulson, the editor; although other senior managers either took their lead from Mr Coulson and continued with his motivation after Mr Coulson's departure; or shared his views themselves.'[10]

Cameron kept Coulson; he may have been bad in the past, but he was too good to lose now. Thankfully, for the Conservative leader and Wapping, the Metropolitan Police and the Crown Prosecution Service had by now dismissed the growing body of evidence about the behaviour of the *News of the World*.

After the all-clear from the PCC, Scotland Yard lobbied the *Guardian* to drop its hostile coverage. On 10 December 2009, the Commissioner, Sir Paul Stephenson, accompanied by his head of public affairs, Dick Fedorcio, visited Rusbridger in the paper's office in King's Cross and told him that Nick Davies's coverage was 'overegged' and had wrongly implied the force was 'party to a conspiracy'. Davies kept going. On 1 February 2010, he revealed that the mobile phone companies Orange, O2 and Vodafone had discovered more than 100 customers had their inboxes accessed by Mulcaire. He also divulged that the Met had finally answered the paper's freedom of information request, revealing that it had found ninety-two PIN codes in Mulcaire's notes. Fedorcio again protested to Rusbridger, writing that Davies 'once again presents an inaccurate position from our perspective and continues to imply this case has not been handled properly and we are a party to a conspiracy'. At a follow-up meeting with Rusbridger on 19 February, John Yates, accompanied by Fedorcio, again sought to persuade the *Guardian* – in Rusbridger's words – that 'Nick's doggedness and persistence in pursuing the story was misplaced.'[11] Rusbridger kept his faith in his old friend.

The Culture Committee was similarly dogged, requesting further details of News International's inquiries and the payments to Goodman and Mulcaire. In November, Rebekah Brooks wrote back enclosing an explanation from Jonathan Chapman confirming the company had settled their claims for unfair dismissal, but only because of technicalities, and again declined to disclose the 'confidential' sums. Asked how many Nevilles the company employed, Brooks replied: 'One.'

Responding to the queries about the internal inquiries, she enclosed Harbottle & Lewis's letter of 29 May 2007 about its review of the emails for Clive Goodman's employment case (see pp. 55–6). Set in the context of an inquiry into the *News of the World*, lawyer Lawrence Abramson's words looked reassuring. They appeared to indicate that a law firm had made a thorough check of Wapping and found no evidence of a wider problem.

Boldly the MPs decided they should hear from Brooks in person. She contemptuously declined the invitation. In a letter to John Whittingdale on 4 January 2010, she dismissed the 'supposed incongruity' between the treatment of Clive Goodman and Matt Driscoll, the 'For Neville' email and misbehaviour by News International journalists, which, she suggested, was not worse than 'any other national newspaper', adding that she would 'ensure the proper journalistic standards continue to be applied across all our titles'. She concluded:

> Given the above, I hope you and your colleagues agree that my attendance before the committee to face questions on the three areas to which you refer would be pointless and a waste of the committee's time. As I have said before, if there are other matters being investigated by yourselves and on which you and your colleagues feel I may have direct knowledge, I remain very happy to be of assistance.
>
> I should conclude that, given my clear commitment to assisting the committee, I am very surprised at the threat of coercion made in your letter which, I am sure you must agree, is inappropriate.

Although the committee clearly wanted Brooks to give evidence, its members capitulated and decided not to summons her. On the day the committee met to discuss the issue, two Labour MPs close to Tony Blair – Janet Anderson and Rosemary McKenna – were absent. The gay Plaid Cymru MP Adam Price – who in September unexpectedly announced that he would leave Parliament at the general election to take up a Fulbright scholarship in the US – claimed that the committee's members had been warned that if they had called Brooks, their private lives would be raked over. He said later: 'I was told by a senior Conservative member of the committee, who I knew was in direct contact with executives at News International, that if we went for her, they would go for us – effectively they would delve into our personal lives in order to punish [us].'[12]

Despite Scotland Yard, News International and the Press Complaints Commission all insisting that nothing was wrong, on 23 February the Culture Committee published a report which damned them all. The PCC, the committee said in 'Press Standards, Privacy and Libel', should have been 'more assertive in its inquiries rather than accepting submissions from the *News of the World* once again at face value', adding that its report was simplistic and surprising: 'It has certainly not fully, or forensically, considered all the evidence to this inquiry.' The Metropolitan Police, the MPs said, had failed to investigate properly the Greg Miskiw contract – which promised to pay Mulcaire £7,000 for a story on Gordon Taylor – or the 'For Neville' email, which were strong evidence of additional lawbreaking: 'These matters merited thorough police investigation, and the first steps to be taken seem to us to have been obvious. The Metropolitan Police's reasons for not doing so seem to us to be inadequate.'

About News International itself, the report could hardly have been more scathing. Although the committee had seen no evidence that Andy Coulson had known about phone hacking, it was 'inconceivable' that no one else at the *News of the World* bar Clive Goodman was aware of the practice. The MPs stopped just short of accusing Britain's biggest newspaper group of lying. They wrote:

> Throughout our inquiry, we have been struck by the collective amnesia afflicting witnesses from the *News of the World*. Throughout, we have repeatedly encountered an unwillingness to provide the detailed information that we sought, claims of ignorance or lack of recall, and deliberate obfuscation. We strongly condemn this behaviour which reinforces the widely held impression that the press generally regard themselves as unaccountable and that News International in particular has sought to conceal the truth about what really occurred.

Press coverage was muted. The *Guardian* reported the committee's acerbic verdict on its front page and the *Independent* across pages 6 and 7, but other papers marginalized the criticism. The *Daily Mail* ran a 154-word story headed: 'Tory Spin Chief Cleared'. The *Sun*'s political editor, Tom Newton Dunn, assisted both the Conservative Party and his employers in a small piece on page 2 which read: 'Labour MPs wanted to smear Tory communications boss Andy Coulson, an ex-editor. But the report found "no evidence" he knew phone hacking was taking place.' *The Times* ran a small story on page 15.

The *News of the World* was apoplectic. In an editorial on 28 February, Colin Myler's paper protested that the report had been 'shamefully hijacked' by Tom Watson and Paul Farrelly. It thundered: 'We'll take no lessons in standards from MPs – nor from self-serving pygmies who run the circulation-challenged *Guardian*.' To add insult to injury, the *NoW* ran a commentary from one of the committee's Tory MPs, Philip Davies, who complained that its work on press freedom should not be overshadowed 'by pathetic and petty Labour politicians who have tried to hijack the report to settle a score with News International for supporting the Conservative Party at the next election'.[13] In a statement, News International said the select committee system had been damaged and diminished by the report, which, it protested, was laden with 'innuendo, unwarranted inference and exaggeration'.[14]

9
A Murder

No one pays like the News of the World *do*
— Jonathan Rees

Despite the underwhelming response to the MPs' report, News International and the Conservative Party knew that another dark story about the *News of the World* was about to surface. On 25 February, Ian Katz, the *Guardian*'s deputy editor, phoned Steve Hilton, David Cameron's director of strategy. Katz wanted him to know that Andy Coulson's newspaper had worked with a notorious private investigator after his release from prison for conspiring to pervert the course of justice. The *Guardian* could not publicly report Jonathan Rees's conviction to avoid prejudicing a new court case – because he was now on trial for murder. The case, which revealed close links between tabloid newspapers and corrupt police, dated back three decades to the late 1980s, when Scotland Yard was awash with bent coppers – and Rees, a Freemason, ran a detective agency in Thornton Heath, south London, with another investigator, Daniel Morgan.

According to his brother Alastair, Morgan, a gregarious 37-year-old with a photographic memory, had become alarmed by Rees's links to corrupt officers and had been trying to sell a story about a police cocaine ring to a reporter on a national newspaper: Alex Marunchak, at the *News of the World*.

At the same time, Morgan had become concerned about the theft of £18,000 in cash Rees had been transporting for a client. Belmont Car Auctions, the client, and Morgan suspected that Rees and his associates – some of whom were moonlighting police officers – had stolen the money.

On 10 March 1987, the two partners of Southern Investigations, Rees and Morgan, met for a drink at the Golden Lion in Sydenham. Rees left the pub. A few minutes later Morgan walked towards his BMW in the car park. He never drove away. His body was discovered in the car park at 9.30 p.m., with a hatchet buried so deep in his face that the only part showing was the haft. Morgan's £900 Rolex watch had been taken but not £1,100 in cash from his pocket.

Morgan's brother, Alastair, spoke to Rees about what had happened but was so unconvinced by his explanation he went to the police incident room at Sydenham, where he was interviewed by a CID officer, Sid Fillery, one of the detectives who had moonlighted for Rees – and was surprised by his casual manner. At Morgan's inquest in 1988, Kevin Lennon, Southern Investigation's bookkeeper, testified that six months before the murder, Rees said he was planning a contract hit: 'My mates are going to arrange it. Those police officers are friends of mine and will either murder Danny or will arrange it.' Asked if he had murdered Morgan, Rees replied: 'I did not.' The inquest returned a verdict of unlawful killing. The coroner pointed out that there was no forensic evidence to link anyone to the murder.

A second murder inquiry failed in 1989, by which time Fillery had left the Metropolitan Police on medical grounds and became Rees's new business partner at Southern Investigations. The most lucrative work was selling confidential data to the media. Much of it came from bent detectives at Scotland Yard, though Rees and Fillery also developed contacts in other forces. In the late 1990s, their best customers were the *News of the World*, the *Sunday Mirror* and the *Daily Mirror*.

In 1997, following pressure from Alastair Morgan, Scotland Yard launched a third murder inquiry, Operation Nigeria, in secrecy. An elite anti-corruption squad, CIB3, planted a listening device in Southern Investigations' office in the hope of recording Rees and Fillery talking about Morgan's killing. Stressing the need to place the bug with great delicacy, a CIB3 report warned: 'Such is their level of access to individuals within the police, through professional and social contacts, that the threat of compromise to any conventional investigation against them is constant and very real.'[1]

Between April and September 1999, the bug unintentionally picked up Rees's conversations with Fleet Street journalists. The Metropolitan Police gave a briefing on the conversations to a reporter, Graham McLagan, who detailed them in the *Guardian* on 21 September 2002. Through his corrupt contacts in the police, Rees had sold a string of juicy stories about ongoing investigations, obtaining information about the former Chilean dictator General Augusto Pinochet, the Yorkshire Ripper Peter Sutcliffe and the neo-Nazi nailbomber David Copeland. He was also in touch with a corrupt VAT inspector who could access business records, two corrupt bank employees (nicknamed Fat Bob and Rob the Bank) who could provide details of personal accounts, and two former police officers working for Customs and Excise. Two blaggers conned phone companies into handing over names and addresses of customers and itemized phone bills. One, John Gunning – later convicted – was skilled at blagging ex-directory numbers from BT. Once, Rees was asked by an unnamed journalist to trace the owner of a Porsche whose registration number he had been given. He had the owner's name and address from the DVLA and his criminal record from the Police National Computer in thirty-four minutes.

While the *Mirror* titles were enthusiastic customers, the *NoW* was paying Rees £150,000 a year and the bug recorded him saying: 'No one pays like the *News of the World* do.' His handler at the paper was Alex Marunchak.

Police would have carried on eavesdropping had they not stumbled on a serious crime. With Austin Warnes, a corrupt police officer in the Met's south-east regional crime squad, Rees had hatched a plot to plant cocaine on a former model, Kim James, so that her businessman husband, Simon James, could gain custody of their child. Drugs were duly planted in Kim James's car and Warnes provided false information about her drugs activities. In September, police raided Southern Investigations. In December 2000, Rees was sentenced to six years, increased to seven on appeal, for conspiring to pervert the course of justice. Warnes was sentenced to four years. As they closed down the corruption ring, police arrested twelve suspects and raided twenty-three premises.

With Rees in jail for a long stretch, the police began a fourth inquiry into Daniel Morgan's murder in early 2002 and arranged for an appeal to be made on BBC TV's *Crimewatch*. Detective Superintendent David Cook, head of the Met's north London murder squad, and the husband of one of the programme's presenters, Jacqui Hames, would make the appeal. The day after it was broadcast on 26 June, Scotland Yard warned Cook that it had picked up intelligence that Rees's partner, Sid Fillery, had been in touch with Alex Marunchak – now editing the *NoW*'s Irish edition – who had agreed to 'sort Cook out'. Surrey Police, where Cook had previously worked, also told him someone purporting to be an 'Inland Revenue inspector' had tried to blag his home address from its finance department.

Unbeknown to Hames and Cook, Glenn Mulcaire had started tracking data about them. Under the heading 3 July, Mulcaire recorded the date Hames had joined the Met in 1977, her payroll and warrant numbers, the name, location and phone number of her place of work and her home phone number and address. Mulcaire recorded Cook's name, phone number, rank and made a reference to his *Crimewatch* appeal.

Hames later said:

> This information could only have come from one place: the MPS [Metropolitan Police Service]. I was horrified by the realization that someone within the MPS had supplied information from my personnel file to Mr Mulcaire, and probably for money.[2]

On 10 July, Cook noticed a van parked opposite his and Hames's home. The following day there were two vans. When he took Hames's son to school, both vehicles started following them. When the vans followed them again soon after, Cook contacted the Met, who asked a policeman to stop one of them on the pretext that it had a broken tail light. Both vans were leased to News International. Police mobilized a witness protection unit and counter-surveillance team to protect the family.

Rebekah Brooks (then Wade) was alerted to the surveillance by police. At a press social event at Scotland Yard in January 2003, Cook, his superior officer, Commander Andrew Baker, and Dick Fedorcio, ushered Wade into a side room and told her of the sinister activity. They added that there was evidence that Alex Marunchak had a corrupt relationship with Jonathan Rees. A former colleague of Rees had claimed that some of his *News of the World* payments were channelled back to Marunchak, who had been able to pay off his credit card bill and his child's private school fees. (Marunchak denies this.) Wade lamely claimed the paper was trying to discover whether Hames and Cook were having an affair (they were married) and defended Marunchak on the grounds that he did his job well. Scotland Yard, ever eager to maintain a good relationship with Wapping, took no further action. Sir John Stevens, the Commissioner at the time, later said he had no knowledge of the meeting.[3]

Hames told the Leveson Inquiry in February 2012:

> The *News of the World* has never supplied a coherent reason for why we were placed under surveillance ... I believe that the real reason for the *News of the World* placing us under surveillance was that suspects in the Daniel Morgan murder inquiry were using their association with a powerful and well-resourced newspaper to try to intimidate us and so attempt to subvert the investigation. These events left me distressed, anxious and needing counselling and contributed to the breakdown of my marriage to David in 2010.[4]

After his release from prison in 2005, Rees was re-employed by the *News of the World*, until the Met charged him with murder three years later. For in secrecy, in 2006, a fifth murder inquiry, Operation Abelard,* had begun away from Scotland Yard, led by Cook and supervised by John Yates. The squad consisted of thirty-five officers, all of whom were asked to declare that they were not Freemasons. Cook built a case which included testimony from career criminals who had turned 'Queen's evidence' and whose sentences were reduced as a result of their cooperation. In April 2008, the police charged Rees, two brothers, Glenn and Gary Vian, and a builder, James Cook,

---

* The names of operations were chosen at random; they have no particular significance.

with Morgan's murder. Sid Fillery – who had been convicted of possessing indecent images of children in 2003 – was charged with perverting the course of justice. In October 2009, the trial began at the Old Bailey. The laws of contempt of court meant the *Guardian* could not report Rees's re-employment by Coulson after his jail term – but, in February 2010, Ian Katz could mention it in a phone call to David Cameron's office. Cameron kept Coulson. He hoped the hacking scandal would die down. He was wrong.

10

Following the Lawyers

I also mentioned surveillance

– Julian Pike, Farrer & Co

While Rees's lawyers sought to throw out the murder charge at the Old Bailey, Max Clifford was pursuing his civil claim for breach of privacy through the courts. As Mark Lewis had done in the Gordon Taylor case, Charlotte Harris asked Scotland Yard to disclose Mulcaire's notes on Clifford, and, just as in the Taylor case, a judge ordered disclosure. But this time, when the documents came through on 7 December 2009, the police had struck out whole sections. Harris recalled: 'The police would only provide documents under court order and when you did get the documents they would be redacted in a random way. The police would have known that journalists at the *News of the World* were named in the top left-hand corner of many of the pages and yet they blacked them out.'[1] She returned to the High Court, where, on 3 March 2010, Justice Geoffrey Vos ordered the removal of the redactions. Harris expected that there would be clear evidence that journalists* at the *News of the World* had ordered the hacking of Clifford's phone. Just as in the Taylor case, News International suddenly became desperate to settle.

Relishing his own negotiating skills – which had squeezed £300,000 out of the *News of the World* for Rebecca Loos's kiss and

---

* At the time of going to press, the names of the individuals who had commissioned the hacking cannot be published, to avoid prejudicing ongoing legal cases.

tell on David Beckham – Clifford lunched Rebekah Brooks in London, and agreed a deal: News International would pay him £220,000 a year for three years and costs of £331,112 – a total of £991,112 – in return for his silence, and for reopening the flow of exclusives. Clifford rang Harris and trilled: 'Poppet, poppet, I've sorted it out with Rebekah. I've done the money! Now you sort the costs out between you.'[2] Harris was devastated that the end of the case might ruin any chance of exposing phone hacking. Nonetheless, she and Jeremy Reed met the News of the World's legal team – Tom Crone and Julian Pike – at Clifford's house in the Home Counties to agree the small print. Clifford emerged from the swimming pool, dried off and went out – leaving the lawyers haggling in the sitting room, underneath portraits of the coiffeured publicist with celebrity clients. Harris said: 'We were being distracted by his dogs the whole time. Tom Crone would be saying things like: "Well, it's obvious you were going to win this case, so you shouldn't be getting the 'no win, no fee' uplift" and these dogs were slavering all over my feet. When Jeremy and I wanted to talk on our own, we would leave the room and go into Max's kitchen and conservatory.'[3] On a handshake, Clifford agreed to keep the deal secret, but abandoned that when, he said, 'News of the World lawyers revealed the details of my settlement.'[4] (How or when the NoW's lawyers did this remains a mystery.) Clifford spoke to the Guardian, and on 9 March Nick Davies and Rob Evans reported the settlement online (and in the next day's newspaper): 'Max Clifford drops phone hacking action in £1m deal':

> The News of the World was tonight accused of buying silence in the phone hacking scandal after it agreed to pay more than £1 million to persuade the celebrity PR agent Max Clifford to drop his legal action over the interception of his voicemail messages.

Clifford was quoted as saying: 'I'm now looking forward to continuing the successful relationship that I experienced with the News of the World for twenty years before my recent problems with them.' The News of the World had paid an extraordinarily large sum to keep a lid on the scandal, but again it had failed. Harris said: 'The difference between Gordon and Max was that while Max settled he didn't shut up. He said to them: "Please give me this amount of money." And then: "Thanks for the money, I'm telling everyone!"[5]

Despite disclosing the payment of more hush money, the *Guardian*'s story was not followed up by any other national newspaper. Most Fleet Street editors knew their own titles had dealings with Steve Whittamore; they may also have thought that the Gordon Taylor story had not come to anything.

The small band of campaigners who wanted to crack open the scandal grew despondent. All the political parties were focusing on the general election in May and almost every national paper had ignored or belittled a year-long Commons inquiry. The trail was going cold. At the *Guardian*'s offices, Alan Rusbridger called his friend Bill Keller, executive editor of the *New York Times*, and urged him to investigate the story – which, for a liberal American paper, was a rich brew of Britain's muckraking tabloids, the royal family, Scotland Yard and Rupert Murdoch. The *Guardian* would offer every assistance.

Keller dispatched three senior reporters – Don van Natta Jr, Jo Becker and Graham Bowley – to the UK almost immediately. Straight off the plane, on 15 March, they met Rusbridger, Nick Davies and the *Guardian* lawyer Gill Phillips in a room on the first floor of Kings Place. Davies spoke for most of the three-hour meeting, taking the American team through the story, and repeating the process at the *New York Times*'s office in Westminster two days later. Over the following months, the Americans would criss-cross Britain investigating, with the help of Davies, whom they dubbed 'Nickypedia' because of his detailed knowledge of dodgy tabloid practices.

Davies himself carried on digging. He contacted celebrities whom ex-*News of the World* employees indicated had been targeted, and urged them to write to Scotland Yard. He also tracked down former reporters, private investigators and friends of Glenn Mulcaire. By this time, he was speaking regularly to Tom Watson, and both were talking to Charlotte Harris at JMW and Mark Lewis, now working for the law firm Stripes. All were on the edge of their respective fields, away from the centre of power: Watson was a backbencher; Lewis and Harris solicitors in provincial general practice rather than

London media firms; Davies was an outlier who rarely visited the *Guardian*'s offices. Together they continued to challenge the official story.

On 4 April, Davies made a startling disclosure. Only eight victims had been named in court in 2006 and John Yates had told Parliament that police could only prove that phone hacking had taken place against a small number of individuals. Yet in an answer to a Freedom of Information request by the *Guardian*, Scotland Yard admitted that Mulcaire's notes contained no fewer than 4,332 names or partial names of people, 2,978 numbers or partial numbers for mobile phones and thirty audio recordings of voicemail messages. Incontrovertibly, the true number of victims might not just be eight, or even scores, but thousands of people, from all walks of life, rich and poor, famous and ordinary – whose messages had been secretly hacked and retailed by the UK's largest news group. He also disclosed the existence of the secret agreement between the Crown Prosecution Service and the Metropolitan Police in July 2006 (see chapter 4) that the case presented in court should be 'deliberately limited' to 'less sensitive' witnesses.

Inside Wapping in spring 2010 executives became aware that the affair was once again becoming volatile. Although Tom Crone and Julian Pike had seen off Gordon Taylor's case and the ancillary ones of Jo Armstrong and John Hewison – as well as Max Clifford's – more cases were coming forward. Just as Goodman and Mulcaire's court proceedings had prompted Taylor's action, and Taylor's had prompted Clifford's, Clifford's now set others in motion. The sports agent Sky Andrew began to sue, represented by Charlotte Harris, and Mark Lewis started to act for Max Clifford's assistant Nicola Phillips.

Although other lawyers had written to police on behalf of Sienna Miller, Chris Bryant and others, Lewis and Harris were by far the most bothersome. Crone and Pike suspected they were having an affair and sharing confidential information from their respective cases. If they could prove that, they reasoned, a complaint of professional misconduct could be made against them – which might prevent them taking any more hacking cases. Secretly, a plan was hatched to spy on the lawyers. Pike explained in 2011:

> For a number of reasons, by the early part of 2010, I had concerns, which had accumulated over the previous months, that Ms Harris and Mr Lewis may be exchanging highly confidential information gained from acting for claimants (and Mr Taylor in particular) in cases against NGN in order to assist other clients in bringing further actions against NGN.
>
> I shared those concerns with NGN and in March, I suggested we should consider again whether Ms Harris and Mr Lewis were in a position to continue acting. I also mentioned surveillance.[6]

In Wapping, Tom Crone initially 'pooh-poohed' the idea, but two days later, on 24 March, he asked the *News of the World*'s news editor, Ian Edmondson, to put in place the arrangements.[7] The man the *News of the World* turned to again was Derek Webb. On 1 April, Webb was asked to drive north from Surrey to a house in Manchester. From the road he videoed a woman with dark hair and followed her and a teenaged girl as they went shopping at a garden centre four miles away. Webb finished his work in Manchester on 3 April, billed the *News of the World* for 9.5 surveillance shifts, or £1,425, and sent his report and video to Wapping. When the film arrived in the *News of the World*, Tom Crone must have been disappointed since Charlotte Harris was blonde and the woman on Webb's video was dark-haired; Webb had gone to Lewis's former home and filmed his ex-wife and their fourteen-year-old daughter Orli. It was a fiasco.

The *News of the World* persisted. On 12 April it sent Webb back to Manchester, where for five days he staked out Harris's office at JMW and that of another firm of solicitors. In 2011, Webb told the Leveson Inquiry: 'This was in the hope that they would be seen together; after a week, I had failed to get a sighting of either and the assignment was terminated.' For the second batch of surveillance, which ended on 16 April, his company, Silent Shadow, billed News International £1,350.

Wapping was not finished with the idea of discrediting Lewis and Harris and on 5 May instructed Julian Pike to commission a private investigation firm, Tectrix, to search publicly available databases, including birth records, for Harris's two children – then aged two and four – to see if Lewis was their father. He was not. Later, referring to both the Webb and Tectrix surveillance, Harris said:

> There can be no justification for this conduct. The motive was to attempt to discredit solicitors who were conducting the phone hacking cases. The reports were prepared in order to find a way to stop us acting in those cases.
>
> From March to the end of May 2010 the intensity of the litigation was increasing. In my view this organization and its lawyers thought that they could still pursue a strategy that would contain their liability and deter others from pursuing them. I had many conversations with Tom Crone at the time. He was absolutely wedded to the defence that there was only one rogue journalist engaged in phone hacking. My correspondence with Julian Pike had ended when we had a telephone conversation in or around May 2010 when he said something like 'I know what you are.' I was not sure what he meant by that at all and I certainly did not know that he had put me under surveillance.[8]

Lewis described the video of his ex-wife's home and footage of her and his daughter as 'sickening'.[9]

Aware that News International had extensive surveillance powers (though oblivious to the operation on the Manchester lawyers), Nick Davies took precautions. He bought untraceable burner phones and shredded documents rather than put them out with the rubbish. At meetings, he and contacts would remove the batteries from their phones to ensure the handsets were not secretly and remotely recording their conversations. As well as being conscious of the danger to his sources, he and his editor were personally fearful. Davies said: 'Alan and I were both worried that the *News of the World* might come after our private lives – they don't just expose, they also distort, so it is a nasty prospect. But we calculated that as long as we kept publishing, they would not go for us, because it would be too obviously vengeful.'[10]

Rusbridger believed that Wapping was seeking to intimidate him:

I think one way they operated was to say things that would get back to you, so they didn't lift the phone directly to you, but they would drop something menacing to your best friend and of course you would hear about it very quickly – or they would indicate that they knew about you. Occasionally Nick would come round and say: 'You've got to be very careful – they are actively going after people.' And at one point I had someone in to sweep my house [for bugs] and within two days someone from News International rang up the press office and said: 'Has Alan Rusbridger had his house swept?' And I thought: That's not a story but they're just letting me know they know. There was definitely a black box operation going on, because other reporters who went to see them would ring me up and say: 'They're really bad-mouthing you and spreading gossip about you.'[11]

Over in west London, Britain's other liberal daily paper, the *Independent*, had shown less enthusiasm for the story. Under its editor Roger Alton – whose earlier editorship of the *Observer* had been criticized by Nick Davies in *Flat Earth News* – there was a feeling that the *Guardian* had overplayed its hand. After the Russian billionaire and former KGB economic attaché Alexander Lebedev bought 'the *Indy*' in March 2010 and Alton left to become executive editor of *The Times*, it became more prepared to challenge News International. During the general election campaign in April, the *Independent*, under its new editor Simon Kelner, ran an advertisement with the slogan: 'Rupert Murdoch won't decide this election. You will.' Furious at the reference to Murdoch's power (or perhaps angered by the suggestion that he would not decide the election), on 21 April James Murdoch and Rebekah Brooks strode into the *Independent*'s offices in Kensington High Street, marched through the newsroom and shouted at Kelner: 'What the fuck are you playing at?' Kelner ushered them into his office, where James gave full vent to his fury. Kelner wrote later: 'He called me a "fucking fuckwit" and became furious at my bemusement that he should find our campaign so upsetting, given that one of his newspapers famously claimed that it did indeed decide elections. Brooks said very little, but, when her boss's rage blew itself out, chipped in with: "We thought you were our friend." Their use of language and the threatening nature of their approach came straight from the "Mafioso for Beginners" handbook.'[12]

Martin Hickman, the paper's consumer correspondent, was one of many reporters who watched stunned as Brooks and Murdoch breezed cockily back out of the building.

11

Our Man in Downing Street

'*Our Only Hope*'
      – *Sun* front page about David Cameron, 6 May 2010

There was no surprise as to which party Rupert Murdoch backed at the general election. Politically, his newspapers tended to operate in unison: in 2001 they all backed Labour, in 2005 all but one backed Labour (the *Sunday Times* tepidly endorsed the Conservatives) and in 2010 they all supported the Conservatives. On polling day, 6 May, the *Sun* ran a stylized front-page picture of David Cameron with the headline: 'Our Only Hope'. Despite an ailing economy and Murdoch's help, the Conservatives fell short of a majority and formed a Coalition with the Liberal Democrats on 11 May.

Cameron now had to decide which members of his team would join him in government. He had received several warnings about Andy Coulson. Paddy Ashdown, the former Liberal Democrat leader, who had been briefed by Alan Rusbridger on the Morgan case, said: 'I warned Number 10 within days of the election that they would suffer terrible damage if they did not get rid of Coulson, when these things came out, as it was inevitable they would.'[1] The Deputy Prime Minister, Nick Clegg, also warned Cameron, only to be told by him that Coulson deserved a 'second chance'.[2] Coulson became the government's director of communications on a salary of £140,000 – more than any other of Cameron's officials, including his chief of staff, Ed Llewellyn. His instincts for the tabloid world outweighed all other considerations.

On 18 May Rupert Murdoch entered Downing Street through a back door. As a former Cabinet Office minister, Tom Watson knew that secret meetings took place between prime ministers and Murdoch. He tabled a parliamentary question asking the new Prime Minister who attended his meeting with Murdoch and what was discussed. On 2 June, Cameron refused to say.

With Cameron ensconced in 10 Downing Street, Murdoch finally launched his long-planned bid for BSkyB. On 10 June News Corp approached the Sky board with a 700p-a-share bid, worth £7.8 billion. Five days later, Sky's independent directors announced the approach and revealed they were holding out for a higher offer. As he prepared to negotiate, Murdoch knew that the deal would have to be approved by both the European Commission, which would have to satisfy itself that it would not harm competition, and the British government, whose decision on its impact on media 'plurality' was politically trickier. With complete control of Sky and News International, News Corp's annual British revenues, £7.9 billion, would dwarf the BBC's £3.6 billion and ITV's £1.9 billion. Murdoch's Conservative friends in the new government were likely to be supportive, but – unfortunately – the 'quasi-judicial' decision would be made by a Liberal Democrat minister, Vince Cable. Cable, the Business Secretary, would have to decide whether Ofcom should assess whether the deal might be against the public interest and should be passed to the biggest business regulator, the Competition Commission. A Competition Commission inquiry would take months to come to a decision and could block the takeover.

News Corp's new lobbyist, Fred Michel, a Frenchman with a jovial manner and good contacts at Westminster, set about contacting Cable. Michel was understandably worried about the Business Secretary: he was not on the Murdochs' social circuit and his party had long been ignored by his newspapers. To Michel's surprise, though, Cable was apparently receptive. On the day the deal was announced, 15 June, Michel wrote to James Murdoch's senior aide, Matthew Anderson, in an email later publicly revealed, along with other contacts between News Corp and the government at the Leveson Inquiry:

Vince Cable call went very well. He did say he 'thought there would not be a policy issue in this case'. We should have recorded him![3]

That day Michel also spoke to Jeremy Hunt, the Conservatives' new Culture, Media and Sport Secretary. Despite concern that the deal would crowd out other media companies, Hunt, a self-made publishing millionaire who admired Murdoch,* was supportive. In fact, Hunt had called Michel. News Corp's lobbyist recorded in an email:

Jeremy just called. He did an interview with FT today, after his chat with JRM [James Murdoch]. He was asked about Sky/NC [News Corp]. Said it was 'a matter for competition authorities but he didn't see any problems'.[4]

In his *Financial Times* interview, Hunt said: 'It does seem to me that News Corp do control Sky already, so it isn't clear to me that in terms of media plurality there is a substantive change, but I don't want to second guess what regulators might decide.' He was also keen to show his support in person. On 28 June, Hunt held a meeting with James Murdoch, at which no civil servant was present and no minutes were taken, and a second meeting with Sky's chief executive, Jeremy Darroch, on 21 July. No minutes had been taken at that meeting either, despite the fact that a civil servant had warned the Culture Secretary that Darroch was likely to ask about media regulation.

Over the following months Michel sought to influence Cable, while also keeping open a back channel to Hunt. Rupert Murdoch and his executives developed ever closer links with David Cameron and his ministers, meeting them far more often than they did representatives of other media groups. Among those with the closest links were Cameron; the Chancellor of the Exchequer, George

---

* In an interview with *Broadcast* magazine in August 2008, Hunt said Murdoch 'has done more to create variety and choice in British TV than any other single person because of his huge investment in setting up Sky TV which, at one point, was losing several million pounds a day.' Hunt's own website quoted *Broadcast*'s verdict: 'Like all good Conservatives Hunt is a cheerleader for Rupert Murdoch's contribution to the health of British television.'

Osborne; the Foreign Secretary, William Hague; and the Education Secretary, Michael Gove.

While News Corp and the Conservatives were weaving themselves ever tighter together through a series of political and personal connections, a collection of disparate phone hacking victims began to launch new phone hacking cases. Crucially, Sienna Miller acted. In October 2009 Scotland Yard had finally informed her that her name was in Mulcaire's files, while adding that there was no evidence her phone had actually been hacked. On 1 June 2010, Miller's lawyer, Mark Thomson, sought an order in the High Court requiring the Metropolitan Police to disclose the evidence about her in Mulcaire's notes. In July, the High Court granted the order and Thomson began preparing a case. For a young woman in the entertainment industry this was a brave step: she was standing up to a powerful man who owned a Hollywood film studio. She said later: 'Everyone was scared of Murdoch, even governments.'[5] Within months, her case would set off a chain of events that would humiliate Murdoch.

Chris Bryant was also preparing to act. In March 2010, Scotland Yard informed the MP that his details had been jotted down by Mulcaire. At the same time the police told him that there was no evidence that his phone had actually been hacked. Bryant consulted his lawyer, Tamsin Allen at the London law firm Bindmans, who by chance had another client whose name and mobile phone number were in Mulcaire's notes: Brian Paddick, a former Metropolitan Police Commander. On behalf of Bryant and Paddick, Allen began planning a judicial review of the police's failure to inform them that they had been victims of a crime.

Andy Coulson's presence in Downing Street at the centre of the new administration had irritated another public figure, Steve Coogan, who believed his phone had been hacked by the *News of the World* under his editorship. In public, the Mancunian comedian played the nerdy radio presenter Alan Partridge; in real life he was feisty, stubborn and intelligent. He suspected that his phone had been hacked because in 2005 someone posing as him had tried to obtain his personal details from his phone company. Coogan said:

It bothered me that he [Coulson] was there. I also felt a certain hubris that came with having no skeletons in my closet. It had been well and truly emptied by all the tabloids. I had a conversation with Matthew Freud whom I had counselled for advice. 'Do you really want to make enemies of these people?' he had asked – advising me that my action was unwise. It made me angry and intrigued me. I don't like bullies; playground ones or Australian ones in suits. Almost everyone in my life cautioned me against it. The only one who said go for it was Martin Sixsmith, a friend, who said: 'You could walk away but you're a bloody-minded northerner, you like a fight.'[6]

The rising number of civil cases appears to have caused anxiety at News International. On 29 July 2010, a senior executive – perhaps unwisely – sent an email asking: 'How come we haven't done the email deletion policy discussed and approved six months ago?' By 4 August, however, the policy was back on track and, in an email referring to 'email deletion', the executive warned colleagues that 'everyone needs to know that anything before January 2010 will not be kept'.[7]* News International's emails contained a hoard of material of use to the police and the civil courts – but News International had no intention of keeping them. When in autumn 2010 the *News of the World* moved from its offices in St Katherine's Dock to nearby Thomas More Square, the company smashed up reporters' old computers and bought new ones. News International said it was a routine technical upgrade.

Over the summer the visiting team of *New York Times* reporters – instigated by Alan Rusbridger – tracked down more than 100 people, mostly journalists and police, and conducted on-the-record interviews with Mark Lewis, Charlotte Harris, Max Clifford and Phil Hall, Brooks's predecessor as editor of the *News of the World*. Many former *NoW* staff were nervous about speaking out, even off the record, but the Americans won their confidence. 'I think a few may have trusted us more because we were US journalists,' Don van Natta Jr

---

* At the time of going to press, the senior executive cannot be named for legal reasons.

said, 'but that wasn't the case with all our sources. Some appreciated the fact that we wanted to get the story exactly right, and that we had the time to really dig into the truth.'[8]

On 1 September, the *New York Times* published its damning, 6,167-word verdict under the headline 'Tabloid Hack Attack on Royals, and Beyond'. Two former *News of the World* staffers were quoted as saying that Andy Coulson knew about phone hacking. One was willing to be named: Sean Hoare, the reporter Coulson had put in the perspex box during the David Blaine stunt (see chapter 2). Hoare had been angered by the company's treatment of Clive Goodman and by his old editor's new berth in Downing Street. With the encouragement of Matt Driscoll, Hoare admitted that he had hacked voicemails at the *Sun* and the *News of the World*, with the management's encouragement. A second, anonymous ex-*NoW* journalist was quoted as saying: 'Everyone knew. The office cat knew.' The Americans spoke to Sharon Marshall (author of *Tabloid Girl*), who said:

> It was an industry-wide thing. Talk to any tabloid journalist in the United Kingdom and they can tell you each phone company's four-digit codes. Every hack on every newspaper knew this was done.

A detective told the Americans that when Dick Fedorcio's public affairs directorate realized the *News of the World* was under investigation following the raids on Goodman and Mulcaire, a police press officer started waving his arms in the air, saying: 'Wait a minute, let's talk about this' and stressed the importance of the Met's long-term relationship with the newspaper. Don van Natta Jr and his colleagues wrote:

> Scotland Yard's narrow focus has allowed *News of the World* and its parent company, News International, to continue to assert that the hacking was limited to one reporter. But interviews with more than a dozen reporters and editors at *News of the World* present a different picture of the newsroom. They described a frantic, sometimes degrading atmosphere in which some reporters openly pursued hacking or other improper tactics to satisfy demanding editors. Andy Coulson ... had imposed a hypercompetitive ethos, even by tabloid standards ...

News International responded with absolute denial and character assassination. Privately, it briefed against Hoare, portraying him as an unreliable witness. In public, it released a statement accusing the *New York Times*, which competes with the *Wall Street Journal*, of carrying out a commercial vendetta:

> The *News of the World* repeatedly asked the *New York Times* to pro-
> vide evidence to support their allegations and they were unable to do
> so. Indeed, the story they published contained no new credible evi-
> dence and relied heavily on anonymous sources, contrary to the paper's
> own editorial guidelines. In doing so, they have undermined their own
> reputation and confirmed our suspicion their story was motivated by
> commercial rivalry. We reject absolutely any suggestion there was a
> widespread culture of wrongdoing at the *News of the World*.[9]

For hours after publication, the campaigners were elated because they thought the story would force the government to announce an inquiry. The *New York Times* had independently corroborated the work of the *Guardian* and gone even further in its depiction of an out-of-control newsroom. Rusbridger's gamble had paid off. Although the US investigation was a feat of newsgathering, it could have been accomplished by any British newspaper; but most had not wanted to look.

Fleet Street had been doubly shamed, but the government refused to act. In Downing Street, a spokesman for Andy Coulson 'emphatically' denied any wrongdoing, adding: 'He has, however, offered to talk to officers if the need arises and would welcome the opportunity to give his view on Mr Hoare's claims.' A spokesman for David Cameron said: 'Andy has made the position clear, and there have been a number of reports over the past few days but none of those reports change anything as far as the Prime Minister is concerned ... He has full confidence in Andy Coulson.'

Tom Watson, Nick Davies and the Manchester lawyers decided that, while News International and the Murdoch-backed government were unlikely to move, it would be harder for the police to ignore new evidence: Scotland Yard was the weakest link. On 3 September, Watson wrote to the Commissioner, Sir Paul Stephenson (publishing the letter on the Labour Uncut website run by his friend Siôn Simon):

Dear Sir Paul,

I write as a Member of Parliament, a former Cabinet Office minister and a member of the Culture, Media and Sport Select Committee which took evidence last year from Andy Coulson and Les Hinton about the *News of the World*'s illegal phone hacking operations.

The Metropolitan Police's historic and continued mishandling of this affair is bringing your force, and hence our democracy, into disrepute.

Former Assistant Commissioner Brian Paddick has requested a judicial review of the Metropolitan Police's investigation (or lack of it – we do not know) into his phone being hacked by newspapers while he was a serving officer. This is extraordinary.

Indeed, it would appear that the Metropolitan Police Service (MPS) may have deliberately withheld from this serving senior officer the information that his phone had been hacked. Please confirm whether this is true.

The phone of a serving Metropolitan Police commissioner was also on a list of numbers intended to be hacked by newspapers. It has been reported that an MPS investigation established that his phone had not been hacked. Please confirm whether this is true.

If it is, please confirm whether the phone of every other name on any list found of numbers intended to be hacked was also investigated.

If not, please confirm who decided, according to what criteria and on what authority, which names to investigate and which to ignore.

MPS officers were on lists of names to be illegally hacked; which were investigated and which were notified? Much anger and concern centres on your force's failure to inform people that their names had been found on these lists. Please confirm exactly how many names were on Mulcaire's and any other lists.

Many Members of Parliament were on these lists. The Metropolitan Police has strongly implied that all Members of Parliament so targeted had been informed. This was not true. Please confirm how many Members of Parliament were on the lists.

Please confirm who decided which Members of Parliament to notify, according to what criteria and on what authority.

Please confirm, in all other cases, who selected which victims should be notified, on what criteria, on what authority and who else had any requisite knowledge. Please confirm who went to seize the materials, where are these materials stored, and what processes the Met go through when answering letters and inquiries about these materials.

The *New York Times* allege key evidence was withheld from the Crown Prosecution Service. Please confirm that all evidence was provided to the Crown Prosecution Service.

Your conduct of this matter is being scrutinized all over the world. So far, it is bringing shame – as has News International – on our country.

I await your early response.*

Yours sincerely, Tom Watson MP

Later that day, 3 September, the police's position was made more uncomfortable by Sean Hoare speaking out again – this time to the British media. On BBC Radio 4's *PM* programme, Hoare left listeners in no doubt about the methods used at Wapping. 'There is an expression called the culture of dark arts,' he said. 'You were given a remit: just get the story. Phone tapping hadn't just existed on the *News of the World*. It was endemic within the whole industry . . . Such was the culture of intimidation and bullying that you do it.'

More senior politicians came forward to say their phone messages had been hacked. Later that day, 3 September, Tessa Jowell, Labour's

---

* John Yates eventually responded on 22 October. In an anodyne letter he said it was 'inappropriate' for the force to comment on the cases of Brian Paddick, Chris Bryant and Brendan Montague (a freelance journalist who had by then joined the judicial review), since they were taking proceedings or on the cases of third parties since the police owed them a duty of confidence. He concluded:

> Finally you raise a number of other issues about the Metropolitan Police Service's handling of this investigation. All I can say on this point is what we have said in public statements, namely that the MPS has a duty to ensure that any inquiries are lawful, proportionate and involve an appropriate use of police resources. We worked closely with both the CPS and Leading Counsel throughout and . . . the DPP has conducted his own review and considered that the case was handled appropriately.

former Culture Secretary, disclosed that the Met had told her in 2006 that her phone had been intercepted twenty-eight times, but later informed her that she was not needed as a witness. On Sunday 5 September, the *Independent on Sunday*'s Matt Chorley disclosed that the phone numbers of Tony Blair's cabinet minister Peter Mandelson and the former Defence Minister Peter Kilfoyle had been found in Mulcaire's notes. Still the government would not budge. Michael Gove, the Education Secretary and a former *Times* journalist whose wife still worked for the title, dismissed the *New York Times* article. Appearing on the BBC's *Andrew Marr Show*, Gove – who had received an advance from Murdoch's HarperCollins for a book he still has not written – said its disclosures 'seem to be a recycling of allegations we have heard before', taking the News International line that they may have been a product of 'circulation wars' in the US.

On Monday 6 September, the Speaker of the House of Commons, John Bercow – who consistently allowed MPs to air allegations about the scandal – granted Tom Watson an 'urgent question', forcing a statement from the Home Secretary, Theresa May. She repeated the official story that two men had been jailed and the investigation had been reviewed by Scotland Yard and the Director of Public Prosecutions. The prosecution of Goodman and Mulcaire, she assured MPs, had 'appropriately represented the criminality uncovered'. In the angry debate that followed, Watson and Chris Bryant attacked the government and police's position and the shadow Home Secretary, Alan Johnson, called for Andy Coulson's resignation.

Making a prearranged appearance before the House of Commons Home Affairs Committee, John Yates said that he was prepared to consider Hoare's evidence. But he added that the law on hacking, RIPA, meant: 'We can only prove a crime against a very small number of people and that number is about ten to twelve people.' Asked whether Lord Prescott, the former Deputy Prime Minister, was one of them, he replied: 'He is not on that list and he has never been hacked to my knowledge and there is no evidence that he has.' The Home Affairs Committee opened an inquiry into the police's handling of the affair.

Scotland Yard's position was being bombarded daily. On Wednesday 8 September, the *Guardian* disclosed that Ross Hindley, the *News of the World* reporter who had transcribed Gordon Taylor's hacked voicemails, offered to talk to detectives. The following day, Nick Davies finally persuaded the second, anonymous *News of the World* reporter who had spoken to the *New York Times* to step out of the shadows. Paul McMullan, the *NoW*'s former features editor, told Davies that phone hacking was 'so routine' at the paper that its journalists didn't realize they were doing anything wrong. 'People were obsessed with getting celebs' phone numbers,' said McMullan, now a pub landlord in Kent. 'There were senior people who were really scared when the Mulcaire story came out. Everyone was surprised that Clive Goodman was the only one who went down.'

That evening, the Speaker granted Chris Bryant another parliamentary debate, during which Tom Watson articulated the all-pervasive fear of News International and redtop newspapers more generally:

> The truth is that, in this house we are all, in our own way, scared of the Rebekah Brookses of this world. It is almost laughable that we sit here in Parliament, the central institution of our sacred democracy – among us are some of the most powerful people in the land – yet we are scared of the power that Rebekah Brooks wields without a jot of responsibility or accountability. The barons of the media, with their red-topped assassins, are the biggest beasts in the modern jungle. They have no predators. They are untouchable. They laugh at the law; they sneer at Parliament. They have the power to hurt us, and they do, with gusto and precision, with joy and criminality. Prime Ministers quail before them, and that is how they like it.

'And yet,' he added, 'I sense that we are at the beginning of the end-game. Things will get better because, in many senses, they cannot get worse.'

That day, 9 September, a News International executive made another request to destroy emails. In an email later disclosed to civil claimants, an employee in Wapping's IT department wrote: 'There is a senior NI management requirement to delete this data as quickly as possible but it needs to be done within commercial boundaries.' A month later, on 7 October, a senior executive again asked – in an email – 'How are we doing with the email deletion policy?'[10]

At Scotland Yard, John Yates went about checking the new allegations in a curious way. He interviewed Sean Hoare under caution, meaning that anything he said could lead to his prosecution: understandably Hoare stayed silent. Lawyers, journalists and politicians were furious, because it looked as if one of Yates's first moves following the *New York Times* article had been to scare off other whistleblowers.

Boris Johnson, the mayor of London, was emphatically unconcerned by the haplessness. The Conservative politician had been warned by detectives in 2006 that he had been targeted by Mulcaire, but he had not sued then or later; and though he was chairman of the Metropolitan Police Authority (which oversaw London's police force) he had also failed to do anything on publication of the Gordon Taylor story in July 2009. Like his fellow Etonian and Conservative David Cameron, Johnson was close to Rebekah Brooks and knew he might need the full-blooded support of News International if he was to fulfil his long-held ambition to become Prime Minister. At the mayor's monthly question time on 15 September 2010, Johnson shrugged off demands to put pressure on Scotland Yard, saying he could not see anything new in the story. He said: 'I think it's patently politically motivated and unless there are significant new facts brought into the public domain that actually change the police case and make necessary a fresh look at it, then I don't propose to change my views.' Looking at his fellow London Assembly members, he laughed: 'This is a load of codswallop cooked up by the Labour Party.'[11]

12

Losing a Battle

I have declared war on Mr Murdoch and I think we're going to win

        – Business Secretary Vince Cable

Two years after he had been turned over by the *News of the World*, Max Mosley was about to strike again. During the summer of 2010, from Monaco, he had been taking a closer interest in the phone hacking story and had started talking to Nick Davies at the *Guardian*. He had also acquired a highly confidential source, Mr X, who had told him that Scotland Yard was holding extensive evidence about illegal newsgathering techniques. Mosley decided the best way to intensify the pressure was through the civil law. Disclosure would unlock the secrets of Mulcaire's files. But there was a problem: money. Many potential litigants were deterred by the prospect of being landed with crippling costs, so Mosley agreed to underwrite the risk for litigants in the judicial review against Scotland Yard and emerging privacy cases against the *News of the World*. If the cases were lost, his costs could run into hundreds of thousands of pounds, but he decided he would risk half his fortune, if necessary, to fight Rupert Murdoch. Ordinarily that money would have gone to his son, Alexander, but he had died in 2008. On 12 September, five days before Mosley returned to London at the end of his presidency of the FIA, Tamsin Allen at Bindmans began the judicial review against the Met at the High Court on behalf of Chris Bryant, Brian Paddick and Brendan Montague; a week later they were joined by John Prescott.

In 2011, Mosley said: 'I saw it as a much bigger thing than giving the *News of the World* a bit of their own back, or privacy generally, because I feel the Murdoch empire is a really sinister presence undermining the whole of our democracy. They are capable of suborning the police, Parliament and the government.' He suspected that the police had been reluctant to inform the victims 'because they knew damn well there would be writs flying down to the High Court and their friends in Wapping would be upset'.[1]

In a memo to the Home Affairs Committee in October, Mark Lewis speculated that Operation Caryatid might have failed because of a lack of resources, high-priority terrorism cases – or the closeness of the relationship between senior officers and *News of the World* executives. With the benefit of legal privilege applying to parliamentary affairs, the lawyer raised another possibility: that Andy Hayman and John Yates, who had both had their phones hacked, had been fearful of press coverage. Lewis wrote:

> At the relevant time, Mr Hayman had reason to fear that he was a target of Glenn Mulcaire and the *News of the World*. It became public knowledge that throughout the period of the investigation into voicemail hacking, Mr Hayman was involved in a controversial relationship with a woman who worked for the Independent Police Complaints Commission and was claiming expenses which were subsequently regarded as unusually high. The same, of course, is also true of John Yates who, we now know, at the time when he responded to the *Guardian*'s stories about Gordon Taylor's settlement with News Group, was involved in a controversial relationship with a woman who worked for the Met press bureau.[2]

Lewis offered no evidence that the officers had been fearful, and Yates and Hayman both denied that their behaviour had been compromised by their relationships.

With pressure building on the police, News International became ever more determined to marginalize its detractors. The company always held champagne receptions at the party conferences, at which there was no shortage of ambitious guests. At the Labour conference at the end of September 2010, despite scorning the party the year before, Wapping's executives were out in force. At a reception on the night of the Labour leader's speech, a member of the *Sun*'s political staff, referring to a planning extension to Tom Watson's family home, told Kevan Jones MP: 'Tell that fat bastard of a mate that we know everything about his little planning difficulty.' At another event, within Watson's earshot, Colin Myler referred to him as a 'fat bastard'. At a Sky reception, a *Times* journalist told the Labour backbencher Stephen Pound that Watson was drinking heavily and about to check in to the Betty Ford clinic.

Watson, an occasionally enthusiastic drinker, gave up alcohol and devoted himself to exposing the company. He still did not know that he had been tailed by Derek Webb in 2009, but the whispering campaign, the unusual characters sitting in cars near his home and the motorbike rider outside his Westminster flat (he knew that the *NoW* sometimes used a motorbike to follow targets) induced in him a degree of paranoia. He kept the curtains and blinds closed, had his laptop computer within his sight at all times, never called key contacts on mobile phones and did not dispose of letters or personal documents in his own bins. He alternated his routes to work.

At the Conservative Party conference in early October, in a meeting with David Cameron's chief of staff, Ed Llewellyn, the *Guardian*'s deputy editor, Ian Katz, again directly raised Andy Coulson's record at the *News of the World* and his employment of Jonathan Rees. (Rees's murder trial at the Old Bailey had become mired in legal argument.)

There was a much bigger game being played at the conference, though: News Corp's takeover of Sky. On 5 October, Fred Michel and Rebekah Brooks held a meeting with Jeremy Hunt – and two days later sent him a briefing document on the bid. While it was politically awkward for Hunt to be seen to be treading on Cable's domain, communications could be discreetly routed through Hunt's special adviser, Adam Smith. Smith had worked for Hunt for years in opposition and knew his mind well. On 8 October, Smith emailed Michel: 'Jeremy's response to this – "persuasive".'[3] Like other ambitious ministers such as Michael Gove, Hunt was keen to ingratiate himself with the Murdochs.

Despite Cable's earlier expression of support, News Corp was becoming concerned that the Business Secretary might succumb to growing opposition to the bid. On 11 October, in a rare show of agreement, the owners of the *Guardian*, *Telegraph*, *Mirror* and *Mail* newspapers, BT, Channel 4 and the BBC's director-general Mark Thompson signed a letter to the Department of Business, Innovation and Skills (BIS) warning that the takeover 'could have serious and far-reaching consequences for media plurality'. A prominent media analyst, Claire Enders, warned that Rupert Murdoch's dominance in Britain would be unmatched.[4]

Cable was doggedly resistant to direct lobbying. After consulting with Lib Dem policy advisers, Fred Michel floated the idea of using editors of *The Times* and *Wall Street Journal* as bait to lobby Cable and his close colleague Michael Oakeshott. After meeting 'Vince's main adviser' (unnamed) on 18 October, Michel emailed Rebekah Brooks:

> It was suggested that we should try a very soft approach with him; get him to meet with James Harding [editor of *The Times*] to get his views on some of the BIS key items like migration cap; and get me to pop in at some stage to give him an update on the current battle we face and inform his views. It would be very much better than a direct lobbying conversation . . . [Oakeshott] would be VERY receptive to a message from Patience [Wheatcroft, then editor of the *Wall St Journal* Europe] on this.[5]

Michel also contacted Alex Salmond, leader of the Scottish National Party, which the Scottish edition of the *Sun* had backed at the general election. In an email to James Murdoch on 1 November, Michel wrote: 'Alex Salmond is very keen to also put these issues across to Cable and have a call with you tomorrow or Wednesday. His team will also brief the Scottish press on the economic importance of News Corp for Scotland.' Salmond later denied he had lobbied the government over the deal.[6]

As the company privately lobbied ministers, News Corp publicly dismissed any suggestion that phone hacking had been widespread at Wapping; to have admitted widespread wrongdoing would have cast a question over the company's ethics. At News Corp's annual meeting in New York on 15 October, Rupert Murdoch told investors:

> We have very strict rules. There was an incident more than five years ago. The person who bought a bugged phone conversation was immediately fired and in fact he subsequently went to jail. There have been two parliamentary inquiries, which have found no further evidence of anything at all. If anything was to come to light, we challenge people to give us evidence, and no one has been able to.

Nearly every claim in that statement was untrue.

The government made a series of policy announcements which helped News Corp. On 14 October, Jeremy Hunt announced a sweeping reform of Ofcom, removing its policy-setting powers on media ownership and transferring them to himself. Ofcom's annual budget was reduced from £142 million to £112 million by 2014–15, 28 per cent in real terms over four years. One in five staff, 170 in all, would lose their jobs. The regulator had been hobbled; now it was the turn of the state broadcaster.

In his first spending review on 20 October, the Chancellor, George Osborne, announced the licence fee would be frozen at £145.50 for six years, a 16 per cent cut to the BBC's budget in real terms. The BBC would also have to take over the £300 million annual cost of running the World Service and contribute £150 million a year towards the roll-out of rural broadband. The government pointed to the fact that the spending of government departments was being cut by 19 per cent (though the BBC's income was raised separately through the licence fee). The government deferred until 2013 Gordon Brown's intention to strip Sky of its exclusive live rights to home tests in the Ashes.

Privately, as Cable's decision drew closer, News Corp's lobbying grew ever more persistent – and threatening. On 27 October at Portcullis House, Fred Michel met the Lib Dem leader Nick Clegg's chief adviser Norman Lamb. According to Lamb, during the meeting Michel made a coded threat to the Liberal Democrats if Cable did not back the bid. Lamb recalled later:

He specifically mentioned the *Sun* and indicated that it had given the Liberal Democrats reasonable coverage since the election. He then implied that if the decision surrounding the bid did not fall in their favour, it would be a pity if things were to change and they were no longer able to report in such a positive way. I cannot remember the exact phraseology but the message was very clear.[7]

In his handwritten note, disclosed to the Leveson Inquiry a year later, Lamb wrote: 'It was brazen: VC refers the case to Ofcom – they turn nasty.'[8]

On 4 November, Cable refused to buckle and asked Ofcom to assess whether the deal threatened 'media plurality'. His decision was a big setback for News Corp and was strongly at odds with the pro-Murdoch decisions made by the Cameron government.

The Murdochs were furious. They lost no time in searching out the reasons for Cable's intransigence. On 8 November, Michel was rebuffed by Cable's adviser, Giles Wilkes, who told him they could not meet to discuss 'the Ofcom business'. Michel told James Murdoch: 'I am also having follow up calls with David Laws and Clegg on this.' That day, Michel met George Osborne's special adviser, Rupert Harrison, and relayed the details to James Murdoch the following morning:

> Confirmed tensions in the Coalition around Vince Cable and his current policy positions. Vince made a political decision, probably without even reading the legal advice, as confirmed to us by [Liberal Democrats] Vicky Pryce and David Laws yesterday. He [Harrison] was very much taken by our commitment to Scotland and Alex Salmond's desire to support us. He thought it was a strong ally to put forward, very contrarian/unexpected. Same for Scottish LibDems.[9]

On 15 November, Michel passed on the bad news to James Murdoch that a scheduled meeting with Hunt could not happen because 'he has received very strong legal advice not to meet us today as the current process is being treated as a judicial one'.[10] Not one for delicacies, James angrily replied: 'You must be f***ing joking. Fine. I will txt him and find a time.'[11] Hunt and James spoke by phone the following day. Faced with the ban on meetings, Hunt apparently told News Corp to pass on information through Adam Smith, his 'special adviser' and trusted aide. Michel emailed the cabinet minister: 'Thanks for the call with James today. Greatly appreciated. Will work with Adam to make sure we can send you helpful arguments. Warm regards. Fred.'[12] Hunt relayed the Murdochs' anger at Cable's decision in a memo to Cameron:

From Jeremy Hunt
To David Cameron
Date 19 November 2010

James Murdoch is pretty furious at Vince's referral to Ofcom. He doesn't think he will get a fair hearing from Ofcom. I am privately concerned about this because News Corp are very litigious and we could end up in the wrong place in terms of media policy. Essentially what James Murdoch wants to do is to repeat what his father did with the move to Wapping and create the world's first multi-platform media operator available from paper to web to TV to iPhone to iPad. Isn't this what all media companies have to do ultimately? And if so we must be very careful that any attempt to block it is done on plurality grounds and not as a result of lobbying by competitors.

The UK has the chance to lead the way on this as we did in the Eighties with the Wapping move but if we block it our media sector will suffer for years. I am sure sensible controls can be put into any merger to ensure there is plurality but I think it would be totally wrong to cave into the Mark Thompson/Channel 4/*Guardian* line that this represents a substantial change of control given that we all know Sky is controlled by News Corp now anyway.

What next? Ofcom will issue their report saying whether it needs to go to the Competition Commission by 31 December. It would be totally wrong for the Government to get involved in a competition issue which has to be decided at arm's length. However I do think you, I, Vince and the DPM [Nick Clegg] should meet to discuss the policy issues that are thrown up as a result.[13]

Hunt was offering to intervene in a strictly controlled quasi-judicial process; to have a word with the judge, because he had made the wrong decision. As it happened, he need not have bothered – because Hunt soon became the judge himself.

At midday on 21 December, the European Commission cleared the Sky bid. At 12.57 p.m. Hunt texted James Murdoch: 'Great and congrats on Brussels. Just Ofcom to go.'[14] The Culture Secretary seemed to regard the regulator as merely a hurdle to be jumped rather than an independent arbiter of what was best for the British media.

At 2.30 p.m., the BBC's business editor Robert Peston published a story highly damaging to Vince Cable. A few weeks earlier Cable had been visited at his constituency surgery by two 'constituents' who were, in fact, undercover reporters from the *Daily Telegraph*, looking for a scoop on tensions in the Coalition. The female reporters recorded their conversation with Cable and must have been surprised by what he told them. 'You may wonder what is happening with the Murdoch press,' he told them. 'I have declared war on Mr Murdoch and I think we're going to win. I didn't politicize it, because it is a legal question, but he is trying to take over BSkyB . . . I have blocked it. His whole empire is now under attack.' The *Daily Telegraph*, whose parent company had signed the letter of opposition to the Sky deal, had not reported Cable's comments, but somehow they had been leaked to Robert Peston. A detective agency later hired by the Telegraph Media Group, Kroll, suspected that Will Lewis, News International's general manager and a former *Telegraph* editor, was likely to have obtained the quotes from a *Telegraph* insider and passed them to his friend Peston. The *Telegraph* insider was later employed at Wapping.[15]

News International issued a statement saying it was 'shocked' by Cable's comments, which, it said, raised questions 'about fairness and due process'. In Downing Street David Cameron and his Chancellor, George Osborne, wondered what to do. After speaking to James Murdoch by phone, Hunt stepped up the pressure by texting Osborne: 'Just been called by James [Murdoch]. His lawyers are meeting now and saying it calls into question legitimacy of whole process from beginning. "Acute bias", etc.' Osborne responded: 'I think you will like the solution.'[16]

At 5.45 p.m., Cameron publicly stripped Vince Cable of responsibility for the bid decision and passed it to Jeremy Hunt. Cameron of course knew of Hunt's warmth for the Murdochs because the Culture Secretary had sent him a memo expressing support for their bid the previous month.

In coming months Hunt's special adviser Adam Smith would pass News Corp's Fred Michel inside information about the progress of the £7.8 billion takeover, exchanging hundreds of text messages and emails. The public and other politicians knew nothing about this: outwardly it was a semi-judicial process.

While Hunt pondered how to get the bid through, the phone hacking scandal veered off northwards: to Scotland. By November, one of the longest-running legal battles in Scottish history, between News International and the socialist politician Tommy Sheridan, was coming to a head. In August 2006 Sheridan had won a defamation case and £200,000 damages against the *News of the World* for its stories about his private life. On the steps of the Glasgow High Court, Sheridan had likened his win to football minnows Gretna beating Real Madrid on penalties, saying: 'They are liars and they have proved they are liars.'[17]

But the following year, 2007, Sheridan and his wife, Gail, had been charged with perjury, accused of lying in his defamation victory. One of the questions at their trial, which began in October 2010, was whether four years previously the *News of the World* had hacked Sheridan's phone and paid witnesses who had testified against him. On 17 November, Bob Bird, the editor of the Scottish edition of the *News of the World*, told the court that emails about the case had been lost while being sent to be archived in India.

From his time at the Cabinet Office, Tom Watson knew the Data Protection Act and demanded the Information Commissioner's Office investigate whether News International had broken the law on the safe storage of personal data and its transfer abroad. The complaint was obscure but it placed News International in a quandary: either it admitted that it had a full archive of emails (potentially revealing its newsgathering crimes) or it risked the ICO seizing its computers, as it had in the raid on Steve Whittamore in 2003.

On 10 December, Sheridan, who was conducting his own defence, called Andy Coulson to the witness stand. During a three-hour inter-rogation, Sheridan asked the Prime Minister's spokesman about Glenn Mulcaire, whose notes contained Sheridan's mobile phone number, address and PIN code. Coulson denied knowing anything about phone hacking. He told the court he had not heard of Mulcaire until he had been arrested. 'I'm saying that I had absolutely no know-ledge of it,' he said. 'I certainly didn't instruct anyone to do anything at the time or anything else which was untoward.'[18]

One of the consequences of the Sheridan case was that the BBC's *Panorama* team began investigating phone hacking. Until then, the Cor-poration had failed to devote much – or indeed any – of its investigative resources to unpicking the scandal, but an experienced reporter, Glenn Campbell, now started looking into the case. From his time as the crime reporter of ITV's *London Tonight* programme in the 1990s, Campbell had excellent contacts inside the Metropolitan Police and other forces. He began delving into the relationship between News International, corrupt former police officers and the private detectives who blagged and hacked personal and financial records. His disclosures would darken the scandal, but his programme was still months away.

Publicly, in December Scotland Yard was still sticking to its position that its inquiries had been complete. Following the *New York Times* investigation, Keir Starmer, the Director of Public Prosecutions, had begun to harbour doubts about the behaviour of Scotland Yard. On 29 October, to the surprise of parliamentarians, he completely reversed his earlier interpretation of the law when he told the Home Affairs Committee that the police and prosecutors should treat all interceptions of phone messages as crimes – regardless of whether they had already been heard. Although RIPA had been untested in the courts, Starmer wrote, 'a robust attitude needs to be taken to any unauthorized interception and investigations should not be inhibited by a narrow approach'.* The change was deeply significant. Scotland

---

* Keir Starmer was later asked by the Home Affairs Committee why in 2009 he had made such a clear statement that it was only a crime to intercept some messages. He

Yard had maintained that it could not bring cases on behalf of many victims because of the narrow interpretation of the law; now that excuse was swept away.

On 5 November, Andy Coulson was interviewed by the police. Unlike Sean Hoare, the Prime Minister's communications director was interviewed as a witness by appointment at his solicitors and not placed under caution. The arrangements suggested that rather than believing Coulson had to explain Hoare's allegations, the police may have hoped he would implicate Hoare. It is not known what, if anything, Coulson said, but John Yates's inquiry singularly failed to establish the facts about phone hacking. Sean Hoare had not repeated his allegations since he had been interviewed under caution and Paul McMullan had not responded to a letter from the Met asking for an interview. (Surprisingly, Yates took no further action.) Despite the cascade of information in the *New York Times*, Scotland Yard had got nowhere.

On 10 December, Keir Starmer reluctantly announced that there was no admissible evidence on which to charge anyone. With a degree of frustration, he said: 'The contents of the reports in the *New York Times* and the associated reports and coverage are not enough for criminal proceedings unless those making allegations are prepared to provide the police with admissible evidence to support their assertions.' The thrust of his remarks was that former *NoW* journalists had failed to stand by their evidence. He and Yates had not yet grasped the obvious fact that the key evidence was not new, but old – and already in the possession of the Metropolitan Police.

As 2010 drew to a close, Tom Watson realized that the prospects of charges being brought were, if anything, diminishing. He fired off a barrage of parliamentary questions, Freedom of Information requests and letters to the Prime Minister, ministers, the Metropolitan Police, the PCC and the Information Commissioner. The few replies he received tended to be bland, cursory or contemptuous. But as a former government minister, he knew how to apply pressure. On

---

replied that he had been trying to reply quickly to a parliamentary inquiry and that 'nobody at that stage went through the documents in detail'.[19]

23 December, he wrote to the country's most senior civil servant, the Cabinet Secretary, Sir Gus O'Donnell.

The previous day O'Donnell had rejected a complaint from Labour's John Denham that Jeremy Hunt's previous support for Rupert Murdoch disqualified him from ruling on the Sky bid. O'Donnell, a loyal and genial mandarin, had consulted government lawyers, who reassuringly advised that Hunt's interview with *Broadcast*, the 'cheerleader' reference on his website and his comments to the *FT* about News Corp already controlling the broadcaster were not an impediment.

Watson – who knew of several meetings between government ministers and News Corp and suspected other secret contacts were taking place – wrote:

Dear Gus,

I have written to you several times in the past few weeks about matters of propriety and the ethics of government. I am now writing to ask about such matters again . . .

Did you know about Jeremy Hunt's 28 June meeting with James Murdoch and his 21 July meeting with Jeremy Darroch when responsibility for ruling on News Corp's proposal to take full control of BSkyB was transferred from Vince Cable to Jeremy Hunt?

What was discussed during Jeremy Hunt's meeting with James Murdoch on 28 June?

Where was that meeting held, and at what time?

As no civil servants were present at the meeting, can you be entirely satisfied that this meeting will not prejudice Mr Hunt's judgement when acting in the quasi-judicial role?

Did Jeremy Hunt discuss News Corp's proposed purchase of the remaining BSkyB shares at his meeting with James Murdoch on 28 June?

In your letter to John Denham yesterday, you said that you took legal advice on the question of whether there was any legal impediment to moving ministerial responsibility for competition and policy issues relating to media, broadcasting, digital and telecoms sectors from BIS to DCMS. You did not say, though, whether you had taken legal advice on Mr Hunt's conflict of interest.

Did you take legal advice specifically about Mr Hunt's conflict of interest?

If you did, did the lawyers know about the 28 June meeting between Jeremy Hunt and James Murdoch in providing this advice?

Did they know about Mr Hunt's 21 July meeting with Jeremy Darroch?

Did they know about his several published highly prejudicial statements?

Did you know about these meetings?

Did you, and any lawyers consulted, know about Jeremy Hunt's formal meetings with News Corp on 10 June and with BSkyB on 10 July?

Did you know about [Culture Minister] Ed Vaizey's lunch with Rebekah Brooks on 12 July?

Did you know about the News Corp dinner attended by Jeremy Hunt and Adam Smith on 20 May?

Are you seriously going to attempt to hold the line that Jeremy Hunt has no conflict of interest? He has made unprecedentedly prejudicial public statements. And, in a short and busy time since taking office:

he has had several formal meetings with News Corp and its subsidiaries;

he has been to their dinners;

his junior minister has been to lunch;

he has had several, unminuted, private, secret, 'informal' meetings with News Corp, the existence of which DCMS ministers have then denied in written answers to Parliament.

Jeremy Hunt is neck deep in News Corp, and you know it.

Remember, nobody expects the Prime Minister to tell the truth or do the decent thing. But the Cabinet Secretary is supposed to be the government's conscience.

I look forward to hearing from you as soon as possible.

Yours sincerely

Tom Watson

Member of Parliament for West Bromwich East

From his time in Gordon Brown's Downing Street, Watson knew

O'Donnell to be a clever operator and had no personal animus against him, but he also realized that he primarily saw his role as protecting the government. Watson knew that the mandarin would be making a calculated decision that there was nothing in his letter that he couldn't ignore, but that there were questions he could not answer and questions to which he probably did not want to know the answer. He wanted to make O'Donnell and others in power nervous.

Despite the hyperactivity, Watson was running out of avenues. He was also struggling personally. His marriage – strained by the Damian McBride affair and his preoccupation with the hacking scandal – had collapsed and his estranged wife had moved back to Yorkshire to be closer to her family.

During the Christmas break, he had taken to walking in the Peak District from where he would phone or text his close friends, David Wild and Siôn Simon. They indulged him as he related his latest idea for the investigation, sometimes listening to him for an hour. Although they did not say so at the time, they became deeply worried about his mental health. He was obsessively memorizing the number plates of suspicious vehicles.

On 27 December, in the peaks of the Yorkshire and Derbyshire border, a phone call transformed the MP's mood. A source, who had detailed knowledge of the information technology of News Corp, contradicted Watson's belief that data had been lost irrevocably. During the Sheridan trial, News International had declared that emails had gone missing while being transferred to India. The insider, who had read about Watson's complaint to the Information Commissioner, patiently explained that personal data would not be archived abroad: News Corp had strict rules on data storage because American law placed draconian sanctions on firms which failed to maintain adequate records. The archives, he said, would be in the UK. There were two servers at Wapping: the first was for all emails; the second allowed executives to share confidential information. An email sent to an executive would be stored on both servers. Were the first server to be destroyed, the second would remain. As they talked for over an hour, Watson tried not to betray his increasing sense of euphoria.

Back in 2005 when Mulcaire and Goodman were hacking phones,

the company felt it was untouchable. It had politicians and police in its pocket, and had no 'predators'; Watson's logic was that with that level of power executives would feel invulnerable and become complacent – and make mistakes. He already knew that Brooks was careless with her digital fingerprints because of the text message about him which she had sent the previous year to someone close to the Prime Minister. If others shared her arrogance, there would be a rich source of information on that second server that the police could use. He did not know at that point that data had been destroyed. But just as he had been losing hope, he was reinvigorated.

13

Out of Control

It doesn't say 'Fulham', it says 'Soham'

— Charlotte Harris

While the police and prosecutors were claiming they were searching for new evidence, the civil litigants had been making progress with the old. In September 2010, with the benefit of the Mulcaire notes disclosed to her by the police in July, Sienna Miller had begun a High Court case against News International. In her court papers, Miller claimed that the *News of the World* had published eleven articles about her and her then boyfriend Jude Law derived from hacking, causing her 'extreme concern about her privacy and safety as well as enormous anxiety and distress'. Whenever she had changed phones, she told the court, Mulcaire had obtained the number's PIN code, as well as phone numbers and PINs for Law and his personal assistant, Ben Jackson, and for her friend Archie Keswick and publicist Ciara Parkes. On 15 December, Miller's lawyer, Mark Thomson, disclosed to the court the name of the commissioning journalist in the top left-hand corner of Mulcaire's notes. It was 'Ian'. On 5 January 2011, the BBC's business editor Robert Peston broke off from the Davos summit in Switzerland to announce that the *News of the World* had suspended Ian Edmondson, the paper's news editor and one of Andy Coulson's signings from the *People*. In a statement, News International said: 'The *News of the World* has a zero tolerance approach to wrongdoing.'

Events now moved quickly and pressure built on News International, Downing Street and Scotland Yard by the day.

The Met's story was at breaking point. The previous February it had been forced to admit that thousands of names were in Mulcaire's notes; now lawyers were claiming one of the commissioning 'corner names' was a senior executive at the *News of the World*. Over coming months more civil litigation threatened to expose further embarrassing evidence and the Max Mosley-backed judicial review would subject London's police force to a forensic examination of its treatment of victims. Two days after the news of Edmondson's suspension, on 7 January, Scotland Yard formally asked News International to hand over any new evidence in its possession about phone hacking.

On 14 January, Keir Starmer announced a 'comprehensive review' by a senior lawyer, Alison Levitt QC, of the evidence held by the police. In a letter to Starmer published the same day, John Yates welcomed the review, saying there remained 'outstanding public, legal and political concerns' surrounding phone hacking.

The following day, News International's IT department deleted a copy of the email chain sent to James Murdoch's laptop during the Gordon Taylor case in 2008. The company later told the Commons Culture Committee that the deletion was part of an 'email stabilization policy and modernization programme which saw a number of users' accounts being prepared for the migration to a new email system'.[1] (On 8 March, the email chain was also deleted from Colin Myler's desktop computer due to 'a hardware failure'.[2])

On 18 January, Steve Coogan and the football pundit Andy Gray lodged an application in the High Court demanding that Mulcaire disclose who had commissioned him. On 19 January, the *Independent* reported that David Cameron had visited Rebekah Brooks at her country home during the Christmas break. Downing Street refused to give any details of the meeting, which it justified on the basis that Brooks was a constituent of Cameron's (though that explanation was undermined when it emerged later that James Murdoch was also present); but it focused unwelcome attention on the social links between the Cotswold set. Brooks and the Prime Minister had been socializing around the time Cameron had handed the Sky decision to Jeremy Hunt. Only those present could say whether Brooks and Murdoch used their personal connection with the Prime Minister to lobby him but for the first time the relationship with News International had become an embarrassment to the government. The heat was now on the Prime Minister as well as his director of communications.

Andy Coulson could take no more. On 21 January, he resigned. In what would become a familiar refrain, he maintained he had done nothing wrong. 'Unfortunately,' he said, 'continued coverage of events connected to my old job at the *News of the World* has made it difficult to give the 110 per cent needed in this role. I stand by what I've said about those events but when the spokesman needs a spokesman, it's time to move on.'

David Cameron said:

> I am very sorry that Andy Coulson has decided to resign as my direc-
> tor of communications, although I understand that the continuing
> pressures on him and his family mean that he feels compelled to do
> so . . . He can be extremely proud of the role he has played, including
> for the last eight months in government.

Piers Morgan tweeted: 'Very sad to hear news about Andy Coulson – good man, good friend. How many times does @*Guardian* want people to quit over the same thing?'

The Conservative blogger Tim Montgomerie suggested that Rupert Murdoch, currently visiting London, had ordered the resignation. Montgomerie said later: 'A very senior cabinet minister who was in a position to know told me that Murdoch was an influence on Andy Coulson's decision to quit. Within minutes Andy Coulson rang to say the suggestion was rubbish.'[3]

Undoubtedly, News Corp was still anxious about the Sky deal, now with the regulator Ofcom. On 31 December, Ofcom had sent its report to Jeremy Hunt, warning that the deal would increase News Corp's share of regular news consumers from 32 per cent to 51 per cent and recommended it be referred to the Competition Commission. Aside from potentially blocking the deal, a Competition Commission inquiry would take at least six months, by which time BSkyB's share price would probably rise and the Murdochs would have to pay more.

Hunt came up with a plan: if News Corp could guarantee the independence of Sky News, Ofcom's objections would be removed and the bid could proceed as planned. The Murdochs took the hint: on 18 January, News Corp submitted concessions – known as 'Undertakings in Lieu', or UILs – which would address Ofcom's concerns without a referral to the Competition Commission. A week later, on 23 January, an email from Michel to News Corp's Matthew Anderson laid bare the astonishing degree of furtive cooperation between Hunt's department and News Corp:

> To: Anderson, Matthew
> From: Michel, Fred
> Date: 23/01/2011
> Time: 8.59pm
> He [Jeremy Hunt] still wants to stick to the following plan:
> – Monday: receive further details on UIL – but no need to meet at this stage
> – Tuesday: Publication of Ofcom report; our submission and announcement that he has received UIL proposal and is looking into it . . .
> – Put the UIL to Ofcom for advice. He said he would be able to send it to them with a specific question to limit their ability to challenge it (ie –'your report demonstrates that Sky News is the core concern; I would like you to consider the following UIL which addresses all of these issues') He said Ofcom would not be able to create major obstacles in that way
> – That in 2 weeks time, he announces he is minded to refer but has received a very substantial UIL and would like to consult publicly
> – He predicts it should all be done by mid-Feb.
> His view is that he announces publicly he has a strong UIL, it's almost game over the opposition . . .
> Fred

On 24 January, the eve of Hunt's announcement to Parliament, Michel sent James Murdoch an email with inside information headed: Confidential – JH Statement.

Managed to get some infos on the plans for tomorrow (although absolutely illegal!). Press statement at 7.30am . . . JH will announce . . . that he wishes to look at any undertakings that have the potential to prevent the potential threats of media plurality identified in the Ofcom report. He will then say that News Corp wished him to consider a UIL, and he has asked Ofcom and OFT to assist him in that process. . . .[4]

The following morning, Hunt announced – just as Michel had been tipped off – that he was halting the referral to the Competition Commission to see if News Corp could come up with satisfactory guarantees for Sky News.

Despite all the troubles that had beset him – the *New York Times* story, Ian Edmondson's suspension, Andy Coulson's resignation – Rupert Murdoch had weathered the storm and his friends in the Conservative Party were being very supportive. Crucially, the fallout from the hacking was not contaminating his wider business ambitions.

On 26 January, Tom Watson decided to step up the pressure on the police. At Prime Minister's Questions he asked David Cameron to strip Scotland Yard of responsibility for investigating phone hacking:

The former investigating officer is now on the payroll of News International and three senior editors have been identified in relation to phone hacking: is it not time that another police force took over the inquiry? You have the power to make it happen, Prime Minister, what are you afraid of?

Cameron's anger rose. 'Let me be absolutely clear,' he said. 'Phone hacking is wrong and illegal, and it is quite right that the Director of Public Prosecutions is reviewing all the evidence.' The Prime Minister added that it was 'not necessarily fair' to say the police had not been active because there had been prosecutions, convictions 'and indeed imprisonments – but the law is quite clear and the prosecuting authorities should follow it wherever it leads'.

That afternoon, four years after the jailing of Goodman and Mulcaire, the Metropolitan Police launched a new inquiry into phone hacking. Operation Weeting had been announced by the Deputy Commissioner, Tim Godwin, while Sir John Stephenson was on sick leave, having an operation to remove a tumour from his leg. Officially, the new inquiry had been prompted by News International handing new evidence to police. Significantly, the Met said that it would be carried out not by the counter-terrorism command (officially, because it was too busy) but by the Specialist Crime Directorate, which dealt with organized crime: John Yates had been taken off the case. In his place was one of the Met's few senior women, Sue Akers, the Head of Organized Crime and Criminal Networks.

A tough woman with a bob of greying blonde hair, Akers had joined London's male-dominated police force as a twenty-year-old in 1976 and risen steadily through the ranks. Now aged fifty-five, she had a reputation as a strict career cop and was, importantly, unsullied by any history of long lunches with Fleet Street editors.

Many newspapers that had ignored the hacking scandal were now forced to report the opening of Operation Weeting. On 27 January, the *Guardian* and the *Independent* made it their splash and *The Times* and the *Telegraph* ran small pieces on their front pages. The mass market papers tucked the story inside, with the *Sun* running sixty-four words at the bottom of page 2. For the next six months, among daily papers, only a few reporters, typically Nick Davies and James Robinson at the *Guardian*, Martin Hickman and Cahal Milmo at the *Independent*, and Ben Fenton at the *Financial Times* would actively pursue the story. Even the Press Association, the national news agency owned by the large newspaper groups, was unenthusiastic. One of its journalists later told Watson: 'You know we're partly owned by News International, don't you?'

The announcement of the inquiry emboldened previously silent victims of illegal newsgathering to speak out. Nick Brown, Labour's former chief whip, revealed his residential landline had been tapped after he had been outed as gay by the *News of the World* ten years earlier: he had had a 'chilling' moment when he heard a recording of his conversation being replayed. A British Telecom engineer had found a manual recorder on the line.[5] (In 2005, Devon and Cornwall Police had contacted Brown to say they were prosecuting an individual for phone bugging and he had been one of the victims, 'but the case collapsed for legal reasons'.)

An aide to David Blunkett, the former Home Secretary, disclosed that he feared that his phone had been hacked around the time of his affair with the publisher of the *Spectator* magazine, Kimberly Quinn, in 2004. Blunkett, a friend of Rebekah Brooks who had been paid up to £150,000 a year for a weekly column in the *Sun*, did not sue. Whatever his attitude towards his own hacking, he was the fifth Labour cabinet minister to suspect or know that his phone had been tampered with by the tabloid press.

At the offices of the *Independent*, Martin Hickman dispatched a journalist on work experience, Louise Sheridan, to the newspaper library at Colindale in north London to comb through back copies of News International titles to identify stories potentially derived from hacking. As she read through the rolls of microfiche, Sheridan found several potential victims, among them Jude Law and his former wife Sadie Frost, whose relationship difficulties had been reported in the *News of the World*. Sheridan also found a story which suggested that phone hacking at Wapping might have extended beyond the *News of the World* – to the *Sun*. On 20 January 2003, in the first week of Rebekah Brooks's editorship of the *Sun*, while the Fire Brigades Union was running a national strike against Tony Blair's government, the paper had exposed an extramarital affair by its leader Andy Gilchrist with a front-page story headlined: 'Fire strike leader is a love cheat'. A former firefighter in North Wales, Tracey Holland, had given the paper an account of the affair. The assumption, inevitably, was that Holland had approached the *Sun* and sold her story, but when Cahal Milmo tracked her down in 2011, she told him: 'When they first came to me it was clear that they knew all about it. They had lots of information about how long we'd been together.' By the time the *Independent* contacted him on 31 January, Gilchrist had already written to Scotland Yard demanding to know whether he was in Mulcaire's files. News International vigorously denied there was any substance to his claims, and the *Sun*'s managing editor, Graham Dudman, maintained the story had been legitimately obtained, though he could not remember how. The *Independent*'s lawyers were nervous, but the paper ran the story on 9 February:

Detectives are looking into allegations that a second newspaper at Rupert Murdoch's News International may have used hacked voice-mails to publish stories about the private life of a prominent public figure. Andy Gilchrist, a former union leader, has asked Scotland Yard to investigate his belief that interception of his mobile phone mes-sages led to negative stories about him appearing in the *Sun* at the height of an acrimonious national strike by the Fire Brigades Union.

News International's new solicitors Olswang dispatched a strongly worded letter complaining about the article, saying the allegations were 'completely false': 'No unauthorized and illegal access to tele-phone messages was employed in respect of the article concerning Mr Gilchrist and there is no evidence to suggest there was. Entirely legitimate means were used throughout.' The letter added the article was 'not consistent with the obligation on the part of your journalists to conduct themselves in accordance with the principles of respon-sible journalism'. News International appeared to be drawing a line: the phone hacking scandal must not infect the *Sun*. The *Independent* offered no correction or retraction and it was not until November 2011 that the words 'the *Sun*' were revealed to be in Mulcaire's notes.

Despite considerable scepticism about its likely effectiveness, Sue Akers had drafted forty-five officers to work on the new inquiry. As they began ploughing through Mulcaire's paperwork, the detectives quickly identified the failings of the original investigation. In its first public update on Operation Weeting on 9 February, Scotland Yard said it had identified a new group of victims previously told by the police that there was 'little or no evidence' about them. As part of 'urgent steps' to inform the misled victims, Akers personally visited John Prescott to tell him he had been targeted in April 2006, the month the *Daily Mirror* had revealed his affair with his diary secre-tary, Tracey Temple. Chris Bryant remarked wryly: 'Until now, it has been the victims that have had to do the investigative work, so it's a welcome development that the police have finally taken on the responsibility.'[6]

While the police had previously handed over hacking evidence only under court order, detectives now started allowing some victims to view the references to them in Mulcaire's notes. As the actress Leslie Ash and her husband Lee Chapman read Mulcaire's references to them, they made a grim discovery. The police had shown them notes on a Leslie Chapman, believing that was Leslie Ash using her husband's surname.

Charlotte Harris, acting for the couple, recalled: 'Leslie Chapman's papers were in front of us and the police were saying of the address: "Yeah, well it's Fulham", but it wasn't a Fulham postcode and I was looking at it, and being so familiar with Glenn Mulcaire's handwriting, I said: "It doesn't say 'Fulham', it says 'Soham'."'[7] The *News of the World* had targeted the father of Jessica Chapman, one of the two children murdered by a paedophile at Soham in 2002. Harris added: 'In my discussions with News International, I kept mentioning it. I told them: "What have you done? Do you know how serious this is? Do you know what's going to happen here?"'[8]

Between January and April 2011, Harris – who had been watched by the *News of the World* in April 2010 – was apparently put under surveillance again, by persons unknown. She discovered this in May when she was handed a twenty-page document containing details about individuals in the scandal, including a section on the private lives of herself, Mark Lewis and Mark Thomson. Harris told the Leveson Inquiry in December 2011:

> There is a section in the report that is headed 'Report III' which contains material on the lawyers involved in the phone hacking cases including me and two others. The material is highly intrusive. The individual who gave me the documents told me that I should 'watch myself' because I was being followed. I read the report immediately. It was clear that an intrusive personal investigation had been conducted on me simply because I was a lawyer involved in the phone hacking cases. The purpose of the report was to obtain information which could be made public in the hope of putting pressure on me presumably to deter me (and my clients) from pursuing claims against the company.

One section of the document, which has not been released publicly in its entirety, read:

The motivation of and association between the key civil lawyers opposing News International is becoming clear. Specifically, the main protagonists are politically motivated with a number being strong Labour supporters, their cases helping promote their professional advancement. The *News of the World* is planning to use these tensions and motivations as a way to force compromise and settlement.

Under the heading '*News of the World* strategy', the document continued: 'The *News of the World* is aware of these facts and is planning to put pressure back on the solicitors by revealing these facts and by linking their political affiliations and career benefits from the cases. They plan to do this publicly and through discreet lobbying.'

As the BBC, ITV and liberal quality papers reported on the progress of Operation Weeting, the number of individuals considering or taking court action against News International reached 115. Twelve cases were under way in the High Court, including those of Sienna Miller, Steve Coogan, the TV presenter Chris Tarrant and the politician George Galloway. (In March 2006, the MP had thwarted a sting by the *News of the World*'s 'Fake Sheikh' Mazher Mahmood when he spotted one of the few tell-tale signs of Mahmood's operation – the metal teeth of his minder.) Given the *News of the World*'s interests, many litigants came from football, including Sky Andrew, Andy Gray and Paul Gascoigne. David Davies, the former executive director of the Football Association, whose flat had been broken into in a burglary in which nothing was stolen, asked police whether he had been targeted.

In February, the lawyers were methodically dismantling the rogue reporter defence with the help of judges in the civil courts. On 1 February the Court of Appeal agreed with Sky Andrew's team, led by Harris, that Mulcaire should divulge who at the *News of the World* commissioned him to hack phones. In a statement to the High Court on 18 February, Mulcaire said: 'Information was supplied to the news desk at the *News of the World*. This was manned by different people . . .'*

For more than a year lawyers had been trying to establish that Mulcaire worked for more than a single reporter and News Inter-

---

* Mulcaire did later provide a list to the lawyers of the civil litigants, but it has not been publicly disclosed so as not to prejudice any possible criminal trials.

national had spent millions trying to suppress that fact. The 'rogue reporter' line had finally collapsed, but the company did not amend its defence in court. It did not want to focus attention on the Sky bid, and whip up more opposition, when it was about to step over the regulatory hurdle put in place by Jeremy Hunt.

On 1 March, News Corp finalized its undertakings, offering to float Sky News on the stock market, with a corporate governance committee to guarantee the independence of its output. Despite the new arrangement, though, News Corp would still own a controlling 39 per cent stake in Sky News in addition to its holding in BSkyB. To seal a £7.8 billion takeover it was making a modest offer to amend the structure of a £60 million-a-year business.

Hunt decided to make the announcement to Parliament on 3 March. As usual, News Corp received the inside track on the announcement before it was made. In the early hours, at 3.52 a.m. on 3 March, Michel emailed James Murdoch:

> Decision made by JH: he is minded to accept in lieu and will release around 7.30am to the market. . . . Release will describe the UIL:
> Spin off
> Shares
> Independent directors . . .[9]

After the Speaker insisted Hunt make an oral statement to the Commons, at 10.49 a.m., Michel informed James Murdoch that patsy questions had been set up:

> Tory backbenchers have now been lined up to ask JH questions which will allow him to reinforce safeguards and strength of UIL . . .
> Don Foster [Lib Dem Culture spokesman] is supporting the remedy and is writing memo to Clegg to support it . . .
> JH will take a call from Salmond today.[10]

Announcing the deal, Hunt said that he was 'minded' to accept News Corp's takeover without a referral to the Competition Commission and put the plan out to public consultation until 21 March. He said: 'Today we are publishing . . . all the consultation documents, all the submissions we received, all the exchanges between my department and News Corporation.' None of the scores of text messages, emails and phone calls between Hunt's department and News Corp were released.

At 6.33 p.m., James Murdoch texted Jeremy Hunt: 'Big few days. Well played.' Two minutes later, Hunt responded: 'Thanks think we got the right solution!'[11]

That night, 3 March, Hunt was interviewed by *Newsnight*'s Kirsty Wark, who asked him when he had last met James and Rupert Murdoch. Hunt struggled to remember, and then said he had met Rupert the previous October and James twice, on 6 and 20 January. But he stressed all the meetings had been minuted.

While News Corp had the government in its pocket, some backbench MPs were still willing to condemn what they saw as a climate of fear and threats in Westminster. In a Commons debate on 10 March, Chris Bryant launched a scathing attack on John Yates and News International. Bryant disclosed that he had been threatened, indirectly, to deter him from speaking out. He said:

> Almost as bad as the original activity – only the tip of which we have yet seen – has been the cover-up. Other Members and former Members of the House have said they were warned off pushing the issue in the House and in select committees. When I raised the question of parliamentary privilege in the House last September, my friends were told by a senior figure allied to Rupert Murdoch and a former executive of News International to warn me that it would not be forgotten.

In a rare public attack by an MP on a senior police officer, he accused John Yates of misleading the Commons by stating that the Crown Prosecution Service had advised police of a narrow interpretation of the law of hacking during the prosecution of Clive Goodman and Glenn Mulcaire, when, Bryant said, that was never the case.

Responding, the junior Home Office minister James Brokenshire read out a prepared speech, reassuring Bryant about the extensive action under way to tackle phone hacking, such as the inquiries by the Metropolitan Police and the Home Affairs Select Committee. For the box-tickers at the Home Office, there was nothing to be concerned about: the authorities were acting. News International declined to comment on Bryant's claims.

While the *Guardian* led its report the following day on Bryant's criticism of John Yates, the *Independent* focused on the threat made to the MP by Murdoch's allies:

> MPs were 'warned off' pursuing the phone hacking scandal in Parliament as part of a cover-up, a Labour frontbencher claimed last night during an incendiary speech in which he accused the country's biggest police force of misleading a Commons committee and its biggest newspaper group of engaging in the 'dark arts' of tapping, hacking and blagging.
>
> Damning the behaviour of the Metropolitan Police and Rupert Murdoch's News International, Chris Bryant claimed his friends had been told by an ally of Mr Murdoch that raising the issue 'would not be forgotten'.

No other newspapers reported Bryant's speech. Nonetheless, it provoked a response. On 17 March, Rupert Murdoch invited the new proprietors of the *Independent*, Alexander Lebedev and his son Evgeny, to a meeting at his flat in St James's, London. After a few minutes of pleasantries, Murdoch turned to the apparent reason for the meeting. Why, he asked, was the *Independent* pursuing the phone hacking story, when there had been no scandal: it was damaging not just to Murdoch but to the whole industry. He appealed to his fellow proprietors to tone down the reporting. The Lebedevs had dealt with far more menacing figures back in Russia; there was no diminution in coverage.

In an attempt to defend his reputation, however, John Yates offered to give further evidence to the Commons Home Affairs and Culture Committees. The result was a disaster. At the Culture Committee on 24 March, Tom Watson asked how Scotland Yard had stored Glenn Mulcaire's notes. Yates replied they were in 'two or three' bin bags. This was the exchange that followed:

WATSON: Were they full?

YATES: I did not see them.

WATSON: Did you or your team examine all of the Mulcaire records?

YATES: At what point?

WATSON: When you were asked to establish the facts?

YATES: No.

Yates, by his own admission, had not bothered to look at the available evidence; he had only checked whether the 'For Neville' email represented 'new' or 'old' evidence. Watson pointed out that the Information Commissioner had discovered that Steve Whittamore had obtained phone numbers of the family of Milly Dowler, who was murdered in 2002 (see chapter 16). Watson asked Yates: 'If it transpires from the review of the Mulcaire evidence that, when Sky News were broadcasting it round the clock, Glenn Mulcaire was instructed to hack the phones of the family members of children killed at Soham, would that warrant adequate use of police resources to investigate?'

Yates replied: 'I am sure that it would, but that is the first I have ever heard of that aspect.' As Leslie Ash and Lee Chapman had accidentally discovered, the name of at least one of the Soham parents was indeed in the Mulcaire files, but John Yates, one of the country's top police officers, did not know that – because he had not checked the evidence.

Outside court, Jonathan Rees said that he should not have been prosecuted, claiming the police had failed to investigate up to forty other potential suspects.

Though a devastating blow for Alastair Morgan and Scotland Yard, the end of the case meant newspapers no longer had to withhold their coverage of Rees's connections to the *News of the World*.

At the BBC, *Panorama*'s Glenn Campbell had already spent five months investigating Rees, with the help of police, Alastair Morgan and Nick Davies. By January 2011, he had gathered enough evidence for an exclusive: as well as hacking phones and blagging bank and medical details, the *News of the World* had been hacking computers.

One especially sensitive target was Ian Hurst, a former intelligence officer in Northern Ireland. While in the British Army's Force Research Unit, Hurst had handled Britain's most valuable agent in the IRA – Freddie Scappaticci, codenamed 'Stakeknife' – who had infiltrated the IRA's notorious 'Nutting Squad', which hunted down, tortured and killed suspected informers. Hurst wanted to expose the dirty work done by the British in Northern Ireland. In 2004, in a book with a former *Independent* journalist, Greg Harkin, *Stakeknife: Britain's Secret Agents in Ireland*, he alleged that in order to maintain Scappaticci's cover the British Army had allowed him to commit murder. In 2006, *Panorama* discovered, Jonathan Rees had introduced the *News of the World* to a computer hacker, who had sent a Trojan virus to Hurst's computer. Once opened, Hurst's emails were faxed to the *NoW*'s Irish edition. News International records showed that the paper paid Rees more than £4,000 for research on Stakeknife.

Panorama filmed Hurst as he was shown faxed copies of the emails that had arrived at the newspaper's office in Dublin. 'The hairs on the back of my head are up,' he said. Hurst subsequently secretly recorded a meeting with the alleged hacker, who explained: 'It weren't that hard. I sent you an email that you opened, and that's it ... I sent it from a bogus address ... Now it's gone. It shouldn't even remain on the hard drive. I think I programmed it to stay on for three months.' Questioned about who had asked him to do the hacking, he replied: 'The faxes would go to Dublin ... He was the editor of the *News of the World* for Ireland. A Slovak-type name. I can't remember his fucking name. Alex his name is. Marunchak.' Marunchak, Rees's handler at the *News of the World*, made no comment to *Panorama*. He later denied its allegations in a statement to the *Press Gazette*.

News International had tried to bully the BBC into dropping *Panorama*, claiming it was trying to damage the Sky bid. In letters to the BBC on 10 and 11 March, Julian Pike of Farrer & Co – who the previous year had threatened to injunct Mark Lewis for representing phone hacking victims – accused the corporation of 'running a campaign' against the takeover. The corporation had 'an obligation to avoid embroiling itself in a political and commercial battle that it should have nothing to do with'. The BBC faced down the complaints and broadcast *Panorama* on 14 March, giving millions of viewers an insight into the range of covert techniques used by News International.

Ten days later, on 24 March, in a highly significant move, an anonymous executive at Wapping (believed to be Will Lewis) asked Harbottle & Lewis for its work in 2007 reviewing the emails for Clive Goodman's employment appeal. Harbottle & Lewis had printed off and kept some copies of the emails. Shockingly, they contained evidence that News International journalists had been bribing Metropolitan Police officers. The payments totalled more than £100,000 – for handing over such sensitive data as the Queen's phone numbers. One anonymous News International executive later told the *Sunday Times*: 'We were sitting on a ticking timebomb.' However, instead of immediately contacting the police, with whom it said it was 'fully cooperating', News International sat on the documents for three months.

Six days after the emails were requested, on 30 March, Rupert Murdoch promoted his son James to the newly created post of deputy chief operating officer of News Corp. Although James would retain control of the company's Asian and European operations (and his chairmanship of News International and Sky), he would now be based at News Corp's headquarters in New York. There, he was expected to join his sister, Elisabeth, in the boardroom. On 21 February, News Corp had bought Shine – her TV production company, maker of *Spooks* and *Masterchef* – for $675 million, sixteen times its most recent annual profits. (Some critics thought Murdoch had overpaid in order to bring Elisabeth back into the fold. Announcing the deal,

Rupert Murdoch said: 'I expect Liz Murdoch to join the board of News Corporation on completion of this transaction.')

Less than a week later, on 5 April, the Metropolitan Police underlined the robustness of its new investigation by making the first arrests for phone hacking for five years: Ian Edmondson and Neville Thurlbeck were held at Kingston and Wimbledon police stations respectively after arriving for interview by appointment. The men, assistant editor and chief reporter, had been central to the news operation at the *News of the World*. They were released on police bail, pending further inquiries.

Despite the embarrassment of having its chief reporter arrested earlier in the day, the *NoW* enjoyed a good night at the British Press Awards, being held – by coincidence – that night at the Savoy in London. The 'Fake Sheikh', Mazher Mahmood, won the award for News Reporter of the Year and the *News of the World* Scoop of the Year for his exposé of corruption in the Pakistani cricket team. *News of the World* staff rose alone to give him, and themselves, a standing ovation, whooping and hollering. As he accepted the scoop award, Colin Myler described the *NoW* as 'the greatest paper in the world'. Many journalists shuffled uneasily in their seats.

News International's journalists tended to dismiss the hacking scandal as celebrities whinging about reporters listening to their gossip – and complained that the police response was disproportionate. On 7 April, the *Sun*'s columnist and former editor, Kelvin Mackenzie, described the assigning of forty-five officers to Operation Weeting as 'incredible', adding: 'Wouldn't it be nice if any of them might be spared from their piddly, politically motivated witch hunt to come round when your tools are nicked from the garden shed?' Roger Alton, executive editor of *The Times*, said: 'With this whole story I just hear the shrill shriek of axes being ground.' Interviewed for the May issue of the *Columbia Journalism Review*, Alton complained: 'People have gone to prison. Coulson's resigned twice. It's not as if any perceived wrongdoing hasn't been sufficiently addressed. For me it's roughly on a par with parking in a resident's parking bay in terms of interest.'

Despite the huffing and puffing of senior journalists, News

International's executives on the tenth floor of Thomas More Square knew total denial was no longer an option. On Friday 8 April they put into action a plan they had been kicking around for weeks. Five years, nine months and eighteen days after Goodman and Mulcaire were jailed for phone hacking, News International admitted for the first time that the rogue reporter defence – advanced by its executives for years – was bogus. But it was still not ready to admit the full scale of the wrongdoing. In a bland press release, the company apologized for phone hacking, admitted its own inquiries had been flawed and announced it would settle several civil cases. Headed: 'News International statement with regard to voicemail interception at the *News of the World* during 2004–2006', the statement carefully limited wrongdoing to Andy Coulson's editorship. It said:

> Following an extensive internal investigation and disclosures through civil cases, News International has decided to approach some civil litigants with an unreserved apology and an admission of liability in cases meeting specific criteria. We will, however, continue to contest cases that we believe are without merit or where we are not responsible. That said, past behaviour at the *News of the World* in relation to voicemail interception is a matter of genuine regret. It is now apparent that our previous inquiries failed to uncover important evidence and we acknowledge our actions then were not sufficiently robust.

At 4 p.m., the BBC's Robert Peston, again using his close contacts at Wapping, named eight individuals whose cases the company intended to settle: Sienna Miller; her stepmother, Kelly Hoppen; Sky Andrew; Andy Gray; Tessa Jowell; her estranged husband, David Mills; Max Clifford's secretary, Nicola Phillips; and John Prescott's chief of staff, Joan Hammell. In all, Peston said, Wapping expected to settle up to ninety-one cases – approximately the number of PINs recovered from Glenn Mulcaire – and had set aside £20 million for the payouts.[1]

In New York that day, James Murdoch explained to Bloomberg interviewer Charlie Rose that everything was going well despite the company's U-turn. 'The interesting thing about this one is,' James explained, 'you talk about a reputation crisis [but] actually the business is doing really well. It shows what we were able to do is really put this problem into a box. If you get everybody sucked into something like that, then the whole business will sputter, which you don't want.'[2]

On Sunday 10 April, in a 159-word comment buried on page 2, Colin Myler publicly apologized to readers for the *NoW*'s hacking of newsworthy individuals, saying: 'What happened to them should not have happened. It was and remains unacceptable.'

News International had now withdrawn from the rogue reporter claim, but had merely retreated to a new line of defence – a few rogue reporters, at the *News of the World*, under Andy Coulson. The *Sun*, *The Times* and the *Sunday Times* largely ignored the ongoing story and Wapping continued to behave firmly towards inquiring journalists: pursuing the scandal would 'not be forgotten'.

Despite its claim to be cooperating fully, the company was still obstructing the police – as it had done in 2006 when its staff frustrated the search of Wapping. On 14 April, detectives from Operation Weeting arrested the *News of the World* reporter James Weatherup at his home and then went to Wapping to seize his computer and other material. By the time they arrived, executives had bagged up his belongings and sent them to the company's lawyers, Burton Copeland (though, strangely, Weatherup's computer – and a hard drive – remained on his desk). Furious, the Met flooded the *News of the World*'s newsroom with uniformed police. Burton Copeland returned the reporter's belongings. Shortly afterwards Sue Akers held a summit with NI's Will Lewis and Simon Greenberg 'to debate our very different interpretations of the expression "full co-operation"'.[3]

Behind the scenes, Scotland Yard had to contend with another problem: political pressure. On 'several occasions' after Sir Paul Stephenson, the Commissioner, returned to work from his leg operation in April, Kit Malthouse, Mayor Boris Johnson's right-hand man, urged him to scale down Operation Weeting, telling him that he should not fall victim to the 'political media hysteria' surrounding phone hacking. Malthouse, Deputy Mayor for Policing, also asked Assistant Commissioner Cressida Dick three times to cut the number of detectives on Weeting. Dick, aware that Malthouse was from 'a particular political party' and appeared to be intervening in 'such a charged investigation', had to ask him to stop on the third occasion. She said later: 'On a couple of occasions, Mr Malthouse, I thought jokingly, said, "I hope you are not putting too many resources into this." On the third occasion when he said it again I said, "That is my decision, not yours, and that is why I'm operationally independent."' Malthouse said he was only trying to ensure that policing was proportionate.[4]

With the Met determined to ensure its new investigation was robust, News International concentrated on what it could achieve. Desperately wanting to settle to prevent executives testifying before a judge, it began picking off the civil claimants and started with Sienna Miller. Newspapers often used her picture to illustrate phone hacking stories and her claims were especially wide-ranging and damaging; among them that the *News of the World* had hacked her computer in 2008, a year after Goodman and Mulcaire's jailing. Despite the strength of her case and the size of the Taylor and Clifford settlements, Miller's lawyers had surprisingly requested only £100,000 damages. News International offered the full amount in a Part 36 offer.

At a High Court hearing on 12 May, Miller's lawyers argued she should be able to fight the case because News International had not yet shown her any internal documents detailing how she was targeted. But Michael Silverleaf, QC for News International, said that the company had been more than reasonable and played down the damage done by the *News of the World*'s stories about her relationship with Jude Law. He told Justice Vos: 'It is hurtful, but it is not that hurtful. It does not belittle her in the public estimation.' What was more, he said, £100,000 was equivalent to the compensation payable for the loss of an eye – and compared favourably to the £60,000 damages awarded to Max Mosley for the *News of the World* story which, Silverleaf said, had 'ruined' his life. Despite her desire to air her case in court, Miller had been put 'in a box' and accepted Wapping's admission of liability and the damages. News International had succeeded in concluding one of the most damaging cases, for an amount far lower than the earlier settlements – and had set the bar relatively low for the emerging cluster of civil cases.

At Bindmans, Tamsin Allen had brought the judicial review on behalf of Chris Bryant, Brian Paddick, Brendan Montague and John Prescott. The essence of the case was that, despite their requests, Scotland Yard had breached their right to privacy by failing to inform them they were in Mulcaire's notes. At a preliminary hearing on 12 May, the Metropolitan Police's QC, James Lewis, tried to strike out the claim, denying there had been a conspiracy to avoid contacting the claimants. The police, he said, had been hampered by the untidiness and complexity of Mulcaire's scribblings. In Bryant's case, for instance, he explained, twenty-three numbers associated with him had been found not on the page with his details but on another page elsewhere in the notes. In court for the hearing, Bryant whispered to Nick Davies and Martin Hickman sitting in front of him: 'They were on the facing page.' Mr Justice Foskett ordered a full trial.

All the while, Operation Weeting was contacting new hacking victims. Wayne Rooney, the Manchester United footballer whose manager, Paul Stretford, had been the target of covert surveillance, tweeted on 28 April: 'Looks like a newspaper have hacked into my phone. Big surprise.'

By May, Tom Watson had been cultivating a high-ranked source, Mr Y. During a meeting at a London apartment, Mr Y alleged that Jonathan Rees, the private investigator recently acquitted of murder, had used blagging, corruption and burglary to acquire personal data about royalty, leading politicians and other senior members of the establishment for the *News of the World* and other redtop newspapers. For the first time Watson glimpsed the real picture of wrongdoing at Wapping, but the more he learned the more he realized that it involved the criminal underworld. At the Birmingham home of his friend Siôn Simon that weekend, the MP was hugely animated as he relayed his discovery, then his tone changed. However ridiculous or melodramatic, he contemplated that he might be killed.

On 11 May, in the House of Commons, Watson challenged David Cameron to call a judicial inquiry. Softly, he said:

The Prime Minister told me that the hacking inquiry should go where the evidence leads. It leads to the parents of the Soham children and to rogue intelligence officers. He knows more sinister forms of cyber-crime. [The Conservative peer] Lord Fowler is calling for a judicial inquiry. Will the Prime Minister please order one now, before the avalanche of new evidence forces him to do so?

Cameron replied there was a real problem of 'interfering' with the criminal investigations and rejected setting up a public inquiry, saying: 'The most important thing is to allow the criminal investigation to take place.' Yes, he seemed to be saying, some bad things have happened, but now they were being investigated.

Those following the scandal knew that, despite the thoroughness of the new phone hacking inquiry, Scotland Yard was not yet doing all it could to investigate the dark arts. For some time the civil lawyers Mark Lewis, Charlotte Harris and Mark Thomson had been cooperating to concentrate their legal firepower; now reporters from competing media groups began to cooperate too. On 20 May, Tom Watson, the *Guardian*'s Nick Davies and BBC *Panorama*'s Glenn Campbell met at Watson's flat in south London, where they discussed News International's use of Jonathan Rees.

On 7 June, at a townhouse in Westminster, another meeting took place, this time between Watson, Davies and Martin Hickman (Campbell was on holiday). They discussed evidence held by Scotland Yard about Rees's work for News International. The allegations were outside the remit of Operation Weeting, the Met's inquiry into phone hacking, and were not being investigated. Knowing that some of the media would not report the story if it appeared only in the *Guardian* and the *Independent*, the trio agreed that Watson would trail the allegations at Prime Minister's Questions the following day, making it difficult for broadcasters to ignore.

On the afternoon of 8 June, Watson said in the House of Commons:

The Metropolitan Police are in possession of paperwork detailing the dealings of criminal private investigator Jonathan Rees. It strongly suggests that he was illegally targeting members of the Royal Family, senior politicians, and high-level terrorist informers yet the head of Operation Weeting has recently written to me to inform me that this evidence may be outside the inquiry's terms of reference. Prime

Minister, I believe powerful forces are involved in a cover-up; please tell me what you intend to do to make sure that that does not happen.

As shock spread across the faces of his colleagues George Osborne and Theresa May, David Cameron replied: 'The police are free to investigate the evidence and take that wherever it leads them, and then mount a prosecution if the Crown Prosecution Service supports that.' He added: 'There are no terms of reference as far as I am concerned; the police are able to look at any evidence and all evidence they can find.'*

Broadcasters covered the speech the following day, repeatedly running Watson's warning about 'powerful forces'. Characteristically, when the *Independent* put the list of Rees's targets to News International later that same day, its spokeswoman, Daisy Dunlop, warned the paper off the story, saying: 'Be very careful before linking those names to News International.' In a statement, News International said: 'It is well documented that Jonathan Rees and Southern Investigations worked for a whole variety of newspaper groups. With regards to Tom Watson's specific allegations, we believe these are wholly inaccurate. The Met Police, with whom we are cooperating fully in Operation Weeting, have not asked us for any information regarding Jonathan Rees. We note again that Tom Watson made these allegations under parliamentary privilege.'

The *Guardian* and *Independent*'s stories disclosed the roll-call of Rees's targets, among them Tony Blair, his director of communications, Alastair Campbell, and his ministers Peter Mandelson and Jack Straw. Several targets had been in charge of media policy: Gerald Kaufmann, the Labour chair of the Culture Committee between 1992 and 2005, and the Tory MP David Mellor, who threatened the press with tighter regulation in the early 1990s. Rees had even tar-

---

* That afternoon, Watson posted on Twitter a letter of 17 May from Sue Akers saying: 'The information regarding Mr Rees may be outside the Terms of Reference of my investigation but the MPS are assessing your allegation along with others we have received to consider a way forward.'

geted the former Commissioner of the Metropolitan Police Sir John Stevens, and John Yates, 'Yates of the Yard'.

While the royal family observed its usual silence, the politicians responded angrily. Peter Mandelson said he was writing to Scotland Yard to ask what information had been held on him by Rees. Jack Straw suspected he may have been targeted by the *Daily Mirror* in 1997 (under the editorship of Piers Morgan) for its 'disgraceful sting' on his teenage son. David Mellor complained: 'Scotland Yard have been extremely tardy investigating these allegations, perhaps because senior officers were more concerned with protecting their own relationships with News International rather than doing their own duty.'[5]

By coincidence, the following day, 10 June, Tony Blair had a scheduled TV interview with the BBC, having given an interview to that morning's *Times* discussing his hopes that the EU would create the new post of President. Unlike his former cabinet colleagues, the former prime minister seemed oddly reluctant to find out about his targeting. He said: 'I assume that if someone's got something they will get in touch with me.'

Later that day, Scotland Yard disclosed that it had begun a 'formal assessment process', Operation Tuleta, to consider potential prosecutions that fell outside the terms of Operation Weeting, such as computer hacking.

Police action against Rupert Murdoch's British news group was growing rapidly: January had brought Weeting; now June brought Tuleta. Eight officers were working on the new inquiry. Overall more than fifty detectives at Scotland Yard were investigating the dark arts of Fleet Street.

15
Summer's Lease

*No other country in the world would allow somebody to
have so much power*
— Chris Bryant, House of Commons, 30 June 2011

Publicly, June was a quiet month: a summer's lull. Though events in the spring had lifted the lid on the scandal, News International had started to weld it back on again. Wapping had made a public apology and concluded the civil cases of both Sienna Miller and Andy Gray (paying him £220,000 in costs and damages). The talk in Westminster was that there was no significant opposition to the Sky takeover. News Corp enjoyed the solid support of the Conservative Party. Privately Will Lewis, Wapping's general manager, was saying that the company's three-year recovery plan was on track.

Inside News Corp there was frustration about how long the Sky deal was taking – Ofcom was being stubborn – but also reassurance that it would soon get its prize. On 3 June, Fred Michel, the ever-persistent lobbyist, emailed James Murdoch to relay the upshot of his latest 'conversations' with 'JH':

> Overall there is a clear blame game going on regarding the delay between lawyers, us and Ofcom. Everyone is getting very heated and his own legal team is not in the best of mood [*sic*] as JH has been pushing them hard this week and become quite impatient in the way they are handling these last stages . . .

He is politically very keen to get this done as quickly as possible and
understands the potential impact this will have on the share price.
He also asked me whether there were any other news which could
conflict with the process in the coming weeks and asked me to keep
him informed as much as possible privately (ie. NI).[1]

As usual, on Wednesday 15 June, Rupert Murdoch hosted his
annual summer party at the Orangery in the grounds of Kensington
Palace in London. The event usually attracted luminaries of politics,
media and the arts. With the allegations swirling around his empire, gossip columnists speculated over who would turn up this year. Downing
Street had refused to say whether the Prime Minister would attend,
but News Corp's chairman need not have worried – David Cameron
arrived discreetly by car at a drop-off point sealed from the public, his
brief emergence captured by a photographer's long lens. The shadow
cabinet was present too: Ed Miliband, the Labour leader (who did not
mention phone hacking during his conversation with Murdoch), the
shadow Chancellor Ed Balls and his wife, the shadow Home Secretary
Yvette Cooper, and the shadow Foreign Secretary Douglas Alexander.
The newly elected Labour MPs Gloria de Piero and Michael Dugher
turned up. Guests drank Moët & Chandon champagne and Becks beer.

On the surface, all was well. But increasingly, Brooks's position
was being questioned by those inside, as well as outside, the company.
In June, according to one well-placed News Corp source, security
staff were ordered to record the times of her entry to and exit from
Thomas More Square and cleaners were warned to avoid disturbing
listening devices placed under her table and by her computer in her
office. The chief executive herself was being bugged.

On the tenth floor, News International's executives could hear the
'ticking timebomb' of police corruption.[2] On 1 April, Harbottle &
Lewis's file on Clive Goodman's employment appeal had been handed
to News International's solicitors, Burton Copeland. At some stage it
was passed to News Corp's solicitors, Hickman & Rose, who, in May
arranged for several of the emails to be reviewed by an eminent barrister. Now in private practice, Lord Macdonald had been the Director

of Public Prosecutions at the time of Operation Caryatid in 2006. Examining the file was not a conflict of interest, Macdonald explained later, because the emails did not concern phone hacking, but bribery of police officers. Macdonald took around five minutes to realize they should be handed to Scotland Yard. 'I have to tell you that the material I saw was so blindingly obvious that anyone trying to argue that it shouldn't be given to the police would have had a very tough task,' he told the Commons Home Affairs Committee. The emails, however, were passed to the police only on 20 June, eleven weeks after they had been retrieved, during which time News Corp's bid for Sky was progressing.[3] In secret, Sue Akers, already leading investigations into phone and computer hacking, began a third inquiry into police corruption. News International agreed to keep quiet about Operation Elveden.

Approaches were made to Tom Watson. By this stage, friends had been telling him: 'You've done a good job, it's time to move on.' But in an attempt to keep the issue to the fore, he had made an inflammatory speech at the GMB conference on 5 June, telling the union's delegates his bins had been rifled during the Damian McBride affair and that the *News of the World* had targeted the parents of the Soham children. (He said: 'You probably didn't know they targeted the Soham parents. That's because it's hardly been written about in a British newspaper. Or ever mentioned by a British broadcaster.')

Two intermediaries close to News International offered him a deal. One told Watson the company would 'give him' Andy Coulson, but Rebekah Brooks was 'sacred', which he took to mean that the company would hand over incriminating evidence on Coulson if he laid off Brooks. He had no idea what the evidence might have been. Over dinner, the other intermediary suggested to the MP that Rupert Murdoch might like to meet him. 'He's a charismatic man,' she said. 'He'd want to square off these difficulties and put matters right.' Watson was not interested in cutting a deal. News Corp was unsurprisingly nervous that it was now the subject of three major criminal inquiries but it did not, however, have to worry about Sky.

A fortnight after the party at the Orangery, in a written statement on Thursday 30 June, David Cameron's government announced its intention to approve the takeover. Ofcom, which previously supported a referral to the Competition Commission, was now satisfied by the undertakings on Sky News. The Culture Secretary, Jeremy Hunt, said that although nothing had arisen out of the 40,000 responses to the public consultation to alter their acceptability, he had decided to insist upon some of the 'constructive changes', such as defining the role of the independent directors in the articles of association of the spun-off company. Hunt, apparently oblivious to Rupert Murdoch's string of broken promises in the past, said News Corp had 'offered serious undertakings and discussed them in good faith'. He added: 'Therefore, whilst the phone hacking allegations are very serious they were not material to my consideration.'

Avoiding a Commons debate by issuing a written statement irritated MPs from all parties, including Mark Pritchard, the independent-minded secretary of the Conservative backbench 1922 Committee. Tom Watson put in a request for an urgent statement from the Culture Secretary, which was granted by the Speaker. During a thirty-five-minute debate on 30 June Jeremy Hunt maintained he had proceeded carefully at all times, following and publishing the independent advice from Ofcom and the Office of Fair Trading; he believed News Corp's promises were serious and robust.

John Whittingdale, the Conservative chairman of the Culture Committee, congratulated Hunt on the 'meticulous care' that he had taken in deciding the bid: could he confirm that every single concern of the regulatory authorities had been addressed? Hunt could. Opposition MPs were furious. Barry Gardiner said: 'He is propping up a crumbling empire. Murdoch is the Gaddafi of News Corporation.' Chris Bryant asked: 'How on earth did we – and I mean all of us, not just the minister – become so spineless as to allow a company whose directors not only failed in their fiduciary duties to prevent criminality at the *News of the World*, but actually participated in its cover-up, to hold dominion over such a vast swathe of the media in this country? No other country in the world would allow somebody to have so much power.' The Labour MP Kevin Brennan interjected: 'Apart from Italy.'

The government had backed the Sky deal despite the new

allegations of criminality engulfing Murdoch's powerful national newspapers. Rupert Murdoch would win his big prize – total control of the UK's biggest broadcaster – after a further, brief eight-day consultation, ending on 8 July. That day, 30 June, in an email headed 'JH Confidential', Michel told James Murdoch: 'JH just told me that he was very keen to make the final decision before the 18th July.'[4]

The Murdochs had reason to celebrate. On Saturday 2 July, another of the dynasty's grand summer events was taking place, at Burford Priory, the Elizabethan home in the Cotswolds of Elisabeth Murdoch and her well-connected husband Matthew Freud. The couple were leading members of the Chipping Norton Set, an informal network of media, political and showbusiness figures living around the Oxfordshire town, whose other luminaries included David Cameron and his wife Samantha, Rebekah Brooks and her husband Charlie, the JCB digger millionaire Sir Anthony Bamford and his wife Carole, and Jeremy Clarkson, the TV presenter and *Sunday Times* columnist.

According to a report in the *Mail on Sunday* later that month, the Murdoch-Freuds' guests included James Murdoch, Rebekah Brooks (though she circulated with diminished effervescence) and Will Lewis. The BBC was well represented by its director-general, Mark Thompson, business editor Robert Peston and creative director Alan Yentob. Among the political rainmakers were the Education Secretary Michael Gove, the Prime Minister's director of strategy, Steve Hilton, the Culture Minister Ed Vaizey – a member of David Cameron's metropolitan Notting Hill Set, who had promised to abolish the BBC Trust – and four Blairite ex-ministers: Lord Mandelson, David Miliband, James Purnell and Tessa Jowell. The current Labour frontbench was represented by Douglas Alexander. Some glamour was provided by the actress Helena Bonham Carter, the explorer Bear Grylls and the TV presenter Mariella Frostrup.[5] Andy Coulson, however, was absent.

The party continued into the next day. The phone hacking affair had fallen quiet – except that Nick Davies had found a new story.

16

A Missing Girl

*This is a watershed moment when, finally, the public starts
to see and feel, above all, just how low and disgusting this
particular newspaper's methods were*

– Hugh Grant, 6 July 2011

As Liz Murdoch and Matthew Freud's guests dispersed on Sunday
3 July, the *Guardian* was hours from breaking a story that would
dominate the headlines for weeks, send media, politics and police into
panic, cost tens of millions of pounds, and wreck multiple reputations. It flashed up at 4.29 p.m. on Monday 4 July on the *Guardian*
website, jointly bylined Nick Davies and Amelia Hill:

> The *News of the World* illegally targeted the missing schoolgirl Milly
> Dowler and her family in March 2002, interfering with police
> inquiries into her disappearance, an investigation by the *Guardian*
> has established.
> Scotland Yard is investigating the episode, which is likely to put new
> pressure on the then editor of the paper, Rebekah Brooks, now
> Rupert Murdoch's chief executive in the UK; and the then deputy
> editor, Andy Coulson, who resigned in January as the Prime
> Minister's media adviser.

The most incendiary detail was in the sixth and seventh para-
graphs: that not only had the tabloid hacked into the missing
thirteen-year-old's phone, it had deleted messages to make space for
more – which could then be mined for stories:

In the last four weeks the Met officers have approached Surrey Police and taken formal statements from some of those involved in the original inquiry, who were concerned about how *News of the World* journalists intercepted – and deleted – the voicemail messages of Milly Dowler. The messages were deleted by journalists in the first few days after Milly's disappearance in order to free up space for more messages. As a result friends and relatives of Milly concluded wrongly that she might still be alive.

Five months later, the *Guardian* would admit that the *News of the World* was unlikely to have caused this 'false hope' moment, which was probably the result of an automatic deletion by the phone company. (See chapter 22.) In July 2011, the Metropolitan Police, Surrey Police, News International and the Dowler family all believed that the *News of the World* had been responsible.

Ten minutes after the story had appeared on the *Guardian* website, Tom Watson (who had been given advance notice of it by Davies) stood up in the Commons chamber and relayed the news. 'In the last few minutes,' he said, 'it has just been revealed by the *Guardian* newspaper that Milly Dowler's phone was hacked by private investigators working for the *News of the World*. As well as being a despicable act . . . it also strongly suggests that Parliament was misled in the press standards inquiry held by the select committee in 2010.' MPs were stunned. David Heath, the Liberal Democrat Deputy Leader of the House, visibly shocked, followed Watson out of the chamber saying: 'Did you really say Milly Dowler's phone was hacked?', then ran off back to his office.

Mark Lewis, now representing the Dowler family, was interviewed by Sky News standing outside the Royal Courts of Justice. 'There are no words to describe how awful this is,' he said. 'The parents were getting through the most awful experience for any parent. It's unimaginable, and yet people in the *News of the World* had no compunction, no fear of anything; no sense of moral right.'

Milly's parents, Bob and Sally Dowler, had experienced nine awful years since their daughter disappeared in Walton-on-Thames, Surrey, on 21 March 2002. Despite a £100,000 reward offer from the *Sun*, detectives could not find her killer and even began to suspect her father, Bob. The Dowlers repeatedly fell victim to hoaxers who claimed to know their daughter's fate. Her body was found in woods twenty-five miles away in Yateley, Hampshire, in September 2002.

In 2010, police finally charged a nightclub bouncer, Levi Bellfield, already in jail for murdering two young women, with her abduction and murder. At his trial in May and June 2011, Bellfield refused to testify but the Dowlers were subjected to a distressing cross-examination by Bellfield's barrister, Jeffrey Samuels, who explored Bob Dowler's private life and read out Milly's letters saying she was a disappointment to her family. During her cross-examination Sally Dowler collapsed in the witness box. On 23 June, Bellfield was convicted of murder, but prejudicial newspaper coverage forced the abandonment of his second trial for the attempted abduction of an eleven-year-old schoolgirl. On Sunday 3 July, as Liz Murdoch and Matthew Freud's guests were waking up after their Cotswolds party, the *News of the World*'s leader column condemned the Dowlers' 'now-infamous courtroom torture'.

The reality was that within days of Milly's disappearance, the *NoW* had put its electronic detectives on her trail, asking Steve Whittamore to trawl phone numbers registered to the Dowlers in Walton-on-Thames. His accomplice John Boyall had blagged two ex-directory numbers from British Telecom, one for the Dowlers' home.

Nine years later, detectives on Operation Weeting had found evidence that the *News of the World* had hacked Milly's phone, at a time when the paper was being edited by Rebekah Brooks, who had since become chief executive of the UK's biggest newspaper group.*

---

* Surrey police later said the *News of the World* had hacked into Milly's inbox by 12 April, within three weeks of her disappearance. On 4 April 2002, it had even published a story based on a hacked voicemail, about a recruitment agency leaving a message on her phone. The paper wrote: 'On March 27, six days after Milly went missing in Walton-on-Thames, Surrey, the employment agency appears to have phoned her mobile.' In the days before the story was published, the *NoW* had bullied the force, refusing to believe its explanation that the recruitment agency message was probably a hoax (it turned out to be a wrong number). The *News of the World* even played a voicemail recording from Milly's phone to Surrey Police. Despite knowing the paper had accessed the inbox – which could have triggered the automatic deletion of evidence

News International said the *Guardian*'s 'allegations' were of 'great concern' and announced that it was launching an internal inquiry.

Radio and TV stations picked up the story. At 6 p.m., it was the second item on the BBC news, by 10 p.m., the first – a position it would retain for a fortnight. After the chimes of Big Ben on Radio 4, the *World Tonight*'s Matt Prodger began his report: 'The allegations couldn't be worse.' On *Newsnight*, Tom Watson attacked the subservience of the three main political leaders towards the Murdochs: all of them had been informed of suspicions that victims of crime were also targets of phone hacking. He said: 'Politicians are frightened of News International. Ed Miliband is as guilty as David Cameron and Nick Clegg.' Jeremy Paxman checked with Watson whether he had just included his own leader in that list. He had.

In the *Independent*'s offices, Martin Hickman and Cahal Milmo confirmed the Met had visited the Dowlers and talked up the story internally. The next morning, Tuesday 5 July, the *Guardian* and the *Independent* splashed the story; the *Daily Telegraph*, *Financial Times* and *Times* ran smaller pieces on their front pages, but the mass market papers buried it inside – the *Daily Mirror* on page 6, the *Daily Star* on 7, the *Daily Express* and *Daily Mail* on 8. The *Sun* carried a six-sentence account on page 2. Soon the blanket coverage on TV and radio made underplaying the story unfeasible.

Overnight in Wapping, News International executives devised a plan. On the morning of Tuesday 5 July, the story was still leading the bulletins, but with Wapping's spin: *News of the World* executives intended to meet the police to discuss the allegations. The BBC's business editor Robert Peston blogged that Brooks still enjoyed Rupert Murdoch's full support and ran supportive quotes from colleagues such as: 'She is committed to finding out the truth of what happened here and leading the company through this difficult time.' (The commentator Toby Young complained on his *Telegraph* blog: 'It reads like a press release that's been handwritten by News International's chief

---

(because murderers sometimes leave taunting messages on victims' phones) – Surrey took no action. Had it done so, it might have stopped the *News of the World*'s phone hacking in its tracks.

executive.') John Whittingdale said the *News of the World*'s misconduct seemed to be 'a very separate question' from the Sky takeover.[1]

The story overshadowed a trip to Afghanistan by David Cameron. At a press conference, the Prime Minister spent fifty-five seconds condemning the hacking, while avoiding mentioning the *News of the World*, News International, Rebekah Brooks or Rupert Murdoch. Referring to 'the allegations', he said: 'If they are true, this is a truly dreadful act and a truly dreadful situation. What I've read in the papers is quite, quite shocking, that someone could do this knowing the police were trying to find this person and trying to find out what had happened.'

At 10 a.m. the next day, as he drank black coffee at the Fire Station pub in Waterloo, Tom Watson was called by Ed Miliband's office, concerned that his comments on *Newsnight* made it look as if he was trying to 'bounce' the party leader into acting. Since winning the Labour leadership in September 2010, Miliband had been accused of being too low-profile. At midday, he took the biggest gamble of his leadership and called for Brooks to 'examine her conscience' and 'consider her position'. He described the hacking as 'truly immoral', adding: 'But this goes well beyond one individual. This is about the culture and practices that were going on at that newspaper over a sustained period. What I want from executives at News International is people to start taking responsibility for this . . .' Party leaders usually bent over backwards to accommodate News International; now Miliband was calling for the resignation of its chief executive. Senior Murdoch journalists were furious. The parliamentary lobby was abuzz with rumours of a row between the Labour Party spokesman Bob Roberts and Tom Newton Dunn, the *Sun*'s political editor. Roberts would not publicly comment, but he reputedly told Newton Dunn not to take Miliband's remarks personally, to which Newton Dunn replied: 'We do take it personally and we're going to make it personal to you. We won't forget.' 'They were very clear with us,' Miliband told the *New Statesman* later, 'that Rebekah Brooks and Rupert Murdoch would be the two people standing at News International when everyone else was gone.'[2]

News International found itself under attack from all sides. While previous polling showed that the public disapproved of phone hacking, the best-known victims had been wealthy celebrities; the targeting of a missing schoolgirl was regarded as heinous. Irate readers berated journalists picking up phones in the *News of the World* newsroom; many were swearing. Reporters felt dreadful. Dave Wooding, the *News of the World*'s associate editor, woke up that morning and 'felt sick'. 'And for the first time in my career – I've been in tabloid newspapers since I left local newspapers – I felt quite ashamed not only to work for the *News of the World*, but to work for a tabloid paper and actually started to think about changing career. [Readers] were all ringing in and Twitter was going into meltdown calling us scumbags . . .'[3] Subscribers complained about the lack of prominence given to the story by *The Times*, which responded by making it its online lead. After being deluged with complaints, the *Sun* disabled the comment section of its website.

In an email to News International staff, Brooks sought to steady nerves. The new 'allegations', she said, had left her 'sickened'. She wrote: 'Not just because I was editor of the *News of the World* at the time, but because if the allegations are true, the devastating effect on Milly Dowler's family is unforgivable.' She explained that executives had no knowledge of the work of Mulcaire, whom she described as 'a freelance inquiry agent'. She continued: 'I am aware of the speculation about my position. Therefore it is important for you to know that as chief executive, I am determined to lead the company to ensure we do the right thing and resolve these serious issues.' At a lunch with advertisers in London, *The Times*'s editor James Harding said that, 'if true', the 'allegations' – which no one had denied – were disgusting, and that his paper would report the story accurately.[4]

Outside his home in Sutton, South London, Glenn Mulcaire said in a statement:

I want to apologize to anybody who was hurt or upset by what I have done. I've been to court, pleaded guilty. And I've gone to prison and been punished. I still face the possibility of further criminal prosecution. Working for the *News of the World* was never easy. There was relentless pressure. There was a constant demand for results. I knew what we did pushed the limits ethically. But, at the time, I didn't understand I'd broken the law at all.

To the incredulity of some, he appealed for the media to respect the privacy of his wife and children.

On the BBC TV show *Daily Politics* at midday on 5 July, presented by Andrew Neil, the Press Complaints Commission's chair, Peta Buscombe, was furious. 'We personally, and the PCC, are so angry because clearly we were misled ... There's only so much we can do when people are lying to us,' she said. The BBC's political editor Nick Robinson, who had seldom covered the controversy, blogged that while the story had previously united those hostile to Murdoch and his switch to the Conservatives, 'now Murdoch, Brooks and Cameron will be aware that for the first time the hacking story may be engaging and horrifying readers'.

In the Commons, Labour MPs began agitating for action. Chris Bryant's request for an emergency debate on whether there should be a public inquiry was granted and scheduled for the following day. In the Lords, the government did not accede to one, but softened its opposition. At Deputy Prime Minister's Questions, Nick Clegg described the hacking of Milly Dowler's phone as 'grotesque': 'If these allegations are true,' he said, 'they are simply beneath contempt.' He, too, rejected a public inquiry.

The story put new pressure on the police. For years, Scotland Yard had stubbornly refused to inspect the evidence, dismissed any suggestion that its inquiry had failed and frustrated the attempts of individuals to discover whether they had been victims of crime. Now its Commissioner, Sir Paul Stephenson – who the previous week had said he would rather his officers were investigating burglaries than phone hacking – was shocked by the same evidence:

My heart goes out to the Dowler family. Whose heart wouldn't with the additional distress this must have caused them? I have to be very careful to say nothing that could prejudice our live investigation but if it proved to be true, then irrespective of the legality or illegality of it, I'm not sure there is anyone who wouldn't be appalled and repulsed by such behaviour.[5]

Shortly after 4 p.m., Cambridgeshire Police confirmed what campaigners had known for months – that the *News of the World* had targeted the parents of the Soham children.

Public protests began. At least five Facebook pages sprang up with titles such as 'Boycott the *News of the World*' and 'Dear NOTW, Millie Dowler is the Final Straw' and, on Twitter, campaigners urged advertisers to shun the paper. Caitlin Moran, *The Times* columnist, advised her 100,000 followers to support a reader and advertiser boycott. A media buying agency, Starcom MediaVest agency, advised clients to avoid that Sunday's *News of the World*, and hinted that the virus could infect the *Sun*. Ford, responsible for about 10 per cent of the *NoW*'s annual advertising revenue, pulled its advertisements from the paper, saying it cared about the behaviour of its partners. Bombarded with protests following Ford's decision, Currys, Npower, Halifax, T-Mobile and Renault began to review their accounts. Tesco said that it would await the results of the police investigation before acting.

One of the difficulties for Wapping was that Rebekah Brooks was heading the company's investigation into its behaviour towards Milly Dowler. Hugh Grant compared the situation to allowing Hitler 'to clean up the Nazi party'.[6] Wapping's spokesman, Simon Greenberg, struggled to explain the anomaly. On *Channel 4 News*, when Jon Snow asked: 'How can she investigate herself?', Greenberg responded: 'When we have got to the facts we will be able to establish exactly how that will be possible.' Alastair Campbell, Labour's former communications director, described Greenberg's media appearances as 'car crash interviews'.[7]

As the outlook for Brooks grew grimmer, the BBC's Robert Peston pitched the news in a different direction. On the BBC's *Ten O'Clock News* that night, he disclosed that News International had passed to Scotland Yard evidence of police corruption at the *NoW* between 2003 and 2007 – during Andy Coulson's editorship. The story deflected attention from Rebekah Brooks, but failed to mention that the evidence came from the emails from the Harbottle & Lewis file, which had been in the company's possession for three months.

Another BBC programme, *Newsnight*, devoted itself to phone hacking night after night. Paul McMullan, the former *News of the World* features executive, began to appear on the show regularly, wearing a crumpled cream suit and surprising viewers with his insouciance. That evening McMullan suggested that phone hacking was commonplace: 'When they first said it's just a rogue reporter, I thought that's so unfair, what about all the legitimate investigations that we've done, where we've had to go into these grey areas and do these things, surely you should be protecting us by saying: "Yes, sometimes we have to do these things" rather than "It's just one person and we didn't know anything about it."'

Wednesday 6 July offered no respite for the Murdochs. Hacking stories dominated most newspapers, though not Wapping's. *The Times* ran a single column down its front page: 'Hacking: Coulson authorized payments to police for stories'. Brooks, it reported, was 'determined to stay in her job and steer the company through the scandal'. A *Times* leader described phone hacking as 'beyond reprehensible', adding hypocritically: 'This is why it is so important that the truth be known.' The *Sun* left the story off the front, writing on page 6: 'Former *News of the World* editor Rebekah Brooks yesterday said she was "sickened" by allegations that a private eye hired by the paper hacked tragic Milly Dowler's phone.'* The *Daily Mirror*, *Mail* and *Express* ran front-page pictures of the Soham girls. The *Guardian* and *Telegraph* revealed that detectives were checking Mulcaire's notes to see whether there was further evidence about the victims of high-profile murders and abductions and were contacting survivors of the 7/7 terrorist attacks in London in 2005.

Graham Foulkes, who had been told by police that his phone was

---

* That morning, the BBC's Nick Robinson reported that News International executives believed they had uncovered the identity of the *NoW* journalist who had sanctioned the hacking of Milly Dowler's phone – and it was not Rebekah Brooks. Although News International claimed to have had no sight of the Mulcaire material, its internal investigation had now apparently found evidence of wrongdoing which cleared its chief executive (who was leading the investigation).

probably hacked as he grieved for his 22-year-old son, who died in one of the 7/7 bombings, told BBC radio: 'The thought that these guys may have been listening to that is just horrendous. It kind of fills you with horror really because we were in a very dark place, and you think that it's about as dark as it can get, and then you realize that there's somebody out there that can make it even darker.'

As public revulsion spread, 60,000 people signed a petition by the online campaigning organization Avaaz calling for a halt to the Sky deal. Attention was now focused firmly not just on the *News of the World*, but on News Corp's wider commercial ambitions.

Shortly before midday the Metropolitan Police publicly announced the launch of Operation Elveden. Confirming that the force had been passed emails by News International, Sir Paul Stephenson said: 'Our initial assessment shows that these documents include information relating to alleged inappropriate payments to a small number of MPS officers . . .'

At its daily briefing for political journalists, Downing Street said that David Cameron stood by his statement on Coulson's resignation in January when he had praised his director of communications. But he was about to do a U-turn on a public inquiry. A hush descended on the Commons at midday, as the Prime Minister told Ed Miliband: 'Yes, we do need to have an inquiry – possibly inquiries – into what has happened. We are no longer talking about politicians and celebrities; we are talking about murder victims – potentially terrorist victims – having their phones hacked into. What has taken place is absolutely disgusting . . .'

Cameron would not commit himself to a judge-led inquiry, nor say that it would be able to compel witnesses to give evidence on oath. Miliband, whose own communications director had insisted in March that the Sky takeover was totally separate from phone hacking, said the public would 'react with disbelief if next week the decision is taken to go ahead with this deal at a time when News International is subject to a major criminal investigation.' Cameron insisted that the behaviour of the newspaper group which had supported him and the commercial ambitions of its owner were separate: 'One is an issue about morality and ethics and a police investigation that needs to be carried out in the proper way – the other is an issue about plurality and competition which has to act within the law.' He declined to call for Brooks's resignation.

Launching his emergency debate at 1.42 p.m. with references to the cases of Milly Dowler and 7/7 victims, Chris Bryant told MPs: 'These are not just the amoral actions of some lone private investigator tied to a rogue *News of the World* reporter; they are the immoral and almost certainly criminal deeds of an organization that was appallingly led and had completely lost sight of any idea of decency or shared humanity.' Frank Dobson, the former Health Secretary, remarked that News International's record would bar it from getting a mini-cab licence. The Conservative MP Zac Goldsmith, whose sister Jemima Khan had been hacked by the *NoW*, said: 'Rupert Murdoch is clearly a very talented businessman and possibly even a genius, but his organization has grown too powerful and it has abused its power. It has systematically corrupted the police and in my view has gelded this Parliament, to our shame.'

Shortly after 2 p.m. that day, Ofcom, which James Murdoch had wanted to neuter, pointed out its duty to ensure the holders of broadcasting licences were 'fit and proper' – adding that it was closely monitoring developments. In early trading in New York, News Corp shares fell by 3.3 per cent to $17.56. More advertisers fled: Aldi, Co-op, Renault, Vauxhall, Virgin Holidays and Mitsubishi (which that evening described the allegations as 'unbelievable, unspeakable and despicable'), all announced they would not advertise in the *NoW*. Other blue-chip advertisers including Procter & Gamble, Coca-Cola, Vodafone and supermarkets Asda and Sainsbury were urgently reviewing their plans. It was turning into a commercial rout.

Soon after 3 p.m. on 6 July, inside Wapping, the *News of the World*'s editor, Colin Myler, told shell-shocked staff he was 'appalled' by the allegations, but assured them they did not work for the same *News of the World* as the *News of the World* in the headlines. Staff at all titles felt under attack. *The Times* journalist Giles Coren tweeted that he had been criticized in a butcher's shop, merely for working for News International.

At 4.30 p.m., as public and commercial opinion swung violently against the *NoW*, Rupert Murdoch made his first public statement since the story had broken forty-eight hours previously. He said: 'Recent allegations of phone hacking and making payments to police with respect to the *News of the World* are deplorable and unacceptable.' He announced that News Corp's response would be managed by his faithful board member Joel Klein, and an independent director, Viet Dinh. Murdoch said: 'I have made clear that our company must fully and proactively cooperate with the police in all investigations and that is exactly what News International has been doing and will continue to do under Rebekah Brooks's leadership.' For now, therefore, Brooks remained in charge. The media commentator Roy Greenslade described the statement as further proof that Murdoch, his old boss, had 'lost his marbles', blogging: 'He has allowed himself to be seduced by Brooks's formidable charms. I cannot imagine him doing anything like this when at the height of his powers.'[8]

Boris Johnson demanded the Independent Police Complaints Commission oversee Operation Elveden. Under the Mayor of London's watch, Scotland Yard had failed to re-investigate hacking properly, and in September 2010 he had dismissed the scandal as 'codswallop'. Now, Johnson said: 'If some police officers were indeed paid as part of this process, there is only one word for this, corruption. It doesn't matter that this happened many years ago, under a different commissioner and indeed mayoralty.'[9]

As detectives redoubled their efforts to inform prominent victims, they visited George Osborne, whose name and home phone number were in Mulcaire's notes. The Chancellor of the Exchequer – who was thought to have been targeted around the time the *News of the World* was hacking the phone of 'Mistress Pain' Natalie Rowe – did not wish to make a fuss. His spokesman said there was no evidence to suggest his voicemail had actually been hacked, and that he was very grateful to the police: 'Frankly he thinks there are far more serious allegations surrounding the whole hacking affair and fully supports the police in their investigations.'

By coincidence, that evening had been scheduled for the launch of a campaign calling for a public inquiry into the scandal: 'Hacked Off' was backed by the Australian journalist John Pilger, Brian Cathcart, professor of journalism at Kingston University, the lawyer Charlotte Harris and Lord Fowler. Hugh Grant, the best-known supporter, gave media interviews on College Green opposite Parliament denouncing Murdoch. In an interview with the American broadcaster CBS, he said: 'This is a watershed moment when, finally, the public starts to see and feel, above all, just how low and disgusting this particular newspaper's methods were. And what will emerge shortly is that it wasn't just this newspaper.' BSkyB shares fell 18p to 827p, while in the US, News Corp stock tumbled by 3.6 per cent.

On Thursday 7 July, the *Guardian* headlined its front page: 'The day the prime minister was forced to act on phone hacking'. The *Daily Telegraph* and *Daily Mail* splashed on suspicions that the *NoW*'s hackers had targeted the families of soldiers killed in Iraq and Afghanistan. Rose Gentle, whose son Fusilier Gordon Gentle was killed in Iraq in 2004, described the possibility as 'a living nightmare'. The potential targeting of servicemen's families was particularly embarrassing for News International, whose papers had supported the British Army and championed the cause of rank and file soldiers in award-winning campaigns. The Royal British Legion dropped the *News of the World* as its partner for its 'Justice for the Brave' campaign, and began reviewing its advertising with News International, saying it had been 'shocked to the core' by the disclosures, which, it said, had affected hundreds of families.

The Times, covering the story in more depth than previously, still subtly deflected the blame for the scandal by partly focusing on the police: 'Parliament puts press and police in the dock over hacking scandal'. The *Sun* found space on its front page for a twenty-three-word story by its political editor Tom Newton Dunn, which read: 'PM David Cameron ordered a public inquiry into newspaper phone hacking yesterday. He said illegal practices by ALL British media must be tackled.'

Despite Wapping's best efforts, the story was highly volatile – and becoming perilous for David Cameron. His friendliness with Brooks and Murdoch was criticized by usually supportive figures. Douglas

Carswell, the Tory MP for Clacton-on-Sea, tweeted: '"I don't think Maggie Thatcher would employ someone like that Andy Coulson", remarked my constituent. Me neither.' The *Telegraph*'s Peter Oborne said that like John Major in 1992, the Prime Minister faced a crisis from which he might never recover.

At 8.30 a.m., Ed Miliband described the possible hacking of the families of dead soldiers as 'grotesque beyond belief', adding: 'The only people in the world who seem to think that Rebekah Brooks should carry on in her position are Rupert Murdoch and David Cameron.'

The government's enthusiasm for the Sky bid was waning. At 11.37 a.m., Labour's leader in the Lords, Lady Royall, said the loss of public and commercial confidence in News International warranted the suspension of the Sky takeover. A government whip, Lady Rawlings, said that Jeremy Hunt was satisfied there were 'sufficient safeguards' to protect Sky News' independence, but added he would need time to respond to the public consultation. 'The Secretary of State will not be rushed, he will be fair,' she said. The government was not changing its mind about the Sky bid but was, seemingly, delaying the timetable. Shortly before 2 p.m., the BBC's Robert Peston tweeted that the government had received 100,000 submissions to the consultation on News Corp's bid, adding – apparently with inside information – 'Culture Sec won't give final decision on bid till Sept at earliest.'

A few newsagents stopped selling the *News of the World*. Andrew Thornton, who banned the paper from his two Budgens in north London, said: 'Their actions have affected people in our community and communities around the country and there must be consequences for the complete lack of morality that seems to be part of the paper's culture.' The *NoW*'s columnists began to heed the public mood. The comedian Dave Gorman quit the paper and the personal finance writer Martin Lewis – the cousin of the lawyer Mark Lewis – cancelled his column that week. One well-known *News of the World* journalist sought to calm the furore. While 'sickened' by the stories about the 'alleged hacking' of Milly Dowler, the showbiz editor Dan Wooton blogged: 'What I have to stress to you is this: I do NOT work for the newspaper you are reading about.'

However, the first of the big supermarkets, the lifeblood of national newspaper advertising, pulled out of the *NoW*: Sainsbury's would not advertise with the title until the end of the police investigation 'due to the rising concerns of our customers'. Asda and Boots followed.*

Scotland Yard announced that to allay 'significant public and political concern', the Independent Police Complaints Commission would indeed oversee its corruption inquiry. The *Evening Standard* carried further details of News International's suspected corruption of the city's police force, stating that officers with access to confidential information had received more than £100,000 in bribes from journalists. It quoted one unidentified source as saying: 'They were running a criminal enterprise at the *News of the World*. Serious crimes have been found.'

Shortly after 4 p.m., *News of the World* staff were called to a meeting with Rebekah Brooks. The last time such a big meeting had been called Andy Coulson had resigned: was she about to go?

Staff on other titles were reading a 968-word email from James Murdoch. It started slowly. The *News of the World* was 168 years old, read by more people than any other English language newspaper and had a proud history of fighting crime, exposing wrongdoing and regularly setting the news agenda – but, sadly, it had failed to hold itself to account. Murdoch wrote:

> Wrongdoers turned a good newsroom bad and this was not fully understood or adequately pursued. As a result, the *News of the World* and News International wrongly maintained that these issues were confined to one reporter. We now have voluntarily given evidence to the police that I believe will prove that this was untrue and those who acted wrongly will have to face the consequences.

---

* With the story at fever pitch, Tom Watson held a press conference with Tommy Sheridan's lawyer Aamer Anwar in Glasgow. Shortly before it took place, the Crown Office in Scotland announced: 'In light of emerging developments regarding the *News of the World*, the Crown has requested Strathclyde Police to investigate the evidence given by certain witnesses in the trial of Tommy Sheridan.' News International was now at the centre of four police inquiries.

This was not the only fault. The paper had made statements to Parliament without being in the full possession of the facts. This was wrong.

The company paid out-of-court settlements approved by me. I now know that I did not have a complete picture when I did so. This was wrong and is a matter of serious regret.

Humiliatingly, James Murdoch was finally admitting that the firm he chaired had misled Parliament, though he was careful to say that he had not known about the extent of the wrongdoing when he authorized the hush payment to Gordon Taylor. (At this stage, the internal documents detailing his involvement with the settlement had not been released.)

He outlined the action he was taking to resolve the problems: News International was cooperating with the police, had admitted liability in civil cases, set up the Management and Standards Committee, and hired Olswang solicitors to examine past failings and recommend new systems. Finally, he got to the news:

Having consulted senior colleagues, I have decided that we must take further decisive action with respect to the paper. This Sunday will be the last issue of the *News of the World*. Colin Myler will edit the final edition of the paper.

This was a bombshell: the UK's top-selling Sunday newspaper was to close. All revenue from its final edition that Sunday would go to good causes. The company hoped to find jobs for many of the paper's 250 staff. Murdoch added: 'I can understand how unfair these decisions may feel. Particularly, for colleagues who will leave the company.'

One of the first journalists in *The Times* to get to the end of the email exclaimed: 'Fucking hell!'

In the *NoW*'s newsroom – where the IT department had disabled the email system – staff were still listening to Rebekah Brooks. After rambling for several minutes, she suddenly announced the closure of the paper.

The journalists were dazed. They headed for the pub, along with a contingent of *Sun* sub-editors. As reporters left Wapping's gates, some were interviewed on live TV, their fate still hanging in the balance. Publicly, they seemed more disappointed than angry. Features editor Jules Stenson said staff showed 'quiet pride' when the announcement was made. 'There was shock, bewilderment, there were a few gasps, there were lots of tears from the staff. It's been reported that there was a lynch mob mentality which is completely untrue; there was none of that.'

Observers started to wonder whether the move was cosmetic. Shortly before the Milly Dowler story had broken, News International had appointed a single managing editor to run both the *Sun* and the *NoW*, increasing speculation that they would merge. Would a *Sun on Sunday* soon roll off the presses? Speaking at the première of a new Harry Potter movie, the TV presenter Jonathan Ross said: 'Clearly this is a cynical move, clearly it is an excuse to carry on.' The National Union of Journalists described the decision as 'an act of damage limitation to salvage Murdoch's reputation and that of News International – both of which are now tarnished beyond repair'. On the BBC's *Question Time* that night, 7 July, Hugh Grant said:

> Clearly the *News of the World* was going out of business anyway. People were not going to buy it on Sunday, advertisers were falling out in their droves – and all credit to them . . . I think we should see this for what it is: it is a very cynical managerial manoeuvre which has put several hundred not evil people (there were certainly a lot of evil people), but certainly non-editorial staff, out of work and has kept in particular one person who was the editor when Milly Dowler was hacked in a highly paid job.

He was loudly applauded. Some weeks later, he said: 'That night a girlfriend of mine had a call, an anonymous call, first on her mobile and then on her home phone. She finally picked it up and it said: "Tell Hugh Grant to shut the fuck up."'[10]

The *NoW*'s closure made front pages around the world, including those of *Le Monde*, *Bild*, *Die Welt*, *El País* and the *New York Times*. In Britain, the *Sun* splashed on 'World's End' and the *Daily Telegraph* 'Goodbye, Cruel World'. Quoting the words of an anonymous *News of the World* staffer, the *Independent* had: 'Newspaper "sacrificed to save one woman"'.

Rupert Murdoch's line had changed, again. For five years News International had insisted there was only one rogue reporter, then only a few rogue reporters. Now it admitted it had been running a rogue newspaper. Murdoch was still not willing to concede, as many people believed, that News International had a rogue chief executive.

17

Sky Plus

I'm not throwing innocent people under the bus
– Rupert Murdoch

If the world's wiliest newspaper proprietor thought changing the defence from one rogue reporter to one rogue newspaper would shut down the hacking scandal and salvage his reputation, he had failed to understand just how disarrayed News Corp and many British institutions had found themselves after the Milly Dowler story. The spasm of outrage that convulsed British public life had shaken an establishment previously too cowed or conflicted to keep Murdoch and his newspapers in check. Politicians, media, police and prosecutors all knew they had failed to act when they should have done, and now, to assert themselves at last, they came to their own conclusion – rather than Rupert Murdoch's – about what should be done.

Startlingly, a wave of openness spread over politics. On Friday 8 July, political leaders who had accepted Murdoch's power began openly questioning his dominance. That morning, in a speech at Reuters' London headquarters, Ed Miliband said: 'If one section of the media is allowed to grow so powerful that it becomes insulated from political criticism and scrutiny of its behaviour, the proper system of checks and balances breaks down and abuses of power are likely to follow. We must all bear responsibility for that.'

In Downing Street an hour later, David Cameron opened a press conference with the words: 'Over the past few days, the whole country has been shocked by the revelations about the phone hacking scandal.' While blaming the police's 'plainly inadequate' investigation in 2006 and the 'failed' Press Complaints Commission, Cameron candidly admitted that politicians had failed to protect the public:

> The truth is, to coin a phrase, we have all been in this together: the press, the politicians of all parties – yes, including me. We have not gripped this issue . . . party leaders were so keen to win the support of newspapers we turned a blind eye to the need to sort this issue, to get on top of the bad practices, to change the way our newspapers are regulated. It is on my watch that the music has stopped.

He confirmed that a judge would preside over the public inquiry.

Coolly, he cut loose Rebekah Brooks, saying that if she had tendered her resignation to him, he would have accepted it. The message to Rupert Murdoch was, finally, that she must go. As to his director of communications, Cameron said that no one had given him 'specific information' about Andy Coulson and he declined to apologize for his hiring. He said: 'He became a friend and is a friend.' The performance of the PR-executive-turned-PM had been assured; he had almost caught up with the public mood. His press conference concluded at 10.23 a.m.

By 10.30 a.m. his friend was in police custody at Lewisham station in south London. Andy Coulson was held on suspicion of conspiring to hack phones and corrupting police. Plain-clothes detectives searched his home in Dulwich, south London, and seized a computer. Four and a half years after his jailing for phone hacking, Clive Goodman, too, had been arrested at his home in Surrey on suspicion of police corruption. Police raided the offices of the *Daily Star Sunday* where he had been working, leaving after two hours with a disc of Goodman's computer activity.

In the City, analysts began to downgrade the likelihood of the Sky deal. At the stockbrokers Panmure Gordon, Alex DeGroote told his clients there had previously been a 90 per cent plus chance of the deal going through, but now it was no better than 50-50. BSkyB shares fell by 4.8 per cent. (They closed the week at 750p, down 11.7 per cent, or £1.8 billion.)

Tony Blair, who had maintained a close relationship with Rupert

Murdoch, described phone hacking as 'beyond disgusting' but sought to widen the scandal beyond his newspaper group. Addressing the centre-left Progress pressure group in London at lunchtime, Blair said: 'I think David Cameron and Ed Miliband are right to say this is not just about News International. It's not just about phone hacking.'

At 4 p.m., *News of the World* journalists were called to another meeting with Rebekah Brooks. Speculation grew that, this time, she really would resign. As News International's IT department again suspended internal email and the Internet, Brooks explained that the paper was closing because advertisers had concluded it was a 'toxic' brand. Ominously, she told staff: 'In a year's time it'll become apparent why we did this.' A journalist complained: 'We're all being contaminated by that toxicity by the way we're being treated,' adding – to applause – 'Do you think we'd want to work for you again?' Brooks responded: 'There's not an arrogance about anyone wanting to work for us at all . . . Sorry if that came across . . . We haven't made the decision on any new publications or strengthening or expanding existing media, it's just too soon.' She revealed she was being removed from the internal Management and Standards Committee. The MSC would now comprise Wapping's general manager Will Lewis, its director of communications Simon Greenberg and News Corp's general counsel in Europe Jeff Palker, reporting to Joel Klein in New York – who in turn reported to Viet Dinh, chairman of News Corp's Corporate Governance Committee. News Corp was taking complete charge of its wayward British subsidiary.

On Saturday 9 July, commentators sought to put the extraordinary events of the previous week into context. Like his former political master, Alastair Campbell sought to implicate other papers, saying the *Daily Mail*'s editor Paul Dacre could soon be under pressure. Campbell blogged:

> When police investigating a murder trial involving Mr Rees raided his home, they found invoices totalling thousands and thousands of pounds relating to inquiries into many public figures for many different papers. The inquiries on me, for example, were made by my former paper, the *Mirror*. As for Glenn Mulcaire, well we know a lot

about him, but there is a lot more to come. So Mr Dacre and his Mail Group, whose coverage of the phone hacking scandal has been minimal until recent days – wonder why? – will be an important part of any serious and rigorous inquiry.[1]

In his evidence at the Leveson Inquiry in February 2012, Paul Dacre denied that the Mail newspapers had ever hacked phones.

Writing for *Newsweek*, the Watergate journalist Carl Bernstein argued that the phone hacking scandal was a surprise only to those who had ignored Murdoch's 'pernicious influence on journalism'. He wrote:

> Too many of us have winked in amusement at the salaciousness without considering the larger corruption of journalism and politics promulgated by Murdoch Culture on both sides of the Atlantic. As one of his former top executives – once a close aide – told me, 'This scandal and all its implications could not have happened anywhere else. Only in Murdoch's orbit. The hacking at *News of the World* was done on an industrial scale. More than anyone, Murdoch invented and established this culture in the newsroom, where you do whatever it takes to get the story, take no prisoners, destroy the competition, and the end will justify the means.'[2]

Rupert Murdoch himself was still in the US, attending the last day of a conference for media magnates in Sun Valley, Idaho. He seemed oblivious to the anger in the country he had called home for many years. Asked by reporters whether he would change his management team, he replied: 'Nothing's changed. We've been let down by people that we trusted, with the result the paper let down its readers.' Brooks, his protégée, enjoyed his 'total' support. He said: 'I'm not throwing innocent people under the bus.'[3]

News International doubled the print run of the final *News of the World* to 5 million. While many readers would buy its farewell edition out of habit or curiosity, for others it had become so tarnished that they would not even accept its charity. Oxfam, the RSPCA, Action Aid, the Salvation Army and other charities refused to accept the proceeds of its final edition. Paul McNamara, the paper's defence correspondent, had to make fifty calls before three – Barnardos, the Forces Children's Trust and the Queen Elizabeth Hospital Birmingham Charity – would agree to take any money. He said: 'I had to beg.'[4]

A surreal atmosphere prevailed inside Wapping, according to one *NoW* journalist working his last day:

> People can't comprehend it and are still very angry with Rebekah. Staff were called together for a group photograph this morning and everyone was quite jovial, then someone called 'smile' and someone else said 'What have we got to smile about?' Someone shouted: 'Because we are the best' . . . The phones on the newsdesk have been ringing all week with people shouting the nastiest, most vile abuse, but today people are ringing up giving their support.[5]

Once the paper was 'off stone', Colin Myler stood on a desk and told staff he could not imagine a more difficult day at work, adding: 'It's not a place we wanted to be and absolutely not a place we deserve to be.' In line with Fleet Street tradition (when printers would whack their hammers against metal benches to mark the departure of a colleague), he 'banged out' each journalist, clattering a plastic ruler against a desk as they filed out. Shortly before 9 p.m., Myler himself emerged from Thomas More Square clutching the *NoW*'s final front page, and – with his staff massed behind him – said to the bank of reporters, snappers and TV crews: 'We're going to do what we should do now and go and have a nice drink – or three.'

The 8,674th edition of the *News of the World* was headlined: 'Thank You and Goodbye'. Its strapline read: 'After 168 years, we finally say a sad but very proud farewell to our 7.5 million loyal readers'. The paper was defiant, proud and a little remorseful, saying:

> We praised high standards, we demanded high standards but, as we are now only too painfully aware, for a period of a few years up to 2006 some who worked for us, or in our name, fell shamefully short of those standards.

A forty-eight page pullout celebrated its front pages, including the sinking of the *Titanic*, the Profumo Affair, the Great Train Robbery, the death of Princess Diana and – in its more prurient modern incarnation – 'Chief of Defence Staff in Sex and Security Scandal' and 'Beckham's Secret Affair'. Missing from the pantheon were David Blunkett's affair and Max Mosley's 'Sick Nazi Orgy'. The paper trumpeted its campaigns on the military covenant and compensation for the 7/7 victims. Mazher Mahmood recalled how he had nailed 'scores of paedophiles, arms dealers, drug peddlers, people traffickers, bent doctors and lawyers'.

News International had worried that the paper's departing journalists would insert rude messages into the final edition. Fleet Street had a history of parting shots: on his last day at the *Daily Express* in 2001, the first letters of leader writer Stephen Pollard's final column spelled out: 'Fuck You Desmond'. Two *Sun* executives combed through the *NoW*'s last edition. They did a good job of checking the news stories, but less so with the crosswords, whose clues included: brook, stink, catastrophe, pest, less bright, woman stares wildly at calamity, criminal enterprise, string of recordings and mix in prison. Answers included disaster, stench, racket and tart. The answers to 1 across, 4 down, 10 across and 7 down were Tomorrow, We, Are, Sacked.

Roy Greenslade felt that the final *News of the World* had played down its 'villainy':

> It's a bit rich to claim integrity while working for a paper that has engaged in the dark arts – entrapment, subterfuge, covert filming, the use of agents provocateurs and phone hacking – for the best part of twenty years.[6]

On Sunday 10 July, the *Mail on Sunday* carried a piece from an anonymous 'News International Insider' claiming that Rebekah Brooks had turned the *Sun* from an 'abrasive, aggressive paper known for breaking big stories' into a title afraid of upsetting politicians, whom she 'love-bombed'. 'She sold the soul of the *Sun* and the *News of the World* to PR snake-oil merchants.' Relationships with PR firms such as Freud Communications – run by Matthew Freud – were so close that 'if they rang the newsdesk with a story, you had to run it'.[7]

John Yates finally admitted that he had made a hash of the phone hacking affair, telling the *Sunday Telegraph*: 'I regrettably said the initial inquiry was a success. Clearly, now it looks different.' His decision not to reopen the case, he said, was a 'pretty crap one', and he now wished he had looked at Glenn Mulcaire's notes. 'In hindsight, there is a shed load of stuff in there I wish I'd known. The Milly Dowler stuff is just shocking beyond anything. It's a tipping point and quite rightly so.'[8]

In Parliament, an anti-Murdoch coalition was cohering around a Labour motion against the Sky bid. The Liberal Democrats, the Conservatives' smaller Coalition partners, were intending to support the symbolic vote in the Commons the following Wednesday. On Sunday, the first signs emerged that the Conservatives were wobbling when Philip Hammond, the Transport Secretary, said: 'If the motion is sensibly formed that would be one thing, but if it called on the government to ignore the law that would not be possible.'

After five days in which his British news operation itself had dominated the headlines, Rupert Murdoch finally arrived in the UK at eleven that Sunday morning. After landing at Luton airport, he went straight to Wapping, carrying a copy of the final *News of the World*, then to his flat in St James's. At 5.35 p.m., Brooks arrived and, surrounded by reporters and camera crews, they walked to a nearby hotel for a meal with James Murdoch. When asked for his priority, Rupert gestured towards Brooks and said: 'This one.' The clip was repeatedly shown on the TV news that evening. Murdoch, the great newsman, was uncharacteristically out of touch with the public mood.

On Monday 11 July, the government swung decisively against the Sky bid, when Jeremy Hunt, later christened the 'Minister for Murdoch' when the extent of his contacts with the company became clear, asked Ofcom to assess whether the *News of the World*'s behaviour undermined News Corp's promises. In a letter to Ofcom's executive director Clive Maxwell, he wrote:

> As you are aware, my consultation on the revised undertakings in lieu offered by News Corporation closed on Friday at midday. I am now considering the responses to that consultation, but as I stated on Friday, I anticipate this taking some time.
>
> However, given the well-publicized matters involving the *News of the World* in the past week, and which have led to the closure of that

paper, I should be grateful if you could let me know whether you consider those revelations and allegations cause you to reconsider any part of your previous advice to me, or otherwise give rise to concerns, on the credibility, sustainability and practicalities of the undertakings offered by News Corporation.

Hunt and the government had long insisted that Ofcom could not consider News Corp's criminal history when assessing the takeover. Political expediency had now changed that. Hunt's message to Ofcom was clear: 'Please now give me an excuse to block this takeover.' The release of the text of the letter sent Sky shares into freefall.

Conservative and Liberal Democrat politicians now started speaking out against the bid – which was still on the table. John Whittingdale, chairman of the Culture Committee – who had deemed the takeover to be an entirely separate issue the previous week – said: 'The best thing would be if it could be put on hold until we have a much clearer idea of who knew what, who was responsible.'[9] After meeting Bob and Sally Dowler in Downing Street, Nick Clegg said: 'I would simply say to him [Murdoch]: look how people feel about this; look how the country has reacted with revulsion to the revelations. So do the decent thing and reconsider, think again, about your bid.' Breaking off from a speech about public service reform in Canary Wharf, east London, at 3.30 p.m. David Cameron said firmly: 'All I would say is this: if I was running that company right now with all the problems and the difficulties and the mess frankly that there is, I think they should be focused on clearing those up rather than on the next corporate move.'

Murdoch was left in no doubt that the government wanted to kill the deal. Shortly before 4 p.m., faced with the prospect of an embarrassing, albeit non-binding Commons vote, News Corp withdrew its commitment to spin off Sky News, forcing the government to refer its bid to the Competition Commission. Though this looked like a defeat, News Corp had merely staged a tactical retreat. A Competition Commission investigation would take months, during which time the political temperature would probably have cooled. The bid was still on the table.

At 4.16 p.m. in a Commons statement confirming the referral, Jeremy Hunt explained:

> Protecting our tradition of a strong, free and independent media is the most sacred responsibility I have as Culture Secretary. Irresponsible, illegal and callous behaviour damages that freedom by weakening public support for the self-regulation on which it has thrived. By dealing decisively with the abuses of power we have seen, hopefully on a cross-party basis, the Government intend to strengthen and not diminish press freedom . . .

MPs were in uproar at his audacity; the Speaker had to call for order.

Disappointingly for News Corp, the bid's referral did not dull the clamour for its death. The Labour Party refused to withdraw its motion, and support for it hardened among Liberal Democrats. Opposition to the deal was bolstered by further reports of the alleged corruption at Wapping. That morning, Robert Peston had revealed that internal emails appeared to show payments of £1,000 to a royal protection squad officer for the phone numbers of senior members of the royal family, their friends and relatives. He quoted a News International 'source' as saying: 'There was clear evidence from the emails that the security of the royal family was being put at risk. I was profoundly shocked when I saw them . . .' In total, Peston said, the paper had paid Metropolitan Police officers £130,000 for information. One million copies of the *Evening Standard* hit the streets of London with a front page reading: 'Queen's Police Sold Her Details to *NoW*'.

Scotland Yard responded angrily to the leaks, which appeared to come from Wapping. In a three-sentence statement authorized by Sir Paul Stephenson, the Met said it believed that information in media stories that day was 'part of a deliberate campaign to undermine the investigation into the alleged payments by corrupt journalists to corrupt police officers' – 'and divert attention from elsewhere'. News International had agreed to keep information confidential so the police could pursue the culprits without alerting them. 'However we are extremely concerned and disappointed that the continuous release of selected information – that is known only by a small number of people – could have a significant impact on the corruption investigation.'

On Tuesday 12 July, at the Home Affairs Committee, senior police officers had to account for their slow progress in bringing Murdoch's hackers to justice. Andy Hayman denied that when he was at the Met there had been any impropriety in his social and professional contacts with NI's executives. Asked whether he had ever received any payment from a news organization while a policeman, he cried: 'Good God, absolutely not.' Pulling an astonished face, he added: 'I cannot believe you suggested that.' Keith Vaz, the committee chairman, considered Hayman's performance 'more Clouseau than Columbo'. (Hayman later described the committee's treatment of him as 'appalling'. 'To be accused, as I was, of being a dodgy geezer, which is probably on the basis of my accent, I think that's a really poor show.')[10] Peter Clarke, the former Deputy Assistant Commissioner who led the 2006 investigation, accused News International of deliberately thwarting its inquiry: 'If there had been any meaningful cooperation at the time we would not be here today. It is as simple as that.'

In a move unthinkable even a week before, the Culture, Media and Sport Committee called Rupert and James Murdoch and Rebekah Brooks to give evidence, the following Tuesday, 19 July. Since buying the *News of the World* in 1969, Rupert Murdoch had appeared before a parliamentary committee only once, at the private session of the Lords Communications Committee in September 2007, when he had confirmed he exercised editorial control over his tabloid newspapers (see chapter 5). John Whittingdale said that a figure like Murdoch being brought before a Commons select committee was 'unprecedented'. BBC political correspondent Laura Kuenssberg described it as 'something we simply could not have imagined seven days ago – even twenty-four hours ago'. Extraordinarily, News International declined to confirm that the Murdochs would attend the hearing.

On Wednesday 13 July, the Commons was braced for a historic day. The Liberal Democrats let it be known that they would vote for the motion against the Sky bid, tipping the voting arithmetic away from Murdoch. Faced with almost certain defeat, the Conservatives announced they would vote with Labour and the Liberal Democrats. Extraordinarily, all three parties were planning to thwart the man who had frightened politicians for decades.

At Prime Minister's Questions, David Cameron acknowledged the scale of the crisis, telling MPs there was 'a firestorm engulfing parts of our media, parts of our police and even our political system's ability to respond'. He called for 'root and branch change' at News International, adding: 'It has now become increasingly clear that while everybody, to start with, wanted in some way to separate what was happening at News International and what is happening at BSkyB, that is simply not possible. What has happened at this company is disgraceful. It has got to be addressed at every level and they should stop thinking about mergers when they have to sort out the mess they have created.'

He had done a complete U-turn on a judicial inquiry, Brooks and now Sky. He was pressed by Ed Miliband to explain what had happened to the warnings passed to his chief of staff about Andy Coulson. Cameron responded that he had hired Coulson on the basis of assurances that he did not know about phone hacking. 'He gave those self-same assurances to the police and to a select committee and under oath to a court of law.' Cameron – who only five days earlier had described Coulson as a friend – added: 'If it turns out he lied, then it will not just be that he shouldn't have been in government, it will be that he should be prosecuted . . . But I can say that I did not receive that information.' The Prime Minister was, in effect, blaming his staff for not passing on the *Guardian*'s warnings about Jonathan Rees.

With the prospect of all three main parties voting, albeit symbolically, against its plans, News Corp finally withdrew the takeover bid. Rupert Murdoch left the announcement to his deputy, Chase Carey, who said: 'We believed that the proposed acquisition of BSkyB by News Corporation would benefit both companies, but it has become clear that it is too difficult to progress in this climate.' The aborted takeover bid had cost £40 million in fees alone. Quoting News Corp sources, Sky's business editor Mark Kleinman reported that on the conclusion of the phone hacking inquiries, the company could revive the bid. Under cover of the announcement, News International slipped out the news that the *NoW*'s lawyer Tom Crone had left the company.

The Commons debate still went ahead. Gordon Brown made a spectacularly angry contribution. Two days earlier, on Monday morning, he had recorded an interview with the BBC's Glenn Campbell in which he had complained about two News International stories. In 2000 the *Sunday Times* had used subterfuge to obtain an 'unfounded' story that he had bought a London flat from the administrators of a collapsed firm of the disgraced tycoon Robert Maxwell for a 'knockdown price'. According to Brown, criminals acting for the *Sunday Times* had successfully blagged details of his bank account from Abbey National, which had subsequently informed him of the 'well-orchestrated campaign of deception'. He also questioned how in 2006 the *Sun* had obtained a story revealing his son Fraser's cystic fibrosis, which had left the Browns 'in tears'. The former Prime Minister said: 'I have not made any allegations about how it appeared. But the fact is, it did appear.'*

Murdoch's newspapers went on the attack. The day before the debate, 12 July, the *Sunday Times* did not deny the subterfuge, but said in a statement: 'We believe no law was broken in the process of this investigation, and contrary to Mr Brown's assertion, no criminal was used and the story was published giving all sides a fair hearing.'[11] The following day, the *Sun*'s front page screamed 'Brown Wrong', adding the strapline: 'We didn't probe son's medical records. Source was dad of cystic fibrosis child.'

Rising to speak at 5.26 p.m., Brown vented a simmering rage that he had held inside himself for months. The phone hacking scandal involved many other forms of illicit and illegal behaviour, he said, including the sending of Trojan viruses to hack computers.

> It was not the misconduct of a few rogues or a few freelancers, but lawbreaking often on an industrial scale, at its worst dependent on links with the British criminal underworld.
>
> Others have said that in its behaviour towards those without a voice of their own, News International descended from the gutter to the sewers. The tragedy is that it let the rats out of the sewers.

His administration, he said, had angered News Corp by ignoring its demands to cut the BBC's budget and by ordering the sale of a

---

* In June 2012, Fife National Health Service Board wrote to Brown telling him it was 'highly likely' a member of staff passed information about his son's diagnosis to the *Sun*.

16 per cent stake in ITV it had acquired to frustrate a takeover by Richard Branson's Virgin Media. (Police informed Branson in 2011 that his phone may have been hacked by the *News of the World*.) By a 'strange coincidence' News International and the Conservative Party had come to share almost exactly the same media policy. Brown said:

> It was so close that it was often expressed in almost exactly the same words. On the future of the licence fee; on BBC online; on the right of the public to see free of charge the maximum possible number of national sporting events; on the future of the BBC's commercial arm; and on the integrity of Ofcom, we stood up for what we believed to be the public interest, but that was made difficult when the opposition invariably reclassified the public interest as the News International interest.

The end of the Sky bid led the TV bulletins and the front pages of Thursday morning's newspapers. The focus was now on whether the Murdochs would attend the select committee the following Tuesday. Rebekah Brooks, a UK citizen, agreed to give evidence, while James Murdoch, a dual UK–US citizen, wrote that 'unfortunately' he was not available to attend on 19 July but would be pleased to give evidence the following month. Rupert Murdoch, an American citizen, said he was unable to make the hearing. 'Dear John,' he wrote to John Whittingdale. 'Thank you for your letter of 12 July, on behalf of the committee, inviting me to give evidence to you on 19 July. Unfortunately, I am not available to attend the session you have planned next Tuesday . . .'

The snub outraged politicians. Downing Street called for the Murdochs to appear, while Nick Clegg said that they would do so if they had 'any shred of sense of responsibility or accountability'. The Culture Committee met to determine its response. While still in session, its decision to compel the Murdochs to attend their hearing was quietly communicated to the Commons authorities, who dispatched the Deputy Serjeant-at-Arms to News International's headquarters. Travelling on the London Underground in an ordinary suit, the ancient-office holder slipped past the reporters milling outside Wapping and arrived unannounced, causing consternation at News International. After refusing to hand over the summons to a security guard, he was asked to sit in a waiting room where he watched Sky News break the news of his visit on giant flat-screen TVs. Eventually he handed the documents to the Murdochs' lawyers.

With the crisis spinning ever more dangerously out of control, News Corp called in the PR and lobbying specialists Edelman. With Edelman in charge, News Corp became slicker. Shortly before 5 p.m., the Murdochs agreed they would give evidence to the select committee after all. Rupert Murdoch called the *Wall Street Journal* to defend News Corp's behaviour, saying it had dealt with the scandal 'extremely well in every way possible' and had made only 'minor mistakes'. He rejected criticism that James had been too slow to clean up the business: 'I think he acted as fast as he could, the moment he could.'

While the committee dominated the news, another drama had been playing out in Scotland Yard. At ten that morning officers had arrested Neil 'Wolfman' Wallis on suspicion of phone hacking. When the Yard's top brass dined with the *News of the World*, it was most often with Wallis, the deputy editor. In August 2009, shortly after the *Guardian*'s Gordon Taylor story, Wallis had left the newspaper to found his own company, Chamy Media. Extraordinarily, between October 2009 and September 2010, he had been given a new job – by the Metropolitan Police. For £1,000 a day, Wallis had been giving media advice to Dick Fedorcio at the time Scotland Yard was refusing to reopen the inquiry and complaining about the *Guardian*'s coverage.

At 4.30 p.m., the Met issued a statement owning up to the misjudgement, explaining that Chamy Media had supplied 'strategic communications advice' two days a month after tendering the lowest fee. During his time advising Scotland Yard, it later transpired, Wallis had been selling stories about its investigations to his old friends in the tabloids. Overall, he received more than £25,000 from the press – more than the value of his police contract. News International reportedly paid him £10,000 for one story. Among the scoops were details of a suspected assassination attempt on the Pope.[12]

Wallis's employment by the Yard was met with astonishment. The government, which had been under intense scrutiny for its own contacts with Wapping, was particularly angry. The Home Secretary Theresa May wrote to Sir Paul Stephenson to get 'the full picture' of the contract. The mayor, Boris Johnson, whose deputy had put pressure on the Met to scale down Operation Weeting, told journalists he had 'a very frank' hour-long discussion with the Commissioner.

That day in the US, Eliot Spitzer, the former New York Attorney General, called for News Corp to be investigated by the US Department of Justice over allegations of 'bribery, illegal wiretapping, interference in a murder investigation, political blackmail, and rampant disregard for both the truth and basic decency'. Spitzer, who had brought a series of prosecutions against investment banks, said that the company could be in breach of the Foreign Corrupt Practices Act, which bars American companies from bribing foreign officials. After receiving a formal complaint from the US Congressman Peter King, the FBI began an investigation into the corrosive allegations that the *News of the World* hacked into the phones of 9/11 victims. The phone hacking scandal was going global.

News Corp's second biggest investor was becoming increasingly concerned. Tracked down by *Newsnight* to his yacht in the Mediterranean, Saudi Prince Al-Waleed bin Talal Al-Saud said Rebekah Brooks should resign if she was found to have been involved in wrongdoing. Sitting on deck wearing sunglasses, he said: 'If the indications are that her involvement in this matter is explicit, for sure she has to go, you bet she has to go. I will not accept ... to deal with a company that has a lady or a man that has any sliver of doubts on her or his integrity.'

The Business Secretary Vince Cable, who had wanted to bring down the Murdoch empire when others were still kow-towing, ruefully reflected on a turbulent ten days in an interview with the BBC Radio 4's *PM* programme that afternoon: 'It is a little bit like the end of a dictatorship when everybody suddenly discovers they were against the dictator.'

18
'We Are Sorry'

We are sorry that we have been caught
– Private Eye, 22 July 2011

Rupert Murdoch had stubbornly clung to Rebekah Brooks, despite having to close a best-selling newspaper and abandoning his £7.08 billion bid for Sky, but on 19 July, he was facing a parliamentary inquisition where her continued presence would be an embarrassment. Even his most supportive investor, Saudi Prince Al-Waleed bin Talal Al-Saud, whose stake he needed in the boardroom, was questioning her record. Now, he sacrificed her.

At 9.57 a.m. on Friday 15 July, Brooks resigned as chief executive of News International. During her two years in charge, the business had repeatedly denied any wrongdoing. In a valedictory email to staff, she again denied that she had done anything wrong. But, she explained, her desire to 'remain on the bridge' was 'detracting attention from all our honest endeavours to fix the problems of the past'. Brooks, who had risen from secretary to chief executive in twenty years, praised Rupert Murdoch's wisdom, kindness and advice, James Murdoch's loyalty and friendship and News International's staff. She wrote: 'I am proud to have been part of the team and lucky to know so many brilliant journalists and media executives. I leave with the happiest of memories and an abundance of friends.' She also left with a reported pay-off of £7 million, a free office and a car.[1]

Politicians welcomed her departure, but it failed to end questions about the company's conduct and Murdoch's power. Indeed the fact that Brooks had stayed in post so long had weakened his position. In her remarks to *News of the World* staff, Brooks had cryptically referred to being 'a conductor' for the scandal; now the Murdochs were left to feel the heat alone.

Brooks's successor was not Will Lewis, the general manager, but the head of Sky Italia, Tom Mockridge. With Brooks gone and Mockridge not yet in charge, the public relations professionals took over. News Corp had failed to grasp the scale or the significance of its difficulty, and now, instead of denial, it offered apology. Over the coming days, the Murdochs and News International would be a picture of contrition. James emailed staff displaying the new emollience (with a hint of the steel beneath): 'The company has made mistakes. It is not only receiving appropriate scrutiny, but is also responding to unfair attacks by setting the record straight.'[2]

News International ran full-page advertisements in national newspapers apologizing for its behaviour and wrote to advertisers outlining its remedial action. Mark Borkowski, an entertainment PR specialist, described the adverts as 'classic damage limitation mode'.[3]

The text of the News International apology read:

We are sorry.

The *News of the World* was in the business of holding others to account. It failed when it came to itself.

We are sorry for the serious wrongdoing that occurred.

We are deeply sorry for the hurt suffered by the individuals affected.

We regret not acting faster to sort things out.

I realize that simply apologizing is not enough.

Our business was founded on the idea that a free and open press should be a positive force in society. We need to live up to this.

In the coming days, as we take further concrete steps to resolve these issues and make amends for the damage they have caused, you will hear more from us.

Sincerely,

Rupert Murdoch.

Private Eye parodied the ad thus:

> We are sorry.
>
> We are sorry that we have been caught.
>
> We are sorry that we had to close down the *News of the World*.
>
> We are sorry that we can't take over BSkyB.
>
> We deeply regret that our share price has gone down as a result of previous wrongdoing by some individuals in our employ.
>
> I was personally shocked and appalled to find out the kind of thing that had been going on in my business.

Another act of contrition took place on the afternoon of 15 July, when Rupert Murdoch met Milly Dowler's parents, Bob and Sally, at a central London hotel. As photographers and reporters waited outside One Aldwych, Murdoch apologized abjectly to the Dowlers. Shortly before 6 p.m. their lawyer, Mark Lewis, emerged to tell reporters that Murdoch was 'very humbled and very shaken and very sincere'. Lewis said: 'I think this was something that had hit him on a very personal level and was something that shouldn't have happened, I don't think somebody could have held their head in their hands so many times and say that they were sorry.'

News Corp exploited Brooks's resignation and the meeting with the Dowlers to dump more bad news. Of all the Fridays in the phone hacking scandal, 15 July was the biggest example of what public relations experts term 'put out the trash day'. For days the company had been stalling requests by the *Independent* and ITN for confirmation that Jude Law had launched a phone hacking lawsuit against the *Sun*. At 7 p.m., News International leaked the story to Sky News, giving the Murdoch outlet an exclusive and burying the story under the bigger corporate meltdown.

Shortly after 9 p.m. UK time, Les Hinton, Rupert Murdoch's loyal servant for fifty years, resigned as chief executive of Dow Jones. Hinton said he had watched events unfold at the *News of the World* with sorrow. 'That I was ignorant of what apparently happened is irrelevant,' he added, 'and in the circumstances I feel it is proper for me to resign from News Corp and apologize to those hurt by the actions of the *News of the World*.' News International also disclosed that its legal affairs director Jon Chapman had left the company.

On Saturday 16 July, journalists and politicians who had dismissed the scandal finally began to grasp the scale of the original wrongdoing and the cover-up, which raised much broader questions about the probity of national institutions. Seeking to explain the disclosures of the past twelve days, the *Daily Telegraph* pointed out in a leader: 'Large swathes of the British establishment have been implicated in this scandal. And the shady characters who have been exposed – policemen, politicians and News International executives – have so far revealed only one aim. That is, to avoid giving a straight answer to the public. The suspicion is that they are living in fear of what might be revealed.'[4]

On Sunday 17 July, Scotland Yard arrested Rebekah Brooks. Her fall had been steep: on Friday morning, she had been running the most powerful media organization in the country; at noon on Sunday she was in police custody, detained on suspicion of phone hacking and corruption. Brooks had turned up by appointment to a London police station expecting only to be interviewed. She no longer had the inside track on police investigations.

The Murdochs, however, could still rely on the assistance of their newspapers. In his column in the *Sunday Times*, Jeremy Clarkson damped down speculation that David Cameron, James Murdoch and Brooks had discussed Sky when they met at her home in the Cotswolds on 23 December, hours after the Conservative leader had stripped Vince Cable of the decision on the bid. Clarkson exclusively revealed what had been discussed: sausage rolls. They had all been planning to go for a walk, he wrote, and Brooks had wondered what they would eat: the Prime Minister had suggested sausage rolls. Clarkson assured: 'In other words, it was like a million other Christmas-time dinners being held in a million other houses all over the world that day. BSkyB was not mentioned. Nor was phone hacking.' As both James and David Cameron admitted later at the Leveson Inquiry, Clarkson was wrong: they did discuss BSkyB that day.

More seriously, the *Sunday Times*'s front page carried an exclusive that directed attention towards the police, revealing that while Sir Paul Stephenson was recuperating from his leg operation in early 2011, he and his wife accepted a twenty-day free stay at the £598-a-night Champneys health spa in Hertfordshire, as guests of its owner, Stephen Purdew, a family friend. While the Commissioner's acceptance of thousands of pounds of free hospitality might have raised eyebrows at any time, what made the story explosive was that Champneys' publicist was Neil Wallis.

Stephenson said he had not known of Wallis's connection to Champneys, but his position came under pressure that afternoon from Coalition ministers, whose own links to Rupert Murdoch had been under intense scrutiny. Nick Clegg, the Liberal Democrat leader, said he was 'incredibly worried' about the impact of the phone hacking scandal on London's police force and offered Stephenson less than full support. The Home Secretary, Theresa May, who had repeatedly rejected calls for a public inquiry, announced that she would make a statement to Parliament the following day about the Yard's relationship with Wallis. By the evening, Stephenson – still recovering from his operation – could take no more. At 7.30 p.m., reporters were summoned to a hastily called press conference. At Scotland Yard, Stephenson, the country's top police officer, announced he was quitting. In a fortnight, the scandal had closed the country's best-selling Sunday paper, sunk a £7.8 billion takeover, forced out Rupert Murdoch's favourite bosses in Britain and the United States, and now cost London's police chief his job.

In his resignation statement, Stephenson insisted he had done nothing wrong, but said that the speculation about the links between senior officers and News International was distracting him from his job. He had known Neil Wallis since 2006, but had 'no reason' to suspect he might have been involved in phone hacking. 'I do not occupy a position in the world of journalism,' Stephenson said. 'I had no knowledge of the extent of this disgraceful practice and the repugnant nature of the selection of victims that is now emerging; nor of its apparent reach into senior levels.' He pointed out that while his force had employed a *News of the World* executive who had not resigned over phone hacking, David Cameron had personally employed a man who had done so, Andy Coulson. The country's most senior police officer had not informed the Prime Minister he was about to resign. Senior officers felt Stephenson was carrying the can for the Yard's close relationship with the press forged during Sir John Stevens's tenure from 2000 to 2005.

Cameron, on an official visit to Africa, said he understood Stephenson's decision and stressed that the police investigations should proceed with 'all the necessary leadership and resources'. He abruptly cut short his African tour to return to the UK to deal with the crisis.

On Monday 18 July, politicians let the spotlight fall on another policeman, John Yates. Boris Johnson, who had failed to challenge the Met over phone hacking when it mattered, said that questions would now be asked about the Assistant Commissioner's relationship with Neil Wallis. Brian Coleman, a fellow Conservative member of the London Assembly, said: 'The Commissioner has done the right thing by resigning and accepting the error of judgement in employing Neil Wallis. Yates, who has shown that his stewardship of the original hacking inquiry was to put it bluntly, inept, should go – and go now.'[5]

Yates tried to cling to his post, telling Sky News at 11.30 a.m.: 'I've done nothing wrong.' But his position became untenable. The Metropolitan Police Authority began examining his decision not to reopen the investigation after the Gordon Taylor story in July 2009: he risked suspension.

Shortly after 2 p.m., John Yates resigned as the country's top counter-terrorism officer. He expressed some regret that victims of phone hacking had been dealt with inappropriately, but added: 'Sadly, there continues to be a huge amount of inaccurate, ill-informed and on occasion downright malicious gossip published about me personally. This has the potential to be a significant distraction in my current role as the national lead for counter-terrorism.'

In another blow to its image, Scotland Yard confirmed that the *News of the World*'s Alex Marunchak had for twenty years worked for the Met as an interpreter for victims and suspects, giving him inside information on police investigations. The language was Ukrainian and the years between 1980 and 2000. With a degree of understatement, Scotland Yard said: 'We recognize that this may cause concern and that some professions may be incompatible with the role of an interpreter.'[6] A few days later the Yard revealed that no fewer than ten of the staff in Dick Fedorcio's Directorate of Public Affairs had previously worked for News International.

The public could see now the close bonds between News International and the Yard. The Independent Police Complaints Commission opened an investigation into the conduct of Sir Paul Stephenson, John Yates, Andy Hayman and Peter Clarke.* Theresa May also announced that Elizabeth Filkin, the former Parliamentary Commissioner for Standards, would investigate Scotland Yard's relationship with the media; Her Majesty's Inspectorate of Constabulary would investigate police corruption; and a body yet to be announced would investigate the powers and effectiveness of the Independent Police Complaints Commission. After many years of denial when no one in authority took responsibility for wrongdoing at News International, there were now no fewer than twelve inquiries: four by the police, four into the police, two by Commons committees, one by News Corp's Management and Standards Committee, and Lord Leveson's public inquiry, which would open months later.

As the clock ticked down to the Murdochs' appearance before the Commons Culture Committee, the first journalist to speak out about phone hacking was found dead at his house in Watford, twenty miles from central London. More than any other former NoW reporter, Sean Hoare had exposed the paper's dark arts. He had been spurned by former colleagues who had been friends (one ex-News of the World executive had slammed down the phone on him, saying: 'Don't ever call me on this number again') and he had been treated as a suspect rather than a witness by the police. His inquest later ruled that he had died of liver failure.

* On 17 August, after just twenty-two working days, the Independent Police Complaints Commission cleared Sir Paul Stephenson, John Yates, Andy Hayman and Peter Clarke of any misconduct in their handling of the phone hacking investigations. The IPCC added that the public would 'make its own judgements' about the wisdom of Stephenson's acceptance of the free stay at Champneys. In 2012, the IPCC said that Dick Fedorcio should face a disciplinary charge of gross misconduct for his employment of Neil Wallis. Fedorcio, who had been suspended for months, resigned.

The *Guardian*'s Amelia Hill, co-author of the Milly Dowler story, revealed that the Metropolitan Police were examining a laptop computer found in a bin at London's Chelsea Harbour, the riverside apartment complex where Rebekah and Charlie Brooks lived. At around 3 p.m. that day – the day after Brooks's release from police custody – the computer had been handed to a security guard. Her husband had tried to reclaim it, but had been unable to prove it was his and the guard had called the police. Within half an hour, two marked police cars and an unmarked forensics vehicle had arrived at the scene.

19
Democracy Day

*I do not have direct knowledge of what they knew and at
what time, but I can tell you that the critical new facts, as I
saw them and as the company saw them, really emerged in
the production of documentary information or evidence in
the civil trials at the end of 2010*

– James Murdoch, 19 July 2011

On the morning of 19 July, all eyes were on the showdown between
Rupert Murdoch and his son and the Commons Culture Committee.
Since taking over the *News of the World* and the *Sun* in 1969, forty-
two years previously, Rupert had dominated the media and politics in
Britain but he had never appeared before a parliamentary inquiry in
public. In the days running up to the meeting, James and Rupert Murdoch were extensively coached by public relations professionals.

Over the previous weekend, Tom Watson had also been working
through lines of questioning. At the offices of Max Mosley's solicitors
Collyer Bristow, the day before the hearing, he had spent four hours
role-playing the questions with Mosley and others. He expected News
Corp's advisers would try to protect Rupert by getting James to
answer most of the technical questions. He believed the way to keep
the focus on Rupert was to concentrate on questions of corporate
governance. Watson hoped that Murdoch would either have to admit
that he had known about the criminality at the *News of the World*
or that he hadn't known about it – either way he was arguably unfit to
run the company. Watson assumed the Murdochs would try to begin

by reading out an opening statement, which would almost certainly apologize for the wrongdoing, express regret and outline measures to ensure it never happened again. Just like the attempt to remove Watson from the committee in 2009, this opening gambit, an apology, would then become the main story for the rolling news channels and divert attention away from the examination of culpability. Committee members were determined not to let this happen. At midday, Watson shut the door of his office in Portcullis House, put on the Doors album *LA Woman* at full blast and paced around rehearsing questions.

At 14.34 in the Wilson Room of Portcullis House, James Murdoch led his father to his chair, which Rupert's wife Wendi Deng pulled out for him. She whispered something in his ear and poured him a glass of water.

James Murdoch began with a note of disappointment, even anger. In his British-American accent, he said: 'Our understanding was that we would be afforded the opportunity to make an opening statement, and we prepared on that basis.' Appealing to the chairman, John Whittingdale, he said: 'We would like the opportunity to make that statement. Would you allow us?' Whittingdale explained that the MPs had discussed that and the answer was no: 'We feel that we have a lot of questions.' Referring to James's email to staff announcing the closure of the *News of the World*, Whittingdale said: 'You made a statement on 7 July in which you stated that the paper had made statements to Parliament without being in full possession of the facts, and that was wrong. You essentially admitted that Parliament had been misled in what we had been told. Can you tell us to what extent we were misled, and when you became aware of that?'

With his fierce eyes, politeness and management-speak voice (which the following day prompted an unkind suggestion that he was 'half Harry Potter, half Hannibal Lecter'),[1] James started reciting what sounded like the statement he had planned to make, referring not to phone hacking (too pithy) but 'illegal voicemail interceptions'. 'First, I would like to say as well just how sorry I am,' James said, 'and how sorry we are, to particularly the victims of illegal voicemail interceptions and to their families. It is a matter of great regret to me, my father and everyone at News Corporation . . .' At that moment, Rupert stretched out his right hand and placed it on his son's forearm. 'Before you get to that,' he told his son, 'I would just like to say one sentence. This is the most humble day of my life.'* The statement flashed up on the rolling news channels.

James responded to Whittingdale's question: 'I do not have direct knowledge of what they [Wapping's executives] knew and at what time, but I can tell you that the critical new facts, as I saw them and as the company saw them, really emerged in the production of documentary information or evidence in the civil trials at the end of 2010 . . . It is a matter of real regret that the facts could not emerge and could not be gotten to my understanding faster.'

This, then, was the Murdochs' defence: they had only realized the previous year that hacking had been widespread at Wapping and that, alas, the company's lawyers, the Metropolitan Police and the Press Complaints Commission had all failed to detect the wrongdoing.

Tom Watson asked Rupert whether he had repeatedly stated that News Corp had zero tolerance towards wrongdoing by employees.

Rupert had.

The MP continued: 'In October 2010, did you still believe it to be true when you made your Thatcher speech and you said, "Let me be clear: we will vigorously pursue the truth – and we will not tolerate wrongdoing"?'

'Yes,' replied Rupert again.

'So if you were not lying then,' Watson said, 'somebody lied to you. Who was it?'

'I don't know,' Murdoch said grumpily. 'That is what the police are investigating, and we are helping them with.'

'But you acknowledge that you were misled.'

'Clearly.'

Watson took him back to 2003, when Rebekah Brooks had admitted the company had paid police for information in the past. Did anyone in News Corp or News International investigate that at the time?

---

* The US satirist Jon Stewart later joked: 'Not so humble you couldn't wait for your turn to talk!'

Rupert paused. 'No.'

'Can you explain why?'

'I didn't know of it,' Rupert replied. 'I'm sorry,' he added. 'Allow me to say something?' He started slapping the table with his hand, which he had a habit of doing when he wanted to emphasize his exasperation. 'And this is not [slap] an excuse [slap]. Maybe it is an explanation of my laxity [slap]. The *News of the World* is less than [slap] 1 per cent of our company. I employ 53,000 [slap] people around the world [slap] who are proud and great and ethical [slap] and distinguished people – professionals in their line. And [slap] perhaps I am spread [too thin] watching and appointing [slap] people whom I trust [slap] to run those divisions.'

Watson continued: had Rupert been informed about the payments to Gordon Taylor and Max Clifford?

'No.'

At what point had News Corp's chairman and chief executive discovered that criminality was endemic at the *News of the World*?

'Endemic is a very hard, wide-ranging word', Murdoch protested. '. . . I became aware as it became apparent.'

James explained that he had settled the Gordon Taylor case after receiving legal advice about the cost of fighting it:

> It was advised that, with legal expenses and damages, it could be between £500,000 and £1 million or thereabouts. I do not recall the exact number of the advice. I think that it was £250,000 plus expenses, plus litigation costs, something like that.

The Liberal Democrat Adrian Sanders asked: 'Was part of the advice that a high payment would ensure the matter was kept confidential?'

'No, not at all. Out-of-court settlements are normally confidential,' replied James, who – at that time unbeknownst to the committee – had been copied into an email chain saying hacking was 'rife'.

Sanders asked whether James was familiar with the term 'wilful blindness'.

'Mr Sanders,' James said wearily, 'would you care to elaborate?'

Sanders explained: 'It is a term that came up in the Enron scandal.

"Wilful blindness" is a legal term. It states that if there is knowledge that you could have had and should have had, but chose not to have, you are still responsible.'

Seemingly perplexed, James responded: 'Mr Sanders, do you have a question? Respectfully, I just do not know what you would like me to say.'

'The question was whether you were aware—'

James snapped: 'I am not aware of that particular phrase.'

Sanders: 'But now you are familiar with the term, because I have explained it to you.'

With his eyes glinting, James replied: 'Thank you, Mr Sanders.'

'I have heard the phrase before,' chipped in his father, 'and we were not ever guilty of that.'

Asked about the frequency of his contact with editors, Rupert said: 'I'm not really in touch.'* He added: 'I have got to tell you that, if there is an editor that I spend most time with, it is the editor of the *Wall Street Journal*, because I am in the same building. But to say that we are hands-off is wrong; I work a ten- or twelve-hour day, and I cannot tell you the multitude of issues that I have to handle every day. The *News of the World*, perhaps I lost sight of, maybe because it was so small in the general frame of our company, but we are doing a lot of other things too.'

Philip Davies, the Conservative MP who the previous year had complained Labour MPs had hijacked the committee's last report on NI, asked: 'Surely in your weekly conversations with the editor of the *News of the World*, with something as big ... as paying someone £1 million or £700,000, you would have expected the editor just to drop it into the conversation at some point during your weekly chat?'

Rupert replied simply: 'No.'

* Murdoch's biographer Michael Wolff claimed the proprietor had misled the MPs over the extent of his involvement in his British newspapers. He said the tycoon would spend up to half his day speaking to his newspaper editors in London: 'His involvement with the papers is total. Rupert sat up there [at the committee] and they [his advisers] said, "You have got to say you are not involved with the newspapers." And that's what he said and that's a lie.'[2]

Davies pressed: 'You wouldn't have expected them to say that to you?'

'No . . . He might say, "We've got a great story exposing X or Y" or, more likely, he would say, "Nothing special." He might refer to the fact that however many extra pages were dedicated to the football that week.'

'But he wouldn't tell you about a £1 million pay-off?'

'No.'

To the suggestion that the *News of the World* had been shut to protect Brooks, Rupert answered: 'The two decisions were absolutely and totally unrelated.'

'So,' asked Davies, 'when you came into the UK and said that your priority was Rebekah Brooks, what did you mean?'

Looking confused, Rupert replied: 'I am not sure I did say that; I was quoted as saying that. I walked outside my flat and had about twenty microphones stuck at my mouth, so I'm not sure what I said.'

'You were misquoted, so to speak?'

Perhaps knowing that the remark had been captured by TV crews, Rupert, looking every one of his eighty years, replied: 'I am not saying that. I just don't remember.'

The Murdochs were struggling to give straightforward answers.

Turning to the unfair dismissal claims by Goodman and Mulcaire, Paul Farrelly MP asked: 'Do you know what sorts of allegations they were making? We can only imagine that they were saying that such-and-such a person knew and such-and-such a person knew. Have you satisfied yourself about what allegations they were making?'

James said:

As to Glenn Mulcaire, I am not aware of allegations at the time and other things. As to Goodman – again, this was in 2007, before I was there – it is my understanding that that is what Harbottle & Lewis were helping to deal with, and that that opinion did satisfy the company at the time and we, the company, rested on that [Harbottle & Lewis] opinion for a period of time.

James had skipped out of trouble, but Farrelly asked if he would give the committee the instructions given to Harbottle & Lewis in 2007.

'If additional detail is required around those legal instructions,' James responded, 'we will consult and come back to the chairman with a way to satisfy you with the information that you'd like to have.'

Asked whether it was 'remotely possible' that the *News of the World*'s editors had not known about illegality at the paper, Rupert replied: 'I can't say that, because of the police inquiries and, I presume, coming judicial proceedings. That is all I can tell you, except it was my understanding ... that Mr Myler was appointed there by Mr Hinton to find out what the hell was going on, and that he commissioned that Harbottle & Lewis inquiry.'

Asked about his relationship with prime ministers and presidents, Rupert joked: 'I wish they would leave me alone.' He was disappointed that his relationship with Gordon Brown had foundered. 'His wife and my wife struck up quite a friendship, and our children played together on many occasions. I am very sorry that I am no longer – I thought he had great values, which I shared with him, and I am sorry that we have come apart.' He added: 'I hope one day that we'll be able to put it together again.'

At 4.54 p.m., two hours and twenty minutes into the session, a member of the public, Jonathan May-Bowles, rose from his chair and shoved a shaving foam plate into the face of News Corp's chief executive. Leaping from her chair with quicker reactions than anyone else Wendi Deng slapped the attacker and threw his plate back at him, smearing him with his own shaving cream. (She was later fêted by admiring newspaper profiles as a 'Tiger wife'. Rupert did not want to press charges but 'Jonnie Marbles' was sentenced to six weeks for assault, reduced to four weeks on appeal. On the steps of the court, mockingly contrite, May-Bowles said: 'I would just like to say this has been the most humble day of my life.')

The proceedings were called to a halt for ten minutes. Tom Watson strolled over to the Murdochs and passed the time of day with them. As he did so, he heard one of Rupert's aides assure him: 'Don't worry, this will play well.' Watson poured the mogul a glass of water and told him: 'Your wife's got quite a right hook.' He asked James if he would like some water too. 'No, Mr Watson,' James replied. Watson poured him a glass of water anyway. At 5.08 p.m. the hearing resumed.

After two sometimes gripping and sometimes dull hours, Whittingdale allowed Watson a final question. 'James – sorry, if I may call you James, to differentiate,' he began. 'When you signed off the Taylor payment, did you see or were you made aware of the "For Neville" email, the transcript of the hacked voicemail messages?'

James replied: 'No, I was not aware of that at the time.' It was an important answer.

The session finished at 5.31 p.m. The committee had failed to land any killer blows. Rupert Murdoch seemed to be a doddery, proud old man and his son had intelligently evaded making any serious admissions. But the answers they gave had stored up trouble for the future. First, they had suggested Harbottle & Lewis had failed to identify the wrongdoing and secondly, and most importantly, James Murdoch said he did not know about the 'For Neville' email, the document which indicated widespread wrongdoing at the company years before the truth was admitted – and during which time it paid off more victims, surveilled its critics and repeatedly misled Parliament.

At 5.43 p.m. the same day, Rebekah Brooks made her first appearance before the Culture Committee for eight years, this time accompanied by her solicitor, Stephen Parkinson of Kingsley Napley. Unnoticed by most of the public, Alison Clark, the former public affairs director of News International, slipped into a seat at the back of the room. Days before, Brooks had been seen in a 'distressed state' visiting the offices of the former Met Commissioner, Sir John Stevens.

John Whittingdale started off by referring to News International's statement in July 2009 which denied point-blank that there 'was systemic corporate illegality by News International'. Whittingdale asked Brooks: 'Would you accept now that that is not correct?'

Like the Murdochs, she said the Sienna Miller case was 'the first time that we, the senior management of the company at the time, had actually seen some documentary evidence actually relating to a current employee'. She added: 'I think that we acted quickly and decisively then, when we had that information.'

Taking his turn to interrogate the executive who had threatened to pursue him, Watson looked at her and said slowly: 'There are many questions I would like to ask you, but I will not be able to do so today because you are facing criminal proceedings, so I am going to be narrow in my questioning . . . Why did you sack Tom Crone?'

The company had not sacked Crone, Brooks said; the closure of the *News of the World* had deprived him of a job.

'As a journalist and editor of *News of the World* and the *Sun*,' Watson asked, 'how extensively did you work with private detectives?'

Not at all on the *Sun*, Brooks replied, but there had been questions at the *News of the World* about Steve Whittamore. Among his customers, she added: 'Certainly in the top five were the *Observer*, the *Guardian*, *News of the World*, *Daily Mail*—'*

So, she had worked with private detectives?

What she had said, she corrected Watson, was that the use of private detectives in the late 1990s and 2000s 'was a practice of Fleet Street'.

The MP asked: 'For the third time, how extensively did you work with private detectives?'

'The *News of the World* employed private detectives, like most newspapers in Fleet Street.'

She could not remember authorizing payments; they would have gone through Stuart Kuttner's office.

'One last question,' Watson said. 'Do you have any regrets?'

'Of course I have regrets,' Brooks replied. 'The idea that Milly Dowler's phone was accessed by someone being paid by the *News of the World* – or even worse, authorized by someone at the *News of the World* – is as abhorrent to me as it is to everyone in this room.'

She sounded contrite about the Culture Committee's withering report in 2010:

> Everyone at News International has great respect for Parliament and for this Committee. Of course, to be criticized by your report was something that we responded to. We looked at the report. It was only when we had the information in December 2010 that we did something about it. But I think you heard today from Rupert Murdoch, who said that this was, you know, the most humble day. We come

---

* The *Guardian* and the *Observer* were not, in fact, in the top five.

before this committee to try and explain, openly and honestly, what happened. Of course we were very unhappy with the criticisms that this committee found against the company. We aspire daily to have a great company, and your criticisms were felt.

She denied that she had a particularly close relationship with David Cameron: 'I have read many, many allegations about my current relationship with the Prime Minister, with David Cameron, including my extensive horseriding with him every weekend up in Oxfordshire. I have never been horseriding with the Prime Minister . . . The truth is that he is a neighbour and a friend, but I deem the relationship to be wholly appropriate, and at no time have I ever had any conversation with the Prime Minister that you in the room would disapprove of.'

George Osborne, she said, had suggested that Cameron hire Andy Coulson as his communications director.

Adrian Sanders pressed the point: 'So you had no conversation with David Cameron about Andy Coulson being suitable for that position?'

'No.'

'None whatsoever?'

'No.'

Sanders changed tack: 'Did you approve the subsidizing of Andy Coulson's salary after he left the *News of the World*?'

'Again, that's not true,' Brooks replied, 'so I didn't approve it.'

The session ended at 7.20 p.m. Brooks had been questioned for one hour and thirty-seven minutes. Like the Murdochs, she had not made any embarrassing disclosures, but the committee had been relatively gentle: she was in enough trouble already.

20

Assault on the Establishment

If it turns out that he knew about hacking, he will have lied
to a select committee, he will have lied to the police, he will
have lied to a court of law and he will have lied to me
— David Cameron, 20 July 2011

After the pantomime and evasions of the Culture Committee, deeper questions were asked about how the scandal had been allowed to happen. Politicians, the police and the media were all to blame. On 20 July, the Home Affairs Committee published its findings. Its report, 'Unauthorised Tapping or Hacking of Mobile Communications', was highly critical of News International and the Metropolitan Police. Even without knowing that News International staff had obstructed the police during their search of the building in 2006, the MPs concluded:

> We deplore the response of News International to the original inves-
> tigation into hacking. It is almost impossible to escape the conclusion
> voiced by [Deputy Assistant Commissioner] Mr Clarke that they
> were deliberately trying to thwart a criminal investigation. We are
> astounded at the length of time it has taken News International to
> cooperate with the police but we are appalled that this is advanced as
> a reason for failing to mount a robust investigation.

Even taking into account the large number of anti-terrorist operations in 2006, the police's failure to investigate the Mulcaire evidence
properly had led to 'serious wrongdoing' and Andy Hayman, the

officer who had dined with the *News of the World* while formally overseeing the inquiry, had an 'apparently lackadaisical attitude' towards contacts with those under investigation. The committee was 'appalled' at Scotland Yard's employment of Neil Wallis. At a broader level, the MPs wrote:

> We are concerned about the level of social interaction which took place between senior Metropolitan Police Officers and executives at News International while investigations were or should have been being undertaken into the allegations of phone hacking carried out by the *News of the World*.

Intriguingly, the committee also wondered why the Crown Prosecution Service had not in its early consultations with the police placed more emphasis on Section 2 of RIPA, which stated that it was a crime to hack messages even if they had already been listened to by their intended recipient. The CPS's role was indeed questionable.

From March 2011, Tom Watson had been using Freedom of Information requests to obtain more details about the relationship between News International and Ken Macdonald, the Director of Public Prosecutions at the time of Operation Caryatid in 2006. While most of these contacts lay buried, occasionally they had surfaced. On 18 October 2005 the *Guardian* ran a diary item from the Society of Editors conference headed 'No Sleep to Bowness'. It reported: 'News International arrived in the Lake District mob handed. They tried to leave that way too. The twin tabloid editors Rebekah Wade and Andy Coulson were last seen at the gala dinner with the Director of Public Prosecutions Ken Macdonald threatening to take him to a nightclub in Bowness.' Watson's FoI requests to the CPS revealed Macdonald had visited the Society of Editors conference as a guest of Les Hinton, then News International's chief executive. Among meetings with other journalists, Macdonald had several with News International's editors. On 17 January 2006, a month after Caryatid began – but before the CPS became involved in March – he was treated to dinner at Gordon Ramsay's Maze by the *News of the World*'s then editor, Andy Coulson. On 10 April 2006, while the police and CPS were discussing what charges might be brought, but before he became aware of the investigation, Macdonald lunched with Rebekah Wade and Trevor Kavanagh at the RAC Club in Pall Mall. His diary contained a reference to a News Corporation reception with Rupert Murdoch at Burlington Gardens on 19 June, in the middle of Operation Caryatid, but Macdonald later said that he did not attend. On 20 February 2007, a month after the jailing of Goodman and Mulcaire, Macdonald again lunched with Rebekah Wade at the RAC Club.

Discreetly, in late April 2006, the Crown Prosecution Service had agreed with the police to exclude sensitive (and thus newsworthy) witnesses from any prosecution. A few weeks later, in May, prosecutors in the case had informed Macdonald, and the then Attorney General Lord Goldsmith, that there was 'a vast array' of potential victims. In a letter to the Home Affairs Committee, Goldsmith said that while legal convention meant he could not contact the police about the inquiry, he pointed out that no such restrictions applied to the Director of Public Prosecutions. Macdonald told the Home Affairs Committee that had the CPS been shown evidence of the hacking of victims of crime, such as Milly Dowler, he was sure that 'firm ... action would have followed'. There was no evidence that Macdonald acted improperly during his meetings with News International (which subsequently employed him to assess the emails about police bribery), but it was clear that the CPS had first been run by a director who was friendly with executives at Wapping and who continued to meet them while the organization was under investigation – and then by a man, Keir Starmer, who had not fully read the paperwork but who, when he did so a year later, totally reversed the narrow interpretation of the law which the police claimed had hindered their inquiry.

Shortly before midday, on Wednesday 20 July, David Cameron faced his last Commons showdown before Parliament went into summer recess. Parliament's sitting had been extended by a day so there could be a debate on public confidence in the media and the police. Cameron outlined the action he had taken, ensuring a 'well led' police investigation, publishing his meetings with the media, and establishing the Leveson Inquiry. He distanced himself further from Andy Coulson, who only a week earlier had been his friend. 'With 20:20 hindsight and all that has followed,' he said, 'I would not have offered him the job, and I expect that he would not have taken it. But you do not make decisions in hindsight; you make them in the present. You live and you learn and, believe me, I have learnt.'

Ed Miliband responded:

Given the New York Times's evidence, the public will rightly have expected very loud alarm bells to ring in the Prime Minister's mind, yet apparently he did nothing. Then in October the Prime Minister's chief of staff was approached again by the Guardian about the serious evidence it had about Mr Coulson's behaviour. Once more nothing was done. This cannot be put down to gross incompetence. It was a deliberate attempt to hide from the facts about Mr Coulson ... He now says that in hindsight he made a mistake by hiring Mr Coulson. He says that if Mr Coulson lied to him, he would apologize. That is not good enough. It is not about hindsight or whether Mr Coulson lied to him; it is about all the information and warnings that he ignored.

The former Labour Home Secretary Alan Johnson asked: 'When the Prime Minister read of the extensive investigation in the New York Times on 1 September last year, what was his reaction and what did he do?'

Cameron replied:

The question I ask myself all the way through is: 'Is there new information that Andy Coulson knew about phone hacking at the News of the World?' I could not be clearer about this: if it turns out that he knew about hacking, he will have lied to a select committee, he will have lied to the police, he will have lied to a court of law and he will have lied to me. I made the decision to employ him in good faith, because of the assurances he gave me. There was no information in that article that would lead me to change my mind about those assurances ...

Cameron maintained that he had been open about the meeting with Rupert Murdoch in May 2010, though he had not divulged it to Tom Watson in June 2010, doing so only the previous week. He said: 'In relation to the meeting I held with Rupert Murdoch, the question is not whether he came in through the back door or front door but whether it was declared in the proper way, and yes, it was.'

Chris Bryant raised News International's refusal to release Harbottle & Lewis from client confidentiality. He asked the Prime Minister: 'Is this not clear evidence that News International, contrary to the pretend humility yesterday, is still refusing to cooperate fully with the investigation?'

Cameron responded: 'The point I would make is that that information, if it's germane to the police inquiry, needs to be given to the police and indeed to the Leveson inquiry.' (The message to Wapping was clear: release Harbottle & Lewis from confidentiality.*)

Asked whether the *Mail on Sunday* was correct to report that he had hired Andy Coulson at Rebekah Brooks's suggestion instead of the ex-BBC journalist Guto Harri, Cameron offered another non-answer. He replied: 'She specifically rejected that point yesterday. Guto now works for my good friend and colleague the Mayor of London, and he does a brilliant job.'

Labour MPs asked Cameron thirteen times whether he had discussed the Sky bid with Murdoch's executives and each time he declined to say, merely repeating that he did not have any 'inappropriate conversations'. While the debate was continuing, the *Guardian*'s political editor, Patrick Wintour, blogged:

> Government officials said during the statement that the Prime Minister did not recall any specific conversations with News International about the BSkyB bid, but said he could not stop News Corporation

* In a letter to the Culture Committee that day, 20 July, Harbottle & Lewis wrote: 'Notwithstanding News International's position to date, we are considering whether we can, consistently with our professional obligations and the constraints currently imposed on us by News International, assist the committee by providing substantive comments on yesterday's evidence. If we take the view that we can properly assist the committee, we will do so within whatever time-frame assists the committee.' It was a threat to speak out.

John Whittingdale, the committee chairman, stepped up the pressure, telling the Commons: 'I hope that in the light of the assurance that Rupert and James Murdoch gave us of their wish to cooperate as much as possible, the firm will review that decision and perhaps release Harbottle & Lewis from the arrangement, so that we can see the correspondence.'

officials from lobbying him about the bid during meetings. The officials stressed that the decision was for the Culture Secretary, Jeremy Hunt, on his own, and he at no point discussed the bid with Cameron. The spokesman said the conversations were 'completely appropriate'.[2]

So, Cameron and News International had discussed the Sky bid.

When he finally sat down at 2.28 p.m., Cameron had evaded the gravest threat yet to his premiership, and at the backbench 1922 Committee that afternoon he received from his MPs forty seconds of desk banging, the traditional seal of approval. After a tumultuous fortnight in which his close relationship with News International had imperilled his position, the Prime Minister had made it through to the summer holidays.

That afternoon Rupert Murdoch flew out of the UK on his private Gulfstream jet. He left behind a country still in shock and working its way through the mess his newspapers had deposited.

Murdoch's editors sought to move the news agenda on to other issues. On 21 July, a cartoon in *The Times* by Peter Brookes titled 'Priorities' showed starving African children with grotesquely swollen stomachs saying 'I've had a bellyful of phone hacking.' (The website Political Scrapbook said it was 'tasteless' to suggest that talking about phone hacking had prolonged Somalia's starvation: 'No one is stopping *The Times* covering both stories.') On the same day, the *Sun* centred its coverage on a story about a Unicef official urging the media to focus on the drought in Africa, headlined: 'UN: forget hacking, kids are starving'. The *Sun* also ran a poll that day: YouGov asked 1,800 people online whether phone hacking was the most important story. Under the headline: 'Is phone hacking getting too much coverage?' the paper disclosed the results: Yes, 59 per cent; No 28 per cent; Not sure 13 per cent.

News Corp responded to two criticisms raised during the Murdochs' appearance before the Culture Committee, terminating its agreement to pay Glenn Mulcaire's legal fees and releasing Harbottle & Lewis from client confidentiality.

However, the efforts were futile, and over coming weeks the company was at the centre of a slew of new allegations.

On 21 July, Colin Myler and Tom Crone struck back at James Murdoch's claim to the Culture Committee that he had not known about the 'For Neville' email when he authorized the pay-off for Gordon Taylor. In a joint statement, the *News of the World*'s last editor and lawyer said:

> Just by way of clarification relating to Tuesday's Select Committee hearing, we would like to point out that James Murdoch's recollection of what he was told when agreeing to settle the Gordon Taylor litigation was mistaken. In fact, we did inform him of the 'For Neville' email which had been produced to us by Gordon Taylor's lawyers.

This was not the only challenge to James Murdoch's assertion that he had little involvement in the Taylor settlement. The lawyer Mark Lewis claimed that during negotiations with Farrer's Julian Pike, Pike had told him that he was negotiating 'with Murdoch'. According to a company official with direct knowledge of the settlement who spoke to the *New York Times*, News International's chief financial officer, Clive Milner, who made the financial arrangements, was told the case was very sensitive and 'the cheque is for James Murdoch'.

In a statement News Corp said: 'James Murdoch stands by his testimony to the committee.'

One more particularly unwelcome victim of phone hacking emerged. At 5 p.m. on 28 July, Nick Davies and Amelia Hill at the *Guardian* disclosed that the *NoW* had hacked the phone of Sara Payne, whose eight-year-old daughter Sarah had been abducted yards from her home in West Sussex in 2000 – prompting Brooks's 'For Sarah' campaign. Despite her concern about the eavesdropping of other parents, Payne still thought warmly of the *News of the World* and had contributed a column for its final edition mourning 'the passing of an old friend'. She wrote: 'God only knows why the *News of the World* has stuck by me for so long and for that you'd have to ask them but the reason I have stayed with them is that they have always been a paper that cares and a voice for the people.'

The betrayal, according to Phoenix Chief Advocates, the charity she ran for victims of paedophilia, had left Payne 'absolutely devastated'. Like the Milly Dowler case, the story could hardly have been more damaging for News International and it put the company back in the spotlight just as it was fading from the news after almost three weeks. The 'Hacked Off' campaign said the allegations indicated 'breathtaking hypocrisy and a complete lack of moral sense'.

News International's spin machine whirred into operation. In a statement issued by her new PR firm, Bell Pottinger (which specialized in representing regimes with reputational issues), Brooks said it was 'unthinkable' that the *News of the World* had hacked Payne. 'The idea of her being targeted is beyond my comprehension,' she said. 'It is imperative for Sara and the other victims of crime that these allegations are investigated and those culpable brought to justice.'

News International said it was 'deeply concerned' by the story.

The following day, Scotland Yard confirmed it was expanding Operation Tuleta into a full-blown inquiry. Senior officers had been reluctant to take action against computer hacking while they devoted such substantial resources to phone hacking. Now, however, the evidence was too strong to ignore: detectives said that it was clear that computer hacking had been happening for much longer than the three months reported by *Panorama* in March. Ian Hurst, whose computer had been hacked by the *News of the World* trawling for the whereabouts of the IRA informer Stakeknife, expressed concern that the Met had been so slow to act, despite having the evidence from the Daniel Morgan trial. The former army intelligence officer said: 'Officers do not appear to have investigated these crimes, which, given everything else that has happened, reinforces my belief that the Met is institutionally corrupt.'

On 1 August, an IT firm used by News International disclosed that Wapping had asked it to delete emails nine times between April 2010 and July 2011. HCL Technologies had 'answered in negative' to one of the requests, in January 2011 – the month Scotland Yard launched its new inquiry. News International, in effect, admitted important data had been deleted, saying in a statement: 'News International keeps backups of its core systems and, in close cooperation with the Operation Weeting team, has been working to restore these backups.'

The following day, Operation Weeting's detectives arrested one of the most important figures at the *News of the World*: Stuart Kuttner, its managing editor since 1987. When he appeared before the Culture Committee in 2009, Kuttner had denied any knowledge of wrong-doing. He was detained on suspicion of phone hacking and police corruption, and released on bail. The police operation had now arrested all but a few of the senior editorial executives at the *News of the World* between 2000 and 2007.

But there was worse to come. On 16 August, the Commons Culture Committee published Clive Goodman's withering 2007 letter appealing against his dismissal. In 2009, after the Gordon Taylor story broke, MPs had wondered why Goodman had been paid off after being jailed; the suggestion that he had a strong case in employment law seemed far-fetched. Now the public learned what News International's executives had known all along: after his sacking Goodman had written to Wapping claiming that phone hacking had been so routine at the *News of the World* that journalists openly discussed it at editorial conferences (see pp. 50–51).

Dated 2 March 2007, the letter preceded all the evidence given by Wapping's executives maintaining that Clive Goodman was a lone 'rogue reporter'. If Goodman's claims were true, Wapping had mounted a cover-up and its executives had told lie after lie. Even if they were false, executives were clearly wrong to tell the Culture Committee that there was 'no evidence' of more widespread wrong-doing. News International – employing Edelman PR – said: 'We recognize the seriousness of materials disclosed to the police and parliament and are committed to working in a constructive way and open way with all the relevant authorities.'*

Publication of the letter at 3 p.m. on the Culture Committee website dominated the TV news bulletins and front pages. (The *Guardian* headline was: 'Explosive letter lifts the lid on four-year hacking

---

* This was questionable since the Culture Committee received two copies of Good-man's letter, one from Harbottle & Lewis and one from News International. The News International version blanked out Goodman's allegations about the discussion of phone hacking and the promise that he could return to his job if he did not impli-cate the paper in court. The version of the letter in chapter 5 is Harbottle & Lewis's.

cover-up'; the *Independent*'s: 'Phone hacking: the smoking gun'.) While the letter itself was deeply embarrassing, it was published alongside a venomous attack on News International by Harbottle & Lewis. Evidently, the law firm had been storing up its anger for two years since December 2009, when in answer to a question about Wapping's internal inquiries, Rebekah Brooks had released to the Culture Committee its letter of 29 May 2007 (see p. 97) about Goodman's employment case.

At that time News International had used Harbottle's letter to suggest that outside lawyers had carried out a thorough review of wrongdoing at the *News of the World* and in July 2011, under pressure for their failure to investigate the criminality, the Murdochs had reinforced that impression. In his interview with the *Wall Street Journal* Rupert blamed the lawyers for making a 'major mistake', and James had told the Culture Committee: 'That opinion was something that the company rested on.'

In its letter to the MPs dated 11 August, Harbottle & Lewis now revealed that it had never been asked to launch an internal investigation at Wapping.* Its bill was £10,294 plus VAT, which hardly indicated that it had been commissioned to carry out a forensic examination of Britain's biggest newspaper group. And if News International really had 'rested on' its letter from 2007, it pointed out, it would not have paid out nearly a quarter of a million pounds to Goodman – since its review had not supported his claim that phone hacking was widespread (though there was evidence of police corruption).

The letter left committee members in no doubt that News International had deliberately exaggerated Harbottle's role in the supposed internal investigation. Even more damningly, the firm delicately indicated that crucial evidence about corruption had been destroyed. It carefully explained that in 2007, after its lawyers had been given remote access to Goodman's emails, they had printed out some for further study and obtained hard copies from the IT department of others they could not open. Harbottle had archived its work, together

---

* In a letter to the Culture Committee on 16 August, Burton Copeland said: 'it was not instructed to carry out an investigation into "phone hacking" at the *News of the World*.'

with the printouts, for four years (during which time News International denied all wrongdoing) until 24 March 2011, when News International asked for the file. Harbottle & Lewis told the Culture Committee that what was of 'principal interest' was not confirmation of its remit or Goodman's letter but the printouts of the emails themselves. Without mentioning the deletion of emails, the law firm wrote: 'It seems that the firm's copies of these documents from News International's own records are now the only remaining copies (on paper or in electronic form) still in existence.' The emails discussing corruption had vanished from News International's servers.

News International's defences were rapidly being overwhelmed. James Murdoch had said the company had been relying upon evidence provided by the police, the PCC and Harbottle & Lewis. But the police were now saying Wapping had frustrated their inquiry; the Press Complaints Commission was complaining it had been misled; and Harbottle & Lewis insisted it had never been asked to conduct a widespread inquiry. Most worryingly, there appeared to be evidence of the deliberate destruction of data, apparently in an attempt to prevent the truth ever becoming known.

In Britain the police investigation and the number of civil cases were growing, but News Corp's greatest problem lay in the United States, where, in July, the Department of Justice had ordered an FBI investigation into whether the company had breached the Foreign Corrupt Practices Act. Under the Act, News Corp's directors could be jailed for five years if they had authorized or known about, but failed to stop, bribery in the UK. By now the American directors had become thoroughly disenchanted with the British newspapers. The profits of the *Sun* and the *News of the World* had dwindled and they were causing serious reputational and shareholder damage. In 2010, News Corp's TV and film interests had sales of $22 billion, the newspapers $6 billion.

The company decided on a three-track approach. Firstly, it would cooperate with the police. In the past it had paid lip-service to helping the police while deliberately obstructing their inquiries; that strategy was no longer working because Scotland Yard, shamed by its incompetence, was mounting a proper investigation. Up to 100 staff from the City law firm Linklaters began interviewing staff on the *Sun*, *The Times* and the *Sunday Times* and reviewing old expenses claims, invoices and emails dating back years. Up to twenty police officers from Operation Elveden embedded with the lawyers asked them to search the company's databases, including the second server the IT whistleblower had tipped off Tom Watson about at Christmas, and about which Watson had subsequently informed Sue Akers. The emails had been forensically recovered.

Secondly, the company stepped up its efforts to settle the rising number of civil cases. On 18 August, it paid Leslie Ash and Lee Chapman a 'healthy six-figure sum' and, on 19 September, it struck a deal to settle the most embarrassing case of all: the Dowlers. Mark Lewis had negotiated a vast settlement – £2 million for the family and £1 million from Rupert Murdoch for a charity of their choice. The settlement strongly suggested that the £20 million Wapping had notionally set aside in April for dealing with the scandal would fall well short of what was needed.

Thirdly, the company stuck by its chief executive, James Murdoch, despite growing questions about his role arising from the evidence of former executives. Appearing before the Culture Committee on 7 September, Myler and Crone (who were in line for large pay-offs following the *NoW*'s closure) appeared reluctant to launch a full-frontal attack on News International, but equally they did not wish to be blamed for the cover-up. They were adamant that James Murdoch had known about the 'For Neville' email when he signed off the payment to Gordon Taylor. 'Mr Murdoch is the chief executive of the company,' Myler said. 'He is experienced, I am experienced, Mr Crone is experienced. I think everyone perfectly understood the seriousness and significance of what we were discussing. There was no ambiguity about the significance of that document.' Looking every part the urbane lawyer with his silvery hair and sharply cut suit, Crone stated laconically: 'We went to see Mr Murdoch and it was explained to him what this document was and what it meant.' Within hours, News Corp released a statement from James Murdoch saying bluntly: 'Neither Mr Myler nor Mr Crone told me that wrongdoing extended beyond Mr Goodman or Mr Mulcaire.' The Culture Committee decided to recall James Murdoch.

Previously, during the cover-up, Wapping had helped erring members of its family, paying off Goodman and Mulcaire and Andy Coulson's salary while he was working for the Conservatives,* but now, in direct contradiction, it terminated its agreement to pay Coulson's legal fees for future civil court cases and said it would 'vigorously contest' employment tribunal claims from Ian Edmondson and Neville Thurlbeck.

In his first public statement since his arrest, on 30 September Thurlbeck indicated that the blame for hacking lay with others:

> I say this most emphatically and with certainty and confidence that the allegation which led to my dismissal will eventually be shown to be false. And those responsible for the action, for which I have been unfairly dismissed, will eventually be revealed.

Ominously, he added: 'There is much I could have said publicly to the detriment of News International but so far have chosen not to do so.'

The company cancelled its receptions at the forthcoming party conferences.

---

* At the end of August the BBC's Robert Peston divulged that after he left the *News of the World*, News International had paid Andy Coulson two years' salary in instalments, as well as his work benefits, such as healthcare, for three years while he was working for the Conservative Party. In July, a senior Conservative Party official had said: 'We can give categorical assurances that he wasn't paid by any other source. Andy Coulson's only salary, his only form of income, came from the party during the years he worked for the party and in government.'[1]

21

A Meeting in the Suburbs

It would be absolute suicide for him to admit that he knew it

– Neville Thurlbeck

In early October 2011, Tom Watson's phone rang. In a soft and pre-cise Wearside accent, the caller said: 'I've got some information for you.' A rendezvous was arranged for the following Monday, 10 Octo-ber, at a 1930s detached house in the London suburbs. For the first time in months, its occupant was wearing a suit. After he brewed some coffee, Neville Thurlbeck told his story.

For two years, much of the media had suspected he was a phone hacker, that he was the Neville in the 'For Neville' email. But although he confirmed he was, he wanted it to be known that he had never hacked any phones, nor ordered any hacking, and he wanted to clear his name.

He was angry with News International. In September, after twenty-one years' service, he had been sacked without a pay-off. On the basis of his £96,000-a-year salary as chief reporter, he calculated he was due a redundancy payment of £245,000.

He gave his account of what had happened. Traditionally, Thurl-beck said, hacking had not been a tactic of the *News of the World*. 'I was aware of somebody who did hacking in the nineties . . . he was juggling two mobile phones and I said: "What are you doing there?" and he told me what he was doing – and he went on to do great things on Fleet Street – but anyway, I said to him: "What do you do that for?" And he said: "Well, you can get good stuff."'

By the early 2000s, Thurlbeck told Watson, phone hacking had become more common at the NoW, after the influx of journalists from other papers: 'At the People, one of our competitors, they couldn't rival us for money, they couldn't compete with the buy-ups but the way they could get stories was by stealing them, by hacking.' While Thurlbeck had been on secret assignments for the News of the World, he recalled his surprise at finding reporters from the People turning up at the same job: they had been hacking his phone.

Referring to Brooks, he told Watson: 'She didn't like you at all. She took an absolute pathological dislike to you ... She saw you as the person that was really threatening. She tried to smear you as being mad. She was briefing. She was saying to Blair: "We've got to call this man off, he's mad."'

When, in April 2008, Scotland Yard disclosed the 'For Neville' email to Wapping, the paper was deeply worried; according to Thurlbeck, Tom Crone had confronted him about the email, saying: 'Neville, we've got a problem because of this, what's this all about?' Thurlbeck said:

I looked at it: 'I don't know, Tom, I never received it. Tom, this had nothing to do with me ...' He said: 'However, this shows that this had gone through the office ... so clearly News International are culpable and we're going to have to settle. And I'm going to have to show this to James Murdoch.'

The reason I can remember him saying that was because I said to him: 'Please, do you have to show him this? Because he's going to assume the worst of me and he's going to think it's all to do with me. Is there any way we can get around this?' And he said to me: 'Nev, I'm sorry but I'm going to have to show him this because it is the only reason why we're having to settle. I've got to show him this.'

Thurlbeck stressed: 'This is not some vague memory. I was absolutely on a knife edge. He [Crone] was going to show this to James Murdoch. There's only going to be one conclusion he's going to jump to which is: "Get rid of Thurlbeck." Tom took it to him. The following week I said to him: "Did you show him the email?" and he said: "Yes, I did." Now Tom can't remember if he showed him it or spoke to him about it, but he said: "Yes, I did."'

Thurlbeck kept his job, but so did the journalist he claimed had been responsible.

When Nick Davies's story about the Taylor settlement broke on 8 July 2009, Thurlbeck recalled 'there was a big outcry' in Wapping and executives again came up with the same solution: redundancy for Neville. Thurlbeck said:

> Tom [Crone], who I've always got on well with, very kindly said to me, very privately: 'You're going to be called into the editor's office and you're going to be made an offer . . .' And I was completely shell-shocked and I said to him: 'What do you mean?' And he said: 'The transcript for Neville.' And I said: 'Tom, I've already explained to you what all that was about.' And he said: 'I know.' So I went in and explained to the boss: 'But I didn't do this. I've explained to Tom the sequence of events. Have you spoken to [the other journalist] about this?' The reply he gave me was: 'Yes, he can't even remember anything about the story.'

Thurlbeck added: 'There was a telephone call, a conference call, between Tom, Colin [Myler] and [the other journalist] . . . and Tom screamed [at the other journalist]: "You fucking liar." And the company was aware at this point that I had been telling the truth and that [the other journalist] had been lying.'

Despite warning the management and supplying emails from the journalist he blamed, Thurlbeck believed that it had been convenient for the management – which stuck by its rogue reporter defence – to allow 'the iron filings of suspicion' to stick to him, Thurlbeck, rather than the other, more senior journalist, whose naming would suggest a wider problem at the paper. Neither Crone nor Myler mentioned the conversation described by Thurlbeck in their evidence to the Commons Culture Committee on 21 July 2009.

Watson asked: 'So they effectively misled the committee. They knew?'

Thurlbeck replied: 'They did. I don't know why. The only reason

I can suggest is that it wouldn't be to their corporate benefit to say: "Oh, no, it wasn't Neville – it was [the other journalist]." There's no corporate brownie points to be won for that. All you're doing is spreading the flame-thrower further and further over your company at the time it was still desperately clinging to the rogue reporter defence. So they sat on this for two years, knowing that he was a hacker.'

Before he finished, Thurlbeck had something to say about James Murdoch, who was due to reappear before the Culture Committee within days – that he could not possibly admit he had seen the 'For Neville' email:

> It would be absolute suicide for him to admit that he knew it, to say: 'I knew that hacking went further than a rogue reporter and allowed the company to provide the rogue reporter defence for so long and not do anything about it,' and now the paper's had to close and the company's been tarred and feathered, then it's suicide for him.

Thurlbeck added: 'He can't.'

In early October, the Management and Standards Committee released Julian Pike of Farrer & Co from client confidentiality.* On 19 October, at the Culture Committee, Pike freely admitted that the 'For Neville' email and the Miskiw contract suggested the *News of the World* had misled Parliament. Asked by Paul Farrelly: 'So it was quite clear to you at the time that the "one rogue reporter" defence the company was still maintaining, including in front of this committee, was not true?', he replied: 'That is correct.'

Farrelly probed: 'You have told us that you were aware from the moment that News International came in front of Parliament that it

---

* It is not known why News Corp released Farrer's from the restrictions of client confidentiality. It may be that Farrer's, considering its reputation had been unfairly tarnished by its work for News International, had threatened to stretch confidentiality to its limits, or it may be that the move was part of the MSC's attempt to distance the company from its former executives and lawyers. At the time of writing, News International has not released Burton Copeland, the firm employed during Operation Caryatid, from the shackles of client confidentiality.

was not telling the truth and did nothing. Does that make you uncomfortable?' 'Not especially, no,' Pike replied.

Most important of all, Pike disclosed the legal opinion James Murdoch had referred to in July when he explained to the MPs why he had authorized such a large payment to Gordon Taylor. Michael Silverleaf's advice in June 2008 (see pp. 66–7) clearly indicated that there had been a culture of wrongdoing in the newsroom of the *News of the World* which extended beyond a rogue reporter.

Knowing the company's lies, Farrer & Co could have declined to act for News International, but it did not: Rupert Murdoch's company was its biggest client.

At News Corp's annual meeting, on 21 October, Rupert Murdoch faced personal criticism of his handling of phone hacking and a vote to oust his sons James and Lachlan from the board, which threatened his dynasty's grip on the company. News Corp switched the meeting from New York, its usual venue, where most investors and business journalists were based, to its 20th Century Fox film studios on the outskirts of Los Angeles. Outside, protestors held up placards saying 'Fire the Murdoch Mafia' and 'Rupert Isn't Above the Law'.

Chairing the meeting, Murdoch appeared to be sharper than he had been at the Culture Committee in July. He stressed the 'legend' of News Corp's transformation from a single newspaper in Australia to a multibillion-dollar digital giant headquartered in New York. He admitted that, regrettably, some of its British newspaper journalists had hacked voicemails but he added: 'We could not be taking this more seriously or listening more intently to criticisms.' He then limited contributions from the floor to one minute each.

The Californian pension fund Calpers, the Australian Shareholders' Association and other shareholders assailed Murdoch about the company's handling of the scandal. The Murdochs survived the rebellion but outside the family's holding, 67 per cent of non-aligned shareholders had voted to depose James Murdoch and 64 per cent his brother Lachlan. Non-family shareholders also opposed (unsuccessfully) Rupert Murdoch's $33 million pay. Following the meeting, a senior analyst from Invesco, Kevin Holt, estimated that News Corp was trading at a 40 per cent discount to its true value because of its recent failures, including a 20 per cent 'Rupert discount' – 'because of the acquisitions and the risk of capital destruction'.[1]

On 10 November, members of the public began queuing at 7 a.m. for a place at James Murdoch's hearing. At 11 a.m., Murdoch took his seat in front of the Culture Committee. In place of the passive-aggressive technocrat who had given evidence in July came a more confident, assured witness, but he still answered questions in an anodyne and obfuscatory manner: he did not want to make good television.

Murdoch's greatest difficulty was how to explain that he had no knowledge that wrongdoing had spread beyond Clive Goodman when he authorized the Taylor pay-off. In July, he had told Tom Watson he had neither seen nor been aware of the 'For Neville' email. Now, he admitted he had been made aware of its existence, but insisted he had not been shown it; nor told it indicated wrongdoing was rife. He also denied seeing the advice from Michael Silverleaf QC, the basis on which his company made the largest privacy settlement in British legal history.

'The facts did not emerge in 2008,' Murdoch said. 'Certain individuals were aware. The leading counsel's opinion was there. The "For Neville email", so called, was there. None of those things were made available or discussed with me and I was not aware of those things.'

Murdoch's insistence that he had not misled the committee logically meant he thought that Myler and Crone had done so, but, asked by Watson, he was reluctant to say so:

WATSON: Mr Murdoch, let me just ask you again: did you mislead this committee in your original testimony?

MURDOCH: No, I did not.

WATSON: So if you did not, who did?

MURDOCH: As I have written to you and said publicly, I believe this committee was given evidence by individuals either without full possession of the facts or, now, it appears – in the process of my own discovery in trying to understand as best I can what actually happened here – it was economical. I think my own testimony has been consistent. I have testified to this committee with as much clarity and transparency as I possibly can, and where I have not had direct knowledge in the past, since I testified to you last time, I have gone and tried to seek answers and find out what happened, and where the evidence is and what is there; and that is what I am here to do.

WATSON: So was it Mr Crone, a respected and in-house legal adviser for many years?

MURDOCH: As I said to you, as I wrote to you, and I issued a public statement, certainly, in the evidence that they gave to you in 2011, with respect to my knowledge, I thought it was inconsistent and not right, and I dispute it vigorously.

WATSON: So you think Mr Crone misled us?

MURDOCH: It follows that I do, yes.

WATSON: And so do you think Mr Myler misled us as well?

MURDOCH: I believe their testimony was misleading, and I dispute it.

Watson pointed out there were allegations of phone hacking, computer hacking, conspiring to pervert the course of justice and perjury facing his company – 'and all this happened without your knowledge?' Murdoch replied: 'As I have said to you, Mr Watson, and to this committee on a number of occasions, it is a matter of great regret that things went wrong at the *News of the World* in 2006. The company didn't come to grips with those issues fast enough . . .'

With an eye on media coverage of the hearing, Watson countered: 'Mr Murdoch, you must be the first mafia boss in history who didn't know he was running a criminal enterprise.'

'Mr Watson, please,' Murdoch replied disdainfully. 'I think that's inappropriate.'

To Murdoch's claim that he had not checked the QC's opinion before authorizing the Taylor settlement, the Conservative MP Damian Collins remarked: 'Honestly, it may not be the mafia, but it is not *Management Today*.' Philip Davies MP found it 'absolutely incredible' that Murdoch would not have checked the QC's opinion before settling.

Murdoch said News International's surveillance of the lawyers Mark Lewis and Charlotte Harris was 'just not acceptable'. Asked about surveillance of members of the Culture Committee, he said: 'I am aware of the case of the surveillance of Mr Watson; again, under the circumstances, I apologize unreservedly for that. It is not something that I would condone, it is not something that I had knowledge of and it is not something that has a place in the way we operate.'

The Liverpudlian MP Steve Rotherham, a campaigner for victims of the Hillsborough disaster, asked Murdoch whether, if the *Sun* had also been hacking phones, he would close that paper too? To the shock of committee members, the media and the paper's journalists, Murdoch replied: 'I don't think we can rule, and I shouldn't rule, any corporate reaction to behaviour of wrongdoing out.'

By sticking to his defence, no matter how questionable, Murdoch had successfully avoided incriminating himself but in doing so had been forced to plead gross ignorance of the working of his company and that he had not bothered to read crucial documents, a damaging admission for the deputy chief operating officer of a global conglomerate.

In its leading article the next day, *The Times* rallied to the corporate flag:

James Murdoch yesterday came to Parliament to answer two sets of questions. The first were about his personal integrity. The second were about the culture of the company in which he is a senior executive. Mr Murdoch was recalled by the MPs to answer allegations that, when he had last appeared as a witness, he misled them. On this, as on other questions that touched on the integrity of his personal conduct, he was clear, consistent and convincing.

22

The Press on Trial

Are these all real headlines?
— Lord Leveson, 29 November 2011

In a light, modern room of the Royal Courts of Justice in London on 14 November, a judge began a hearing with a sensational mix of celebrity, sex, power and crime; this time the press was on trial. The inquiry was launched in July under pressure by the Prime Minister, who asked Lord Leveson to recommend a better system of press regulation which would banish once and for all intrusion, exaggeration and fabrication. Although the scandal had begun with a single Wapping title, the Prime Minister had put all newspapers in the dock. The press had uncovered scandals in public life, but had fallen short when it came to policing itself. Lord Leveson said his task was to answer the question: 'Who guards the guardians?'

Robert Jay QC, the inquiry's counsel, outlined its concerns about the failure of the police, politicians and the Press Complaints Commission to control the sometimes overweening and destructive power of newspapers. He made plain the chasm which separated the modest charges brought during the original investigation in 2006 and the suspected scale of News International's actual phone hacking. There were twenty-eight 'corner names' in Glenn Mulcaire's notes. The *News of the World*'s hacking operation had begun by 2002, at the latest, and police believed it continued until 2009. Jay said: 'It is clear that Goodman was not a rogue reporter. Ignoring the private corner name and the illegibles, we have at least twenty-seven other News

International employees. This fact alone suggests wide-ranging illegal activity within the organization at the relevant time . . .'

Turning to the power of newspapers over politicians, Jay asked whether there was a quid pro quo for electoral endorsements, 'namely the bestowing of commercial favours by government'. He said: 'The unaccountable power of the press, or of certain parts of it, is a consistent theme here, and if that power is concentrated in a limited number of individuals the problem is capable of being visualized as all the more menacing.'[1]

A grotesque parade of invasions of privacy filled the inquiry's first weeks, as victims of press misbehaviour – many of whom had silently despaired at the inability of newspapers to correct the slurs – told their stories directly to the public for the first time. News International's titles the *Sun* and the *NoW* often featured, but so too did many of Britain's other large newspaper groups, particularly the other tabloid operators: Express Newspapers, Associated Newspapers and Trinity Mirror.

The treatment meted out to Kate and Gerry McCann, for instance, was inhumane. Venting years of frustration in Court 73, the McCanns recounted how British journalists, desperate for new angles in the aftermath of their daughter Madeleine's disappearance in Portugal on 3 May 2007, recycled reports from the Portuguese press stating that they themselves were under suspicion, without apparently making any checks. Gerry McCann, on 23 November, said: 'I do not know whether they [Portuguese police] were speaking directly to the British media, but what we clearly saw were snippets of information which as far as I was concerned the British media could not tell whether it was true or not, which was then reported, often exaggerated and blown up into many tens, in fact hundreds of front-page headlines.' A meeting with newspaper editors stating there was no evidence to support their involvement had 'very little effect'. Newspapers fought a subsequent libel case brought by the McCanns. Eventually the *Daily Mail* settled without an apology and Express Newspapers paid £550,000 to Madeleine's Fund and on 19 March 2008 printed a grovelling apology on the front page of the *Daily Star* and *Daily Express* disowning the smears:

... there is no evidence whatsoever to suggest that Mr and Mrs McCann were responsible for the death of their daughter, that they were involved in any sort of cover-up and there was no basis for Express Newspapers to allege otherwise. Equally, the allegations that Mr and Mrs McCann may have sold Madeleine or were involved in swinging or wife swapping were entirely baseless. Naturally the repeated publication of these utterly false and defamatory allegations has caused untold distress to Mr and Mrs McCann. Indeed, it is difficult to conceive of a more serious allegation.

The McCanns had treated all publications equally for fear of alienating their rivals, but on the first anniversary of Madeleine's disappearance they gave an exclusive interview to *Hello!* to publicize a new European alert system for missing children. At the *News of the World*, which had put up a £250,000 reward for Madeleine's safe return, Colin Myler was straight on the phone. Gerry McCann recalled:

I think it would be fair to say that Mr Myler was irate ... and was berating us for not doing an interview with the *News of the World* and told us how supportive the newspaper had been, the news and rewards. And at a time of stress for us on the first anniversary – where we were actually launching a new campaign ... he basically beat us into submission, verbally, and we agreed to do an interview the day after.

Five months later, on 14 September 2008, under the headline: 'Kate's Diary: In Her Own Words', the *NoW* published extracts from Kate McCann's personal diary in which she had recorded her intimate thoughts about Madeleine. The Portuguese police had seized the diary and a copy had fallen into the hands of a Portuguese journalist, who had sold it for €20,000 to the *NoW*.

Kate McCann said:

I felt totally violated. I'd written those words and thoughts at the most desperate time in my life, most people won't have to experience that, and it was my only way of communicating with Madeleine, and for me, you know, there was absolutely no respect shown for me as a grieving mother or as a human being or for my daughter, and it made me feel very vulnerable and small and I just couldn't believe it.

Stars who for years had felt intimidated or harassed by press intrusion made the point that, while their jobs put them on the public stage, they had not courted tabloid interest, nor did they believe that it should open the gates to their private life. Hugh Grant said 'hundreds' of people in the public eye would willingly never be mentioned in newspapers again. Listing a series of false and prying stories, he mentioned an 'interview' with him in the *Sunday Express*, explaining: 'I had not even spoken to a journalist. It was completely, as far I could see, either made up or patched and pasted from previous quotations I might have given in an interview.'

A *Mail on Sunday* report in February 2007 about his relationship with Jemima Khan being in jeopardy because he had been receiving late-night calls from a posh woman might have come from hacking his phone, he said. While he had indeed been receiving calls from a plummy-sounding studio executive's PA while he was in Los Angeles – late at night British time – he had not been having an affair with her. He successfully sued for libel. 'But thinking about how they could possibly have come up with such a bizarre left-field story, he said, I cannot for the life of me think of any conceivable source for this story in the *Mail on Sunday* except those voice messages on my mobile telephone.' That evening the *Mail on Sunday* accused him of 'mendacious smears'.

Illustrating his concern that the press had not reformed, the actor said that in March 2011 the *Sun* and the *Daily Express* had reported his medical symptoms – 'dizzy and short of breath' – during an emergency visit to Chelsea and Westminster Hospital. He suspected that a member of the hospital's staff was receiving a retainer from a newspaper or picture agency. 'You know: "If anyone famous comes in, tell us and here's 50 quid or 500 quid."'

Dressed in black with little make-up, the actress Sienna Miller recalled how the *Daily Mirror* had cropped a photo of her at a charity ball to make it look as if she was drunk. She sued, won her case and the paper subsequently printed an apology:

Sorry, Sienna. On Saturday 12 March, we printed pictures of Sienna Miller, who is an ambassador for the Starlight Children's Foundation charity, at the Starlight Children's Foundation charity for terminally ill children. We said that Sienna's boozy antics had shocked guests at the event and thereby suggested that she had behaved in an unprofessional manner. We are happy to make clear that Sienna was not drunk and did not behave unprofessionally. In fact in the pictures Sienna was on the floor playing with a seriously ill six-year-old child. We have apologized to Sienna.

She believed that the paper had calculated the cost in money and reputation of printing an apology before misreporting the story.

Miller's most significant evidence, given on 24 November, was on the hacking by News International. She could not understand how photographers and reporters kept popping up wherever she went, before she had even arrived. She felt 'constantly very scared and intensely paranoid' because every area of her life was 'under constant surveillance'. She said: 'I felt I was living in some kind of video game.'

J. K. Rowling, the author of the Harry Potter novels, recalling that a reporter had slipped a note into her daughter's school satchel, said: 'It's very difficult to say how angry I felt that my five-year-old's school was no longer a place of complete security from journalists.' In 2003, she felt she was being blackmailed when the *Sun* allegedly offered to return a stolen copy of her fifth Harry Potter book – yet to be published – in exchange for a photo opportunity.

When she asked why a photographer from a Scottish tabloid was lurking outside her home, she was told: 'It's a boring day at the office.' Giving evidence on 24 November, she said: 'There wasn't even a sense there was a story. So my family and I were literally under surveillance for their amusement ... It's a very unnerving feeling to know that you're being watched.'

The behaviour of freelance paparazzi and staff photographers was a frequent complaint. The singer Charlotte Church recalled that as a teenager she was constantly chased by reporters and photographers, some of whom tried to take pictures up her skirt. Between the ages of sixteen and eighteen, she was followed by up to eight photographers a day.

Kate McCann said snappers would spring out from behind hedges to give her a fright, and newspapers would then carry those pictures with captions saying she looked 'frail' or 'fragile'. As a 21-year-old Sienna Miller had been regularly chased down the street by packs of up to fifteen photographers, and had been spat at. The police had told Hugh Grant that the paparazzi were increasingly recruited 'from the criminal classes' who would 'show no mercy, no ethics, because the bounty on some of these pictures is very high'.

Church was traduced by Rupert Murdoch's titles, despite agreeing, aged thirteen in 1999, to sing at his wedding to Wendi Deng. According to Church, she was given a choice of rewards by Murdoch's office: £100,000 or positive coverage in the tycoon's papers. (News International denies that this offer was made.) On the advice of her management, she agreed to take the positive coverage and duly sang the song Murdoch wanted, 'Pie Jesu', though pointing out to him that it was a funeral song.

If the promise of positive coverage was made, it was not honoured. The *Sunday Times*, Church said, had fabricated 'horrific' comments by her that after 9/11 New York firefighters did not deserve their heroic status, when what she had actually said was that they had been demeaned by the National Television Awards where they had been asked to present the Best Soap category. Unusually, no one from her management or Sony had taped the interview. 'I was only fifteen and to be exposed by a newspaper of this type to ridicule and derision upon such a sensitive subject was a terrible experience. That article then went over to the *New York Post* and the headline was: "Voice of an angel spews venom". And of course because of the massively sensitive nature of this subject, there was a massive backlash against me in America . . .'

On 11 December 2005, the *News of the World* published the most grievous story, about her father having an affair. Headlined: 'Church's three in a bed cocaine shock', its first line was: 'Superstar Charlotte Church's mum tried to kill herself because her husband is a love rat hooked on cocaine and three-in-a-bed orgies.'

Church told Lord Leveson:

I just really hated the fact that my parents, who had never been in this industry apart from in looking after me, were being exposed and vilified in this fashion. It had a massive impact on my family life, on my mother's health, which the *News of the World* had reported on before then, on her mental state and her hospital treatment. We also think the only way they could have known about that hospital treatment was either through the hacking or possibly through the bribing of hospital staff. So they knew how vulnerable she was and still printed this story, which was horrific.

Testifying on the same grim day for News Corp as Church, 28 November, Anne Diamond explained she had experienced years of negative stories in Murdoch publications. At a social function in the 1980s the TV presenter had told Murdoch that his newspapers seemed intent on ruining people's lives. She said that her subsequent experiences made sense after she saw a Channel 4 documentary in 2011 in which Murdoch's former butler, Phillip Townsend, said that Murdoch had called together a number of his newspaper editors and 'possibly indicated to his editors that I was a person from that point on to be targeted'. Diamond said: 'When you look back now in the knowledge of what Mr Townsend had said . . . well, it would suggest it becomes evident from that point onwards there were consistent negative stories about me in Mr Murdoch's newspapers.'

Hours after visiting a private clinic in 1986 fearing that she was losing her first baby at eight weeks of pregnancy, Diamond recalled, a *Sun* reporter called asking if she was pregnant. Not having told her parents, and not being sure that the baby would survive, she denied she was pregnant. 'They ran the story anyway . . .' While she was in labour in hospital, an administrator told her a reporter for the *Sun* had been caught impersonating a doctor and ejected from the hospital. In December 1987, *Today* (Rupert Murdoch's now closed fifth national newspaper) printed the details of Diamond's new home: 'It wasn't just a dreadful invasion of privacy of my new home, it was a burglar's charter.'

In 1991, when Diamond lost her new baby to cot death, she and her then husband wrote to every newspaper editor asking them not to cover Sebastian's funeral in a small family church. All journalists stayed away apart from a freelance photographer, who took pictures from the road. Diamond said:

Within a few hours of the funeral, the editor of the *Sun* [Kelvin Mackenzie] rang my husband and said: 'We have a picture. It's an incredibly strong picture. We would like to use it.' And my husband said: 'No, we've asked all of you to stay away. No.' And the editor said: 'Well, we're going to use it anyway. We'll use it without your permission.'

The next day the *Sun* put the story on the front page and rang to say that it had received such an enormous response that it wanted Diamond to launch a fundraising campaign. She felt 'emotionally blackmailed' but relented, because she knew 'the power of the press'. *

Recalling how he had been tricked into discussing an affair, Steve Coogan reflected in his witness statement: 'Strangely I don't think it was a malicious personal vendetta against me. My feeling is that it was a dispassionate sociopathic act by those who operate in an amoral universe where they are never accountable.'

At the Leveson Inquiry, newspaper proprietors, editors and reporters were finally held to account. Almost all the titles had some explaining to do. One of the greatest twists was the *Guardian*'s handling of the Milly Dowler story in July 2011. On 10 December 2011, the paper explained that the *News of the World* might not, after all, have been responsible for deleting messages from Milly Dowler's phone, which had led her parents to believe she might be alive. News International journalists leapt on the admission. On 13 December, the *Sun*'s managing editor, Richard Caseby, accused the *Guardian* of 'sexing up' its coverage of the Dowler story.[2] After the paper's columnist Marina Hyde wrongly reported that the *Sun* had door-stepped one of the Leveson Inquiry's junior counsel, a couriered parcel arrived from Wapping for Alan Rusbridger containing a toilet roll and a note which read: 'I hear Marina Hyde's turd landed on your desk. Well, you can use this to wipe her arse.'

---

* She was right. Within days, the *Sun* had raised £100,000 for cot death research. In the twenty years since Diamond fronted the 'Back to Sleep' campaign urging parents to ensure babies slept on their backs, the number of cot deaths in the UK fell from 2,500 to 300 a year.

For the newspaper industry, the witnesses broadly divided into those who admitted they had done wrong and those who did not. Among the innocent was Kelvin Mackenzie, the former *Sun* editor. On 9 January 2012 Mackenzie agreed that his policy while editing the *Sun* was that if something sounded right he would 'lob it in'. He told the inquiry: 'I didn't spend too much time pondering the ethics of how a story was gained nor over-worry about whether to publish or not. If we believed the story to be true and we felt *Sun* readers should know the facts, we published it and we left it to them to decide if we had done the right thing.' He denied Murdoch had ever urged his editors to go after Anne Diamond: 'I have had the advantage as distinct from Ms Diamond of working with Rupert Murdoch for thirteen years closely. And I have never heard him say: "Go after" anybody under any circumstances, whether it is a prime minister, a failing breakfast show host, or anybody.'

On 12 January, Richard Desmond, proprietor of Express Newspapers, asked what interest he took in the ethical conduct of his papers, replied: 'Well, ethical, I don't quite know what the word means.' He apologized for their treatment of the McCanns, but maintained that his newspapers had been 'scapegoated' over their coverage of their daughter's disappearance: 'If there were 102 articles on the McCanns, and thirty-eight bad ones ... you could argue there were sixty-eight or seventy good ones.' He suggested the McCanns had been 'quite happy to have articles about their daughter' on the front page. Robert Jay, the inquiry's counsel, described that as a 'grotesque characterization'.

One of Desmond's former reporters, Richard Peppiatt, spilled the secrets of the *Daily Star* in spectacular fashion and repented of his role in its bias, exaggerations and fabrications. Peppiatt, who freelanced full-time at the paper for two years, on £118 a day, until March 2011, said its reporters wrote to its 'ideological perspective on certain issues, say immigration or national security or policing':

> And so whatever a story may be, you must try and adhere to their ideological perspective. Say there is a government report giving out statistics. Well, you know, any statistics which don't fit within that

framework you ignore or sort of decontextualize and pick maybe the one statistic which does. If there's something that comes out saying crime has gone down, you then go and look for the statistic which says knife crime has gone up 20 per cent . . .

Some stories were 'dictated more from the accounts and advertising departments than the newsroom floor', such as one he wrote about Marks & Spencer's skinny pants.* To the amusement (and horror) of the inquiry, he read out the headlines of false *Daily Star* stories: '"Chile mine to open as theme park"; "Angelina Jolie to play Susan Boyle in film"; "Bubbles to give evidence at Jacko trial" . . . "Brittany Murphy killed by swine flu" – wasn't the case; "Macca versus Mucca on ice", which was that Paul McCartney and his ex-wife were apparently going to showdown on *Dancing On Ice*, never transpired. Then we have the likes of "Muslim-only public loos" . . . completely untrue as well.'

Lord Leveson, apparently not a *Daily Star* reader, interrupted: 'Are these all real headlines?' Peppiatt replied: 'These are real headlines.'

Those who had written raucous accounts of press misbehaviour, but who were now testifying in a wholly new context, suggested that what they had written previously was little more than gossip. Giving evidence via videolink from New York, Piers Morgan was asked about *The Insider*, the account of his tabloid days editing the *News of the World* and the *Mirror*. The inquiry wanted to know about the time that Rupert Murdoch rang up and suggested he drop the Kray story (see p. 16). In his statement, Morgan wrote: 'This is my recollection of the gist of our conversation, almost ten years later on. I did not make a contemporaneous note. Mr Murdoch's recollections and impressions may well differ from mine.' He added: 'I would note that my books were not intended to provide a historical record.'

He said he did not believe that phone hacking took place during his editorship of the *Daily Mirror* between 1995 and 2004, but could

---

* Published on 23 July 2010, it read: 'All the girls are talking about vampire hunk R-Patz – now us fellas have our own R-Pantz. Marks & Spencer are launching a range of slim-fitting undies with blokes who wear skinny jeans in mind.'

not explain how he came to hear a tape-recording Paul McCartney had left for his wife Heather Mills after a row. Suddenly 'the insider' seemed not to know much at all.

Sharon Marshall, who had delved into the devious ways of hacks in *Tabloid Girl: A True Story*, suggested her account had been based on personal recollections and chats with old hacks in the pub. In her foreword to the book, published in 2010, she had written: 'This is what happened when I worked in the tabloid press. Look back through the newspaper archives and you'll see my name on these stories. I wrote them. They're true. I'm not proud of everything we did, but I loved the tabloid journalists I worked with. Every single double-crossing, devious, scheming, ruthless, messed up, brilliantly evil one of them.' Now, she explained when she said 'devious' she was referring to nothing more than probably apocryphal examples of hacks trying to claim camels on expenses and that 'accordingly, no reliance can be placed upon those stories as providing a statement or an indication of general practice in the journalism industry'.[3]

While the inquiry was wary of eliciting any evidence which might compromise the ongoing police investigations, *News of the World*'s former executives were called to account for the cover-up. Out of a job and with their paper closed, they no longer had to lie.

Tom Crone, who had stuck doggedly to the rogue reporter defence, now recanted. Giving evidence on 14 December, and still playing the part of the respectable lawyer, he said languidly: 'I can't remember when and by whom the rogue reporter explanation was first put out, but I was of the view that it was erroneous from the start.'

Did that ever cause him concern? 'Yes,' he replied. 'My feeling is I thought it would probably come back to bite the people who were saying it, which was the company, sure.'

At the meeting on 10 June 2008 at which James Murdoch authorized the Gordon Taylor payment, he said he had taken in a copy of Michael Silverleaf QC's damning opinion on a culture of illegal news-gathering at the organization, as well as spare copies of the 'For Neville' email. Jay asked: 'Did you supply any of those documents to Mr Murdoch?' Crone replied:

I can't remember whether they were passed across the table to him, but I'm pretty sure I held up the front page of the email ... I'm also pretty sure that he already knew about it. What was certainly discussed was the email. Not described as 'For Neville', but the damning email and what it meant in terms of further involvement beyond – further involvement in phone hacking beyond Goodman and Mulcaire. And what was relayed to Mr Murdoch was that this document clearly was direct and hard evidence of that being the case.

On 15 December, Colin Myler – who was shortly to accept a new job as editor of the New York *Daily News*, rival to Murdoch's *Post* – disputed that there had been an attempt to conceal the truth. 'I don't think there was a cover-up,' said the editor who two years previously had told a parliamentary inquiry that there was 'no evidence' phone hacking extended beyond Clive Goodman. Lord Leveson inquired: 'It might be slightly semantic, mightn't it, Mr Myler? What one person might describe as a cover-up another person would describe as an attempt to limit reputational damage?'

Myler replied: 'Absolutely, sir.'

Giving evidence, Stuart Hoare, brother of the late reporter Sean Hoare, said:

The reality was that phone hacking was endemic within the News International group (specifically Sean identified that this process was initiated at the *Sun* and later transferred to the *News of the World*) ... undoubtedly, one of the major issues during Sean's employment with the *News of the World* was that the news desk was out of control and that stories were obtained with very little or no ethics because of the pressure put on journalists to deliver.

In his written testimony on 19 December, Matt Driscoll agreed:

It seemed to me that any methods that could stand a story up were fair game. It was also clear that there was massive pressure from the top to break stories. It was largely accepted that this pressure came from the proprietors and editors on the basis that big, sensational stories sell papers and therefore make more money.

19. The Golden Lion pub in Sydenham, east London, in whose car park Daniel Morgan was murdered in 1987.

20. Jonathan Rees, whose office was bugged by the Metropolitan Police, said: 'No one pays like the *News of the World* do.' Andy Coulson's *News of the World* re-employed Rees after he was jailed for conspiracy to pervert the course of justice.

21. At the time of his murder, Morgan was increasingly concerned about the links between Rees, his business partner at Southern Investigations and corrupt police.

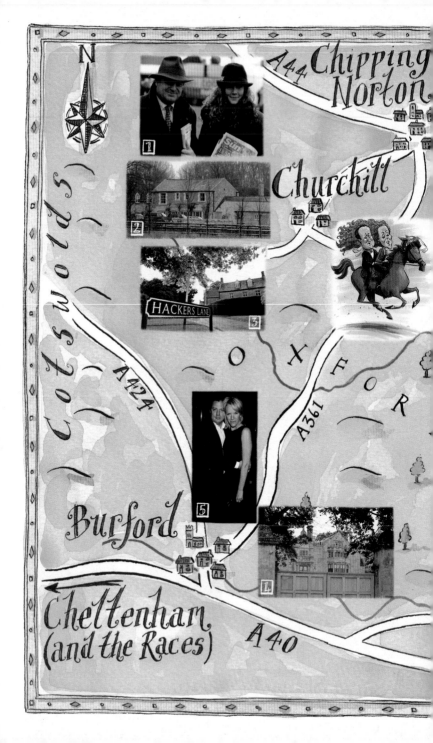

THE COTSWOLD TRIANGLE

1. Charlie and Rebekah Brooks at Newbury Races, 26th November 2011
2. The Brooks' country home in Churchill
3. Hacker's Lane, Churchill
4. Burford Priory, country residence of Matthew Freud and Elisabeth Murdoch
5. Murdoch and Freud, hosts of the party on 2nd July 2011
6. David Cameron's constituency home in Dean

A44

Dean

6

A44 Oxford

River Evenlode

Blenheim Palace

SHIRE

Witney
(David Cameron's Constituency)

A40 Oxford

```
0   1   2   3   4   5   6   7  Km
0       1       2       3      4  Miles
```

22. Flanked by *News of the World* staff outside Thomas More Square, Wapping, on 9 July 2011, Colin Myler holds its 8,674th edition bearing the legend, 'The world's greatest newspaper 1843–2011'.

23. Britain's top policeman, Sir Paul Stephenson, resigned as Commissioner of the Metropolitan Police after accepting an £11,000 free stay at Champneys health spa – whose PR advisor was Neil Wallis.

24. Hours after the *News of the World*'s presses rolled for the last time, Murdoch shrugged off demands for Rebekah Brooks to resign. Asked for his priority, he pointed at her and said: 'This one.' Brooks went five days later.

25. Scotland Yard detectives search Andy Coulson's home in south London following his arrest on 8 July 2011 on suspicion of phone hacking and corruption. In January 2012, Coulson put the five-bedroom house on the market for £1.6m.

26. In the House of Commons on 20 July, the Prime Minister said that 'in hindsight' he wished he had not appointed Coulson as his director of communications: 'You live and you learn – and believe me, I have learnt.'

27. Protesters gathered outside the Houses of Parliament as Rupert and James Murdoch appeared before MPs on 19 July 2011. Millions around the world watched the hearing live on television.

28. 'Before you get to that, I would just like to say one sentence … This is the most humble day of my life.'

29. A comedian, a film star and the former head of world motorsport – Steve Coogan, Hugh Grant and Max Mosley – railed against tabloid tactics at Parliament's joint committee on privacy on 5 December 2011.

30. J. K. Rowling felt like she was being 'blackmailed' by the *Sun* in 2003 over a leak of her new book, *Harry Potter and the Order of the Phoenix*.

31. In exchange for singing at Rupert Murdoch's and Wendi Deng's wedding in 1999, Charlotte Church was promised 'good press': it didn't happen. After settling her case in February 2012, she said: 'In my opinion, they are not truly sorry, only sorry they got caught.'

32. Sienna Miller could not understand how reporters and photographers knew about her life. 'I felt like I was in a video game.' Her legal case against News International uncovered a crucial weakness in the company's story.

33. Milly Dowler's parents, Bob and Sally, arrive at the Leveson Inquiry at the Royal Courts of Justice in London, with the combative Mark Lewis (in the orange coat). Lewis and Charlotte Harris (plate 12) were the first lawyers to challenge News International over phone hacking.

He added:

> I feel that for many years some newspapers have been on course for destruction. Editors were handed far too much power and their egos were allowed to run wild. Some that I worked for often became pampered peacocks who only wanted to hear the word 'yes' and would shout and scream if they heard anything else. No doubt the power and lucrative lifestyle that gives them front-row seats and free holidays helped to corrupt them ... As a result of this aggressive and grotesque arrogance, those in charge – the proprietors and the editors – came to believe that they could do and say whatever they wanted and remain untouchable.
>
> In my years at News International, I came to believe – along with other journalists – that the newspaper group were indeed confident that they were untouchable because they were sure they had the government and police fighting their corner. Thus, they felt that they were almost beyond the reach of the law. These powerful contacts were the reason why some on the *News of the World* felt they could leave their morals and their respect for ethics at the door when they clocked in each morning. The next front page was all that mattered, however it was obtained.

23
Darker and Darker

Hugely in the national interest

– Mr Justice Vos

In 2012, News International's problems deepened – and spread to its other businesses. In secrecy in January, Ofcom – the regulator the Murdochs wanted to hobble – had begun 'Project Apple', an inquiry into whether the stream of disclosures about criminality in News Corp's newspapers rendered Sky unfit to own a broadcasting licence.

At Wapping journalists could no longer ignore the flagrant wrongdoing and the cover-up. In a New Year's edition of BBC radio's *What the Papers Say*, David Aaranovitch, *The Times*'s star columnist, admitted:

> If we had been covering it in any other public body we would have been down on those people [News International executives] like a ton of bricks . . . Our dark cousins in the tabloids are the people, by and large the people who have subsidized [us] and that does create some really awkward problems for an editor at *The Times* if he wants to lam into his colleagues at the *News of the World* . . .[1]

Confronted with overwhelming evidence of the wrongdoing of its parent company, *The Times* admitted its failings in a 1,800-word leader on 17 January – while paying a sour compliment to the investigative journalism which had unpicked its deceit:

As the evidence of wrongdoing came to light, News International, Rupert Murdoch's company that also owns *The Times*, was unable or unwilling to police itself. This was a disgrace. It was, of course, the press that put Fleet Street in the dock. The dogged investigative reporting that unearthed the phone hacking scandal deserves respect, even if the story was exaggerated and key details misreported.

In his evidence to Lord Leveson that day, *The Times*'s editor, James Harding, said: 'I certainly wish we had got on the story harder, earlier.' However, he disagreed with Aaranovitch that the failure to cover the story properly was linked to the Murdochs' ownership; instead Harding blamed a failure to understand its significance.

He was also forced to confront *The Times*'s hacking of the police blogger 'Nightjack' (see pp. 78–9). Confronted with a standard question about computer hacking, Harding told the Leveson Inquiry in a statement on 14 October: '*The Times* has never used or commissioned anyone who used computer hacking to source stories. There was an incident where the newsroom was concerned that a reporter had gained unauthorized access to an email account. When it was brought to my attention, the journalist faced disciplinary action.' Harding's statement was disingenuous since he knew that there was more than a mere 'concern' that hacking had been used against Nightjack.

Over the coming weeks the truth was slowly dragged out of *The Times*. Its legal director, Alastair Brett, and its managing editor, David Chappell, had known by 4 June 2009 that Foster had used hacking, but the paper had published his story days later regardless after seeing off a legal attempt by Horton to prevent its publication. In that High Court case, *The Times* had made no mention of the hacking to the judge, Mr Justice Eady, who was told that a journalist had identified Horton by painstaking detective work. At the Leveson Inquiry on 7 February 2012, Harding said he did not think the paper's testimony to the High Court had been truthful, but he insisted that he had not personally known about the hacking until several days after publication of the story – despite being alerted to it in an email prior to publication (which he claimed he had been too busy to read). Harding disciplined the journalist over the incident, but promoted him a year later. Cheeks flushed, Harding told Lord Leveson: 'When you look back at all of this, sir – I really hope you understand – it's terrible. I really hope you appreciate that. I know that as keenly as you do.' Operation Tuleta, the Metropolitan Police's inquiry into computer hacking, began investigating the Nightjack affair.

Sky News was also forced to admit in April that it too had hacked email accounts – despite originally telling the Leveson Inquiry that it had never hacked – and had in fact done so twice. One of the accounts belonged to a woman, Anne Darwin, who was later convicted of an insurance fraud. Sky said the hacking was in the public interest.

In the courts, News International strove to avoid any civil trial for breach of privacy that would put its executives in the witness box and lead to the disclosure of incriminating documents. On a single day, 19 January, the company settled thirty-seven cases, paying, among others, John Prescott £40,000, Chris Bryant £30,000 and Sara Payne undisclosed damages. In an accompanying statement of brazen doublethink, News Group Newspapers said: 'Today NGN agreed settlements in respect of a number of claims against the company. NGN made no admission as part of these settlements that directors or senior employees knew about the wrongdoing by NGN or sought to conceal it. However, for the purpose of reaching these settlements only, NGN agreed that the damages to be paid to claimants should be assessed as if this was the case.' News Group was, in essence, admitting responsibility for its actions, but at the same time maintaining the legal fiction of its innocence.

Claimants said they were settling because Part 36 offers from News International exposed them to substantial legal costs; and because the Metropolitan Police and the Leveson Inquiry were now properly investigating what had been done to them. Many, however, were still disgusted by their treatment. In a statement after his case was settled for £130,000 on 19 January, Jude Law said:

> For several years leading up to 2006, I was suspicious about how information concerning my private life was coming out in the press.

I changed my phones, I had my house swept for bugs but still the information kept being published. I started to become distrustful of people close to me. I was truly appalled by what I was shown by the police and by what my lawyers have discovered. It is clear that I, along with many others, was kept under constant surveillance for a number of years.

No aspect of my private life was safe from intrusion by News Group newspapers, including the lives of my children and the people who work for me. It was not just that my phone messages were listened to. News Group also paid people to watch me and my house for days at a time and to follow me and those close to me both in this country and abroad.

I believe in a free press but . . . they were prepared to do anything to sell their newspapers and to make money, irrespective of the impact it had on people's lives.

At the same hearing, News International brought into doubt its commitment to openness by opposing a request by the remaining litigants to examine three desktop computers and six laptops belonging to former employees. Wapping's lawyer, Dinah Rose, said the searches were a waste of time since the company was settling civil cases, telling the court: 'We accept we are the villains. We have the horns and the tails.' Rejecting her argument, the judge, Mr Justice Vos, replied that News International should be regarded as 'deliberate destroyers of evidence'. Documents he had seen, he said, might lead a court to conclude that it 'deliberately concealed and told lies and deleted documents and effectively tried to get off scot-free'. He told Rose:

I am rather hesitant, as you probably notice, about acceding to the 'Oh, it is all very expensive and difficult and time consuming and the trial is only around the corner,' because if I had acceded to that last year none of us would be sitting here in the present situation and you just seem a little over-sensitive about these laptops . . .

He said that finding out what had happened at News International was 'hugely in the national interest'.

On 9 February, News International settled another batch of cases, paying Steve Coogan £40,000, Simon Hughes £45,000, Sky Andrew £75,000, David Blunkett's* former friend Sally King £110,000 and Sheila Henry, the mother of 7/7 terrorist victim Christian Small, undisclosed damages.

Michael Silverleaf QC – still working for News International – expressed its 'sincere apologies' for the damage and distress. Charlotte Church – who had wanted her case to be heard in court until NI made it clear that it would seek to cross-examine her mentally fragile mother, Maria – questioned that sincerity. Outside court, the singer, whose family had received £600,000 in costs and damages, said:

> I have discovered that, despite the apology which the newspaper has just given in court today, these people were prepared to go to any lengths to prevent me exposing their behaviour, not just in the deliberate destruction of documents over a number of years but also by trying to make this investigation into the industrial scale of their illegal activity into an interrogation of my mother's medical condition, forcing her to relive the enormous emotional distress they caused her back in 2005. It seems they have learned nothing . . . In my opinion they are not truly sorry, only sorry they got caught.

As the FBI stepped up its investigations under the Foreign Corrupt Practices Act in the US,† the Met's detectives embedded with News Corp's Management and Standards Committee uncovered the payment of tens of thousands of pounds of bribes to police and public officials – by journalists on the *Sun*. Officers from Operation Elveden, the corruption investigation, had arrested one *Sun* journalist on 7 November 2011, the Thames Valley reporter Jamie Pyatt. Pyatt – who had broken the story that Prince Harry had dressed in Nazi regalia for a fancy dress party – was detained on suspicion of paying

---

* In the House of Commons register of interests, Blunkett disclosed that in July 2011 News International paid his family an undisclosed fee for 'intrusion'. In January 2012, the former Home Secretary registered that he was on a rolling six-month contract worth £49,500 advising News International one day a month on 'corporate social responsibility'.

† 'The FBI made it perfectly clear that if the British police drop the ball on this they will pick it up and run with it,' said one legal source familiar with the US investigation.[2]

bribes to police. That arrest had caused serious concern among *Sun* journalists because it suggested that the management was now actively seeking to turn over reporters to Scotland Yard. One colleague commented: 'They have opened up a Pandora's box.'[3] At a meeting with staff, the *Sun*'s editor, Dominic Mohan, a former showbusiness reporter who had once mockingly thanked Vodafone for its help on stories,* reassured staff that Rupert Murdoch had personally committed himself to the paper's future.

As the Metropolitan Police increasingly focused on Operation Elveden, the *Sun*'s worst fears began to be realized. At dawn on 28 January 2012, around forty police officers arrested four *Sun* staff at their homes and searched the paper's offices in Wapping. The arrested men were senior managers: the news editor, Chris Pharo; the former managing editor, Graham Dudman; Mike Sullivan, the crime editor; and Fergus Shanahan, the executive editor (who in 2009 had described Tom Watson as an 'unsavoury creature lurking in the shadows'). To the fury of *Sun* journalists, an anonymous member of News Corp's Management and Standards Committee told the media the arrests were part of a process of 'draining the swamp'.[4]

A fortnight later, on Saturday 11 February, the Metropolitan Police were back, arresting five staff, again on suspicion of bribing public officials: deputy editor Geoff Webster; chief reporter John Kay; chief foreign correspondent Nick Parker; picture editor John Edwards; and deputy news editor John Sturgis. Three other people were also detained: a Surrey Police officer, a member of the armed forces and a Ministry of Defence employee.

The police were usually lauded by the *Sun*, who sponsored the police bravery awards, but not this time. On Monday 13 February,

---

* When editing the *Sun*'s showbusiness column 'Bizarre', Dominic Mohan had mentioned mobile phone security at a party for the most bogus showbusiness stories, the Shaftas. On 1 May 2002, the *Guardian*'s media diary reported a snippet headlined: 'Ring, a ring a story': 'How appropriate that the most glamorous event in the showbusiness calendar should be sponsored by a phone company. Mohan went on to thank "Vodafone's lack of security" for the *Mirror*'s showbusiness exclusives. Whatever does he mean?' Mohan later told the Leveson Inquiry that he could not be 100 per cent sure that stories which had appeared in the *Sun*'s 'Bizarre' column had not come from phone hacking.

the paper – presumably with Rupert Murdoch's blessing – carried an article by its long-time political pundit Trevor Kavanagh headed: 'Witch-hunt has put us behind ex-Soviet states on Press freedom'. Outraged, Kavanagh complained that the arrests had infringed the journalists' privacy:

> Wives and children have been humiliated as up to twenty officers at a time rip up floorboards and sift through intimate possessions, love letters and entirely private documents . . .
>
> Their alleged crimes? To act as journalists have acted on all news-papers through the ages, unearthing stories that shape our lives, often obstructed by those who prefer to operate behind closed doors.
>
> A huge operation driven by politicians threatens the very founda-tions of a free Press. Before it is too late, should we not be asking where all this is likely to lead?

Sensing perhaps the demoralization of his journalists, Rupert Mur-doch flew into London on 19 February and, to cheers in the *Sun*'s newsroom, announced the launch of a *Sun on Sunday*. The euphoria was short-lived.

Making her second of three appearances before the Leveson Inquiry, on 27 February, Sue Akers steelily pointed out that the bribes under investigation by the Yard were not for stories in the public interest but for 'salacious gossip' and that the *Sun* had tried to cover its tracks by channelling payments to friends and relatives of public servants. Damningly, she said the police had found a 'network of cor-rupted officials':

> The payments have been made not only to police officers but to a wide range of public officials. There are other categories as well as police: military, health, government, prison and others. This suggests that payments were being made to public officials who were in all areas of public life. I have said that the current assessment is that it reveals a network of corrupted officials. When I say 'network' I don't necessarily mean that the officials are in contact with each other; more that the journalists had a network upon which to call at various strategic places across public life.

There also appears to have been a culture at the *Sun* of illegal payments, and systems have been created to facilitate those payments, whilst hiding the identity of the officials receiving the money.

At Scotland Yard, 169 police and support officers were working on the three linked investigations into News International, making it the biggest criminal inquiry in the country.

The Met knew that the phone hacking, computer hacking and bribes would not have been uncovered if journalists, lawyers and politicians had believed its repeated assurances that its original investigation had been adequate. On 7 February, the police abandoned its defence against the Max Mosley-funded judicial review and admitted it had behaved unlawfully towards the claimants – John Prescott, Chris Bryant, Brian Paddick, Ben Jackson and HJK – by failing to inform them they were victims of Glenn Mulcaire. It apologized and agreed to pay their costs. Lord Prescott welcomed the decision, saying: 'Time and again I was told by the Metropolitan Police that I had not been targeted by Rupert Murdoch's *News of the World*.'[5]

Operation Elveden reached further into the *Sun* and government departments, Her Majesty's Customs and Revenue, the National Health Service, the armed forces and the police. On 19 April 2012, detectives arrested Duncan Larcombe, royal editor of the *Sun*, on suspicion of conspiracy to corrupt and conspiracy to cause misconduct in a public office. On the same day, police arrested a member of the armed forces. Over coming months (see Appendices), Neil Millard, a *Sun* reporter, and an unidentified 36-year-old male *Sun* journalist, were held on suspicion of corrupting public officials.

At the same time, officers from Operation Tuleta began to investigate suspicions that *Sun* journalists had been involved in the downloading of data from stolen mobile phones. They arrested *Sun* reporter Rhodri Phillips, Nick Parker, the chief foreign correspondent, and an unidentified 37-year-old male *Sun* journalist, on suspicion of handling stolen goods.

Tuleta was examining more than fifty computers and other electronic devices, including those of the former Prime Minister, Gordon Brown, and the former Labour aide Derek Draper. Ironically, it was

Draper who had received the rumour-mongering emails sent by Damian McBride which so damaged Brown's administration, months before News International decisively switched to the Conservatives – the party which was prepared to grant its parent company complete control of Sky. Another computer being examined belonged to the Labour MP Peter Hain, the former Secretary of State for Northern Ireland.

By July, Tuleta was investigating '101 separate allegations of data intrusion including allegations of phone hacking, computer hacking and improper access to banking, medical and other personal records'.

Working from information supplied by News Corp's Management and Standards Committee, the Met's inquiries began reaching into other newspaper groups. Operation Elveden (see Appendix 2) arrested a former reporter at the *Daily Mirror*, Greig Box Turnbull; the *Sunday Mirror*'s crime reporter, Justin Penrose, and Tom Savage, deputy news editor of the *Daily Star Sunday*. The corruption inquiry was spreading into Trinity Mirror and Express Newspapers.

Sue Akers told the Leveson Inquiry on 20 July:

> The police intention has always been to go where the evidence takes us. Our ongoing investigation has more recently revealed that in some cases, a public official has been identified not only in relation to accepting payments from NI, but also in relation to payments from other newspapers. In one case the public official was a prison officer at a high security prison during the period when the payments were made and related stories published. The individual's former partner appears to have facilitated the payments into their bank accounts.

In total, detectives had arrested thirty-eight News International staff. They had also arrested at least seven current or ex-police officers and at least eight suspects linked to the armed forces, Ministry of Defence, Prison Service, Customs & Revenue and the National Health Service. Five people were suspected of being 'conduits' for illegal payments.

While the police investigation continued, the Murdochs had to face the verdict of others. On 1 May, the House of Commons Culture Committee published its report, 'News International and Phone

Hacking', damning Murdoch and News International, and criticizing the police and CPS. Keir Starmer and John Yates, while not involved in the key events at the time, the MPs said, 'both bear culpability for failing to ensure that the evidence held by the Metropolitan Police was properly investigated in the years afterwards . . .'. The MPs accused Les Hinton, Colin Myler and Tom Crone of misleading them (which they denied in public statements).

Witheringly, the committee described Rupert Murdoch as 'not a fit person to exercise the stewardship of a major international company', a conclusion potentially of interest to Ofcom. Rupert, the report noted, had 'excellent powers of recall and grasp of detail when it suited him', adding: 'On the basis of the facts and evidence before the committee we conclude that, if at all relevant times Rupert Murdoch did not take steps to become fully informed about phone hacking, he turned a blind eye and exhibited wilful blindness.' The five Labour MPs and the Liberal Democrat, Adrian Sanders, approved that verdict on Rupert, but it was opposed by the four Conservative members, who described it as 'partisan'.

James Murdoch, the committee said, had demonstrated 'wilful ignorance' about what had been going on at the *News of the World*, which 'clearly raises questions of competence'.

On News Corp, the committee said it was guilty of 'huge failings of corporate governance':

> Corporately, the *News of the World* and News International misled the committee about the true nature and extent of the internal investigations they professed to have carried out in relation to phone hacking; by making statements they would have known were not fully truthful; and by failing to disclose documents which would have helped expose the truth.

In contrast to its attack on the Culture Committee's report in 2010, News Corp accepted some of the findings – but it could not countenance criticism of its leaders. It said in a statement:

> Hard truths have emerged from the select committee report: that there was serious wrongdoing at the *News of the World*; that our

response to the wrongdoing was too slow and too defensive; and that some of our employees misled the select committee in 2009. News Corporation regrets, however, that the select committee analysis of the factual record was followed by some commentary that we, and indeed some members of the committee, consider unjustified and highly partisan. These remarks divided the committee along party lines.[6]

By now the Murdochs had begun to distance themselves from their newspapers. On 29 February, News Corp announced that James was standing down from the chairmanship of News International. On 3 April he gave up the chairmanship of BSkyB,* so that, he said, 'there is no false conflation with events at a separate organisation'.

The corporate retreat continued over the summer. On 28 June, News Corp announced it would split itself into two companies – an entertainment division and a publishing division. The entertainment division, with revenues of $23 billion, would contain the fast-growing 20th Century Fox, Fox, Sky and other TV networks, while the sluggish publishing division, with revenues of $8 billion, would contain HarperCollins, the American and Australian newspapers and News International. While Rupert Murdoch said he would chair both companies, significantly News Corp added that he was not planning to become the chief executive of the publishing division. The phone hacking scandal had broken up News Corp.

On 20 July, the 81-year-old took a further step back, when he resigned from his directorships of the News International companies NI Group Ltd, News Corp Investments and Times Newspaper Holdings. The media commentator Steve Hewlett said: 'For Rupert Murdoch to make this move away from these titles, which he has invested forty years of his life in, is plainly significant.'[7]

*

* On 20 September 2012, the media regulator Ofcom said Sky passed its 'fit and proper' test and would retain its broadcasting licence. However Ofcom savaged James Murdoch's record on phone hacking, saying that his behaviour was 'difficult to comprehend and ill-judged', raising questions about his 'competence'.

As it continued its probing in the spring, the Leveson Inquiry demanded the release of contacts between the government and News Corp and – seemingly in an act of revenge against the Cameron administration for opening the inquiry – Rupert Murdoch released them. Out in the open, finally, were the secret contacts which took place behind closed doors and away from the public's glare between a powerful company and craven ministers. On 24 April, the day James appeared before Lord Leveson, the inquiry released some of the private correspondence between the Department of Culture, Media and Sport and Fred Michel, including his receipt of information about the market-sensitive Sky deal. There were gasps in Court 73 as Robert Jay read out passages such as Fred Michel's quoting of Jeremy Hunt's 'we will get there in the end' to 'Managed to get some infos on the plans for tomorrow (although absolutely illegal!) . . .' and James Murdoch's response to Hunt's refusal to meet him ('You must be f***ing joking').

James maintained there was nothing wrong with the level of contacts: News Corp, he said, had been simply wishing to put its case to the government, while Hunt had always behaved appropriately. 'He,' James said of Hunt, 'only took the advice of Ofcom and the OFT at every turn.'

James dismissed any suggestion that there had been a carve-up. News Corp's newspapers had not backed the Conservatives because they were more likely to support the Sky takeover, he insisted: 'We never made a crass calculation about what the newspapers did.'

Following the disclosure of the contacts between the government and News Corp in James Murdoch's evidence, Labour called for Hunt's resignation. Forced to give a statement to the Commons the following day, 25 April, the Culture Secretary admitted things had gone awry – and announced the resignation of his adviser, Adam Smith. Hunt maintained that he had acted properly, saying: 'Throughout I have followed due process, seeking the advice of independent regulators – something I did not have to do – and after careful consideration, acting on their advice.'

He added:

Transcripts of conversations and texts published yesterday between my special adviser, Adam Smith, and a News Corporation representative have been alleged to indicate that there was a back channel through which News Corporation was able to influence my decisions. That is categorically not the case. However the volume and tone of those communications were clearly not appropriate in a quasi-judicial process, and today Adam Smith has resigned as my special adviser. Although he accepts that he overstepped the mark on this occasion, I want to set on record that I believe that he did so unintentionally and did not believe that he was doing anything more than giving advice on process.

Hunt said that Adam Smith's role as a go-between between the department and News Corp had been approved by the department's most senior civil servant, Jonathan Stephens, the Permanent Secretary. However, the following day when he appeared before the Commons Public Accounts Committee, Stephens refused ten times to say that he had approved the arrangement.

On 25 and 26 April, Rupert Murdoch appeared at the Leveson Inquiry – the second time he had submitted himself to a public examination in Britain. As at his first appearance, before the Culture Committee in July, he could not remember key details, peppering his testimony with 'I do not recall' and 'I did not ask.' To the amusement of Murdoch-watchers, he strenuously denied that he used his newspapers to advance his business interests ('We have never pushed our commercial interests in our newspapers') or that he sought to influence politicians ('I have never asked a Prime Minister for anything').

He also used the occasion to settle old scores, criticizing former editors who had later questioned his methods. He said that Andrew Neil 'seems to have found it very profitable to get up and spread lies about me', while former *Sun* editor David Yelland 'was drunk all the time he was at the *Sun*, which we didn't notice'. Colin Myler 'would not have been my choice' for editor of the *News of the World*.

Asked by Robert Jay, 'Were it not for the *Guardian*, do you accept, the phone hacking story would never had entered the public domain?', Rupert mischievously replied: 'I don't know. The *Independent* seemed to be pretty active.' Tackled on this book's statement that he had contacted Tony Blair to ask Gordon Brown to call off Tom Watson, he interrupted, to laughter: 'I'm not planning on reading it.' But no, he said, he had not contacted Blair.

Finally, Rupert admitted there had been a cover-up at the *News of the World* – but he said it was an internal cover-up which stopped him from learning what had happened. There was a 'clever lawyer' who had been a drinking buddy of the journalists and 'one or two very strong characters' who prevented the truth about the scale of hacking from coming out, he said. (Tom Crone later said: 'It is perhaps no coincidence that the two people he has identified in relation to his cover-up allegations are the same two people who pointed out that his son's testimony to the parliamentary select committee last year was inaccurate.')

What he said, however – the usual denials and memory loss – was less important than Robert Jay's disclosure that during the Sky bid Jeremy Hunt and Adam Smith and News Corp's James Murdoch and Fred Michel had exchanged more than 1,000 emails and text messages, including 799 text messages between Adam Smith and Fred Michel.

The government had been rocked again, not just by the disclosure of the emails but the vehemence and anger with which they were reported by non-Murdoch newspapers, who could see again all too painfully just how special was the relationship between Murdoch and the government compared with what they once believed had been their own warm contacts.

Despite apparently clear breaches of the ministerial code, which required ministers to take responsibility for their special advisers, David Cameron refused to sack Jeremy Hunt or to set up an inquiry into his conduct; instead he said the minister would clear his reputation at his own appearance at the inquiry. Labour claimed that the Prime Minister was using his cabinet minister as a firewall – to protect himself.

On 31 May, when Hunt finally appeared, the inquiry released the text messages between him and James Murdoch and other government ministers which strongly suggested that the minister had been privately backing News Corp. They included Hunt's text to James Murdoch on 3 March: 'Thanks think we got the right solution', the behind-the-scenes messages between Hunt and George Osborne, and Hunt's text to James Murdoch congratulating him on European clearance of the bid on the day he took charge of the semi-judicial process. Hunt's texts to News Corp had been sent from his mobile phone and his emails from his private Gmail account, putting them both out of the reach of civil servants.

Hunt accepted that the level of contact between Adam Smith and Fred Michel was inappropriate but again denied Smith had been an unofficial back channel. The Culture Secretary said:

> The context of our approach on this was that we had inherited responsibility for a deal where we believed we were at serious risk of judicial review by News Corporation over the way that the Government [Vince Cable] had handled the bid, and I was absolutely determined to make sure that it was an open and transparent process and a process that was fair to them.

But he added that 'we weren't expecting 542 text messages to Mr Smith, including, I think – to my astonishment – 35 text messages in just two days at one point in the process and however many, 140 or so, phone calls.'

Within minutes of Hunt's five-hour evidence ending, David Cameron gave him his backing and said there was no need for an inquiry.

With Cameron refusing to jettison his Culture Secretary, the wider issue became Rupert Murdoch's interference in British politics.

The inquiry heard from three former prime ministers – Tony Blair, Gordon Brown and John Major.

Blair, a former barrister well versed in giving technically accurate answers which left room for the sceptical to form their own impressions, denied he had done a deal with Murdoch to lay off media policy in return for his newspapers' support. Appearing on 28 May, Blair said: 'We would never have given assurances to Mr Murdoch or anybody else that we were not going to change policy without their permission.'

He denied that he had agreed a deal with Murdoch at Hayman Island in 1995, or on an earlier occasion, at Mosimann's in London on 15 September 1994, when he had dined with Rupert Murdoch and Andrew Neil, the editor of the *Sunday Times*. Neil had written in his book *Full Disclosure*: 'Blair indicated that media ownership rules would not be onerous under Labour, Rupert that his newspapers were not wedded to the Tories.'

Jay asked: 'Is it possible you said that?'

Blair replied: 'I think "onerous" is not the way I would have put it. I can't specifically remember what was said, but it's perfectly possible, if that issue came up, I would have said: "That's not an issue we're going to be taking on."'

Blair said later that if the government had introduced media reform 'everything else would have been pushed to the side, and it would have been a huge battle with no guarantee of winning'.

Asked whether he had phoned Brown in the hope that Brown would ask Tom Watson to back off, he replied: 'Absolutely not true.'

But he said that after leaving office his 'working relationship' with Murdoch had improved. This was not surprising since in an interview with *Vogue* published in September 2011, Murdoch's wife, Wendi Deng, had let slip that Tony Blair was godfather to their nine-year-old daughter, Grace. *Hello!*'s coverage of the ceremony on the banks of the river Jordan in March 2010 had pictured the official godparents, the actors Nicole Kidman and Hugh Jackman, but not Blair, described by Deng as one of their 'closest friends'. His role as godfather had remained a closely guarded secret until the interview. Initially, Blair's office had refused to deny or confirm he was a godparent.

Gordon Brown, appearing on 11 June, restated his view that the Conservatives had got into bed with News Corp on media issues, including Sky. Jay asked the former prime minister: 'Did you sense, in your dealings with News International, that they were trying to persuade you to pursue media policies which were favourable to their interests but contrary to the public interest?'

Brown implied that there was no need for the Murdochs to lobby, because they had announced their commercial agenda 'in public'.

John Major flatly contradicted Murdoch's assertion that he had never asked a prime minister for anything. Giving evidence to the inquiry on 12 June, Major said that while he was prime minister, Murdoch had, at a dinner on 2 February 1997, asked him to change government policy on Europe: 'If we couldn't change our European policies, his papers could not and would not support the Conservative government.' Major added: 'As I recall, he used the word "we" when referring to his newspapers. He didn't make the usual nod towards editorial independence.'

On 15 June, David Cameron appeared before Lord Leveson and promptly demonstrated his faulty memory. (The *Independent* the next morning headlined its front page: 'Camnesia' with a list of his comments: 'I don't recall . . . I don't remember . . . I can't remember every conversation I've ever had . . . I don't really remember the specifics . . . I don't recall the specifics . . . I can't remember the exact sequence of events . . . That's not something I recall directly . . . I don't recall exactly the conversations that took place . . . The issue here is I don't particularly remember this note . . . I didn't recall its existence . . . I don't recall discussing it with him . . . I don't recall any discussions about it . . . I've obviously racked my brains to try and remember.'

Among the twenty topics he could not remember were: whether he discussed the BBC or Ofcom with James Murdoch at lunch in May 2009; what he discussed with James Murdoch at the George members' club in September 2009 when he learned the *Sun* was about to support the Conservatives; how many conversations he had with Rebekah Brooks about Andy Coulson; and what Nick Clegg had said to him about Coulson before he took him into Downing Street.

As part of his evidence, Cameron disclosed that while he was in opposition he had met Brooks nineteen times, James Murdoch fifteen times and Rupert Murdoch ten times. But he said on the links between the Conservatives and the Murdochs before the general election: 'There was no overt deal for support, there was no covert deal, there were no nods and winks. There was a Conservative politician, me, trying to win over proprietors, but not trading policy for that support.'

Often, the Prime Minister looked pained and embarrassed.

*

Six years after staging the raid on Clive Goodman, on 15 May 2012, the Crown Prosecution Service brought the first criminal charges in the affair. Rebekah Brooks and five other News International staff were accused of mounting a cover-up in the days following the Milly Dowler story in July 2011. All six were charged with conspiracy to pervert the course of justice. Specifically, the police accused Brooks and her personal assistant Cheryl Carter of conspiring to remove seven boxes of material from the archive of News International. Brooks, her husband Charlie, Ms Carter, Mark Hanna, head of group security at NI, her chauffeur Paul Edwards and Daryl Jorsling, a free-lance security guard, were accused of conspiring 'to conceal material from officers of the Metropolitan Police Service'. The Brookses, Hanna, Edwards and Jorsling allegedly plotted to conceal documents, computers and other electronic equipment from the police.

Within hours of the charges being announced, the Brookses were holding a press conference in front of banks of TV cameras and journalists. With his wife by his side, Charlie said: 'I feel today is an attempt to use me and others as scapegoats, the effect of which is to ratchet up the pressure on my wife, who I believe is the subject of a witch hunt. There are 172 police officers, about the equivalent of eight murder squads, working on this, so it doesn't surprise me that the pressure is on to prosecute, no matter how weak the cases will be.' Rebekah expressed her anger 'that those close to me have unfairly been dragged into this'. She added that the prosecution was a 'weak and unjust decision'.

On 30 May, Strathclyde Police turned their attentions to Andy Coulson, arresting him at 6.30 a.m. and driving him to Glasgow where late at night he was charged with committing perjury during Tommy Sheridan's trial in 2010. Unlike other alleged offences during the scandal, Coulson was alleged to have committed the offence while working for the Prime Minister.

On 24 July, the Crown Prosecution Service brought phone hacking charges against seven of the *News of the World*'s senior staff: Rebekah Brooks, Andy Coulson, Greg Miskiw, James Weatherup, Ian Edmondson, Stuart Kuttner and Neville Thurlbeck. They were accused of conspiring to hack the phones of 600 people between 2000 and 2006. They were also accused of conspiring to hack the phones of a combination of a pool of twenty-three newsworthy individuals, including Brad Pitt and Angelina Jolie – the first time they had been named as victims – Sienna Miller, Jude Law and David Blunkett. Specifically, Brooks was charged with plotting to hack the phone of Milly Dowler and the Fire Brigades Union leader Andy Gilchrist, the latter between 3 December 2002 and 22 January 2003, covering the first week of her editorship of the *Sun*.

Glenn Mulcaire was charged with conspiring to hack the phones of Milly Dowler, Andy Gilchrist, Delia Smith and the former Home Secretary Charles Clarke.

In a statement, Coulson said he would fight the allegations: 'At the *News of the World* we worked on behalf of the victims of crime, particularly violent crime, and the idea that I would sit in my office dreaming up schemes to undermine investigations is simply untrue.' Brooks said: 'I did not authorize, nor was I aware of, phone hacking under my editorship.'

Saying he would clear his reputation, Thurlbeck added: 'I have always operated under the guidance and advice of News International's lawyers and under the instructions of the newspaper's editors.'

Prosecutors cleared the *News of the World* reporter Ross Hall, a sports reporter, Raoul Simons, a *Times* journalist, and Terenia Taras, a former partner of Greg Miskiw.

Chris Bryant MP said: 'People thought we'd seen it all already. Actually, we're still only at the beginning of Act 5. It's not until all these prosecutions are completed will we know the full truth.'[8]

The trials are expected to take place at the end of 2013.

In September 2012, David Cameron promoted Jeremy Hunt to Secretary of State for Health.

24

A Corrupt Business

I would argue that Rupert Murdoch with his take-no-prisoners attitude to journalism created the kind of newsroom climate in which hacking and other things were done with impunity on an industrial scale

– Andrew Neil

What began with the battle of Prince William's wounded knee had turned into the worst scandal in British public life in decades, touching almost every pillar of British society: the royal family, the government, the civil service, the courts, the police, the Crown Prosecution Service and, of course, the media.

All News International's titles and many others on Fleet Street had been tainted, but two facts separated Rupert Murdoch's newspapers from others: the hard evidence and the cover-up. When detectives raided Glenn Mulcaire's home on 8 August 2006 they found 11,000 pages of notes indicating that the *News of the World* had been systematically engaged in a campaign of illegal phone hacking. The Metropolitan Police failed to tackle that properly for five years, until 2011. Rather than a fearless, impartial investigator, it was meek and malleable. Its senior officers were lunched by the newspaper executives they should have been investigating and, both before and after leaving office, eagerly accepted their largesse. Less senior officers have now been arrested for directly accepting corrupt payments for the supply of stories. Scotland Yard's reputation for competence and probity has been badly damaged; urgent questions remain about the murder of Daniel Morgan (and in Scotland about the conviction of Tommy Sheridan, which looks increasingly unsafe).

But Scotland Yard was not the only force to fail. If Devon and Cornwall's inquiry in 2002 had succeeded, if Surrey Police had prosecuted the phone hacking identified that same year, or if, the following year, the Information Commissioner's Office had prosecuted the most prolific law-breaking journalists, thousands of people might have been saved from the illegal intrusions into their lives – intrusions which were seldom in the public interest and which often carried a high personal price. Deliberately denuded of the power to levy fines or seize documents, the Press Complaints Commission proved itself inadequate to its task.

Many institutions failed – but there were individual failures too. The holders of high office failed in their duty to protect the public:

- the Scotland Yard detectives who ignored the bulk of the wrongdoing
- the PCC chairwoman who did not understand how the press operated
- the Assistant Commissioner who did not open the bags of evidence
- the Director of Public Prosecutions who did not read all the paperwork
- the London mayor who did not challenge his police force
- the Queen's solicitors who knowingly acted for a lying corporation
- the national newspaper editors and BBC executives who avoided the story
- the cabinet minister who did not take into account a history of broken promises when backing a £7.8 billion takeover
- the Prime Minister who did not listen to warnings about his director of communications, and whose government prostrated itself in front of a foreign tycoon

Incompetence alone cannot explain all of these failures. Fear allowed the phone hacking scandal to happen – fear of public humiliation for an indiscretion, fear of battling against an unremittingly hostile press, fear of not winning that glowing electoral endorsement. In a press whose political leanings were fixed – to the left the *Mirror*, the middle the *Independent* and *Guardian*, and the right the *Daily Mail*, *Express* and *Telegraph* – Rupert Murdoch decisively held the balance of power. He was the ultimate floating voter and five successive governments courted his support. All prime ministers from Margaret Thatcher to David Cameron turned a blind eye when they should have intervened.

From the start of his career in 1950s Australia, Murdoch manipulated politicians and broke rules and promises to accumulate money and power. It may not be possible to prove beyond reasonable doubt that he knew about the wrongdoing in Britain, but many, including the authors, think he is, at best, guilty of wilful blindness. As the head of the company, he shaped its culture. While he depicted phone hacking as an aberration set apart from an otherwise virtuous organization, seasoned Murdoch-watchers identified it as part of a pattern – the greatest manifestation of a win-at-all-costs culture which bent and broke the rules at will, as the former *Sunday Times* editor Andrew Neil pointed out:

> You create a climate in which people think it's alright to do certain things. And I would argue that Rupert Murdoch with his take-no-prisoners attitude to journalism – the end will justify the means, do whatever it takes – created the kind of newsroom climate in which hacking and other things were done with impunity on an industrial scale.[1]

In a sense, what is most revealing is not that his company was breaking the law at will and paying off police and officials, but its prolonged and determined cover-up. In 2006 News International's representatives blocked police officers executing a search warrant and withheld important evidence. In 2007, Murdoch's close executive, Les Hinton, failed to tell the Commons Culture Committee about Goodman's claims that hacking was routine, and failed to call in the police to investigate those claims; instead he sanctioned a large confidential payment to Goodman. When alerted to evidence of more widespread wrongdoing in 2008, with the 'For Neville' email, James Murdoch did not correct Hinton's testimony, nor inform the police. Instead, he authorized another large hush payment, to Gordon Taylor. In 2009, under James Murdoch's chairmanship, News International impugned the reputation of an honest journalist, repeatedly misled Parliament, surveilled an MP, began a smear exercise and intimidated and lied. In 2010, executives ordered the systematic destruction of evidence, ordered surveillance on lawyers challenging the company, and secretly paid off another high-profile victim, Max Clifford. News International fought civil claimants all the way, denying everything they could, at every turn. Even if the Murdochs did only learn of the extent of the criminality at the end of 2010, as they claim, they did not then inform the police, nor correct four years of misleading evidence to MPs, nor apologize to journalists and the public. Only journalistic, parliamentary, police and judicial inquiries prised out the truth. At all times until very recently – and then arguably only under the pressing need to avoid the possible jailing of its directors – News Corp acted to conceal rather than uncover its past.

By dogmatically sticking to the lie of the rogue reporter defence for five years, the Murdochs have ultimately paid a far higher price: the resignation of many senior executives; the closure of a best-selling newspaper and the loss of 150 loyal journalists; the failure to take over the whole of Britain's biggest television network; the arrest of most of the most senior journalists on the *Sun*; at least $224 million (and counting) in compensation, legal fees, internal investigations and redundancy payments; some of the worst publicity imaginable for a global corporation; and shareholder revolts which threaten the family's control of News Corp. Perhaps worst of all, they have lost most of their lucrative power to influence British politics and policing. Everyone who kow-towed before, who pushed for a place at their side, is going to be wary even of being seen in their company now. Like the paper they closed, the Murdochs have become toxic.

And it is going to get worse. Phone hacking cases are still mounting. By September 2012, 174 individuals had begun new civil lawsuits against the *News of the World* and a further 137 claims were before News International's compensation scheme. Criminal trials of Murdoch's British executives, including the Prime Minister's friends Rebekah Brooks and Andy Coulson, are expected to lead to fresh bouts of bad publicity, further disclosures and, possibly, lengthy custodial sentences for former employees. Other newsgathering techniques could be even more troublesome. An increasing number of investigative journalists and parliamentarians are looking at other forms of intrusive surveillance, former contracted private investigators and staff members are speaking out, there is an ongoing FBI investigation in the United States – and the British police are investigating the 'network of corrupted officials' run by the *Sun*. In the margins of the scandal, whispered voices speak about the involvement of rogue intelligence officers, secret political campaigns and commercial espionage. Computer hacking, centred on the activities of politicians and intelligence agents in Northern Ireland, along with the theft and downloading of politicians' mobile phones, could yet provide the murkiest chapter.

Put simply, the phone hacking scandal is about corruption by power. Some of Murdoch's enforcers departed from the company line (it's all about business) and pursued personal agendas and vendettas, even threatening minor politicians and storming into the offices of smaller newspapers. Their arrogance was so stratospheric they discussed their crimes even though they knew they were being recorded. They thought they could destroy the evidence, threaten and cover up; they thought they were cleverer than everyone else – they thought they were untouchable. From the criminal underworld to the headquarters of London's police force, from the decks of yachts in the Mediterranean to farmhouses in the Cotswolds and the deep-carpeted rooms of Downing Street, they had spun an invisible web of connections and corruption. They had privileged access to government ministers, state secrets, tax, health and vehicle data, to the records of phone companies and banks, to the intimate personal information of members of the public. They listened to phone messages, of course, but they also blagged, bribed, spied and bullied, and imposed their will through blackmail, corruption and intimidation. The names of their agents spoke of the darkness: Silent Shadow and Shadowmenuk. Rupert Murdoch was not running a normal business, but a shadow state. Now exposed to the daylight, it has been publicly humbled, its apparatus partially dismantled and its executives in retreat, at least for the moment. It stands shaken and ostensibly apologetic but it is still there, and Rupert Murdoch is still in charge.

Appendix 1 – Confirmed or Suspected Phone Hacking Victims

NAME/RELEVANCE AT TIME OF HACKING

Prince William
Prince Harry
Jamie Lowther-Pinkerton, royal aide
Paddy Harverson, royal aide
Helen Asprey, royal aide
Sarah Ferguson, ex-royal
James Hewitt, former boyfriend of Princess Diana
Paul Burrell, butler to Princess Diana
Guy Pelly, friend of Prince Harry
Frederick Windsor, royal
Cherie Blair, wife of Prime Minister Tony Blair
Alastair Campbell, communications director to Tony Blair
Carole Caplin, fitness adviser to Cherie Blair
John Prescott, Labour Deputy Prime Minister
Joan Hammell, chief of staff to John Prescott
Joyce Matheson, aide to John Prescott
Tracey Temple, girlfriend of John Prescott
David Blunkett, Labour Home Secretary
Matthew Doyle, aide to David Blunkett
Sally King, friend of David Blunkett
Andrew King, husband of Sally King
John Anderson, father of Sally King
Charles Clarke, Labour Home Secretary
Stephen Byers, Labour Trade and Industry Secretary

Tessa Jowell, Labour Culture Secretary

David Mills, lawyer and Tessa Jowell's husband

Denis MacShane, Labour minister

Joan Smith, girlfriend of Denis MacShane

Elliot Morley, Labour minister

Chris Bryant, Labour MP

George Galloway, Labour MP

Claire Ward, Labour MP

Neil Kinnock, former Labour leader

Glenys Kinnock, Labour MEP and wife of Neil Kinnock

Hilary Perrin, Labour regional organizer for London

Janet Woolf, former girlfriend of Labour Mayor of London Ken
Livingstone

George Osborne, Conservative MP

Natalie Rowe, former friend of George Osborne

Boris Johnson, Conservative MP

Lord Blencathra, Conservative Chief Whip

Emma Noble, former daughter-in-law of former Conservative
Prime Minister Sir John Major

Mark Oaten, Liberal Democrat MP

Simon Hughes, Liberal Democrat MP

Tommy Sheridan, Scottish Socialist MP

Anne Colvin, witness in perjury trial of Tommy Sheridan

Nigel Farrage, leader of UK Independence Party

Ian Blair, Commissioner, Metropolitan Police

John Yates, Assistant Commissioner, Metropolitan Police

Andy Hayman, Assistant Commissioner, Metropolitan Police

Brian Paddick, Deputy Assistant Commissioner, Metropolitan Police

Ali Dizaei, Commander, Metropolitan Police

Mike Fuller, Commander, Metropolitan Police

David Cook, Detective Chief Superintendent, Metropolitan Police

Jacqui Hames, wife of David Cook

Yousef Bhailok, secretary-general of Muslim Council of Britain

Andy Gilchrist, trade union leader

Gordon Taylor, trade union leader

Jo Armstrong, lawyer

John Hewison, lawyer
Michael Mansfield, lawyer
Graham Shear, lawyer
Robin Winskell, lawyer
Kirsty Brimelow, lawyer
Sir Richard Branson, entrepreneur
Gary Hersham, estate agent
Brad Pitt, actor
Angelina Jolie, actress
Jude Law, actor
Sadie Frost, former wife of Jude Law
Ciara Parkes, publicist to Jude Law
Ben Jackson, personal assistant to Jude Law
Sienna Miller, actress
Hugh Grant, actor
Jemima Khan, girlfriend of Hugh Grant
Darren Day, actor
Sid Owen, actor
Lacey Turner, actress
Laila Rouass, actress
Cornelia Crisan, friend of actor Ralph Fiennes
Edward Blum, film director
Steve Coogan, comedian
Lisa Gower, former partner of Steve Coogan
Dan Lichters, friend of comedian Michael Barrymore
Bobby Davro, comedian
Trudi Nankeville, wife of Bobby Davro
Sir Paul McCartney, singer
Heather Mills, former wife of Paul McCartney
Charlotte Church, singer
Maria Church, mother of Charlotte Church
James Church, father of Charlotte Church
Richard Reardon, Charlotte Church's priest
James Blunt, singer
Pete Doherty, singer
Kerry Katona, singer

Brian McFadden, singer and ex-husband of Kerry Katona
Claire Powell, agent of Kerry Katona
Meg Matthews, ex-wife of singer Noel Gallagher
Lisa Brash, former girlfriend of singer Robbie Williams
Kelly Hoppen, interior designer
Tara Palmer-Tomkinson, socialite
Elle Macpherson, model
James Burke, model
Laura Rooney, dancer
Delia Smith, chef
Max Clifford, publicist
Nicola Phillips, PA to Max Clifford
Michelle Milburn, theatre agent
Edwina Pitman, art gallery worker
Alan McGee, record label manager
Chris Tarrant, TV presenter
Ulrika Jonsson, TV presenter
Lance Gerrard-Wright, husband of Ulrika Jonsson
Dannii Minogue, TV presenter
Brendan Minogue, brother of Dannii Minogue
Leslie Ash, TV presenter
Lee Chapman, husband of Leslie Ash
John Leslie, TV presenter
Abi Titmuss, model and girlfriend of John Leslie
Andy Gray, TV presenter
Suzanne Dando, former girlfriend of Andy Gray
Jamie Theakston, TV presenter
Matthew Robertson, husband of TV presenter Davina McCall
Lauren Pope, TV personality
Ruth Badger, TV show contestant
Jade Goody, TV show contestant
Jeff Brazier, boyfriend of Jade Goody
Simon Bridger, friend of Jade Goody
Danny Hayward, friend of Jade Goody
Kate Jackson, TV producer
Duncan Foster, TV director

Rebekah Brooks, newspaper editor
Brendan Montague, freelance journalist
Kelvin Mackenzie, journalist, the *Sun*
Daniel Boffey, journalist, the *Observer*
Ted Hynds, journalist
Tom Rowland, freelance journalist
Dennis Rice, journalist, *Mail on Sunday*
Amanda Hobbs, wife of Dennis Rice
Louise Artimati, sister of Dennis Rice
John Blake, publisher
David Davies, football executive
Sven-Göran Eriksson, football manager
Wayne Rooney, footballer
Paul Stretford, agent to Wayne Rooney
Ryan Giggs, footballer
Sol Campbell, footballer
Ashley Cole, footballer
Peter Crouch, footballer
Abigail Clancy, wife of Peter Crouch
Kieron Dyer, footballer
Jermaine Jenas, footballer
Noel Whelan, footballer
Chris Kiwomya, footballer
Neil Ruddock, footballer
Paul Gascoigne, footballer
Jimmy Gardner, friend of Paul Gascoigne
Ted Beckham, father of footballer David Beckham
Michael McGuire, football agent
Phil Hughes, agent for footballer George Best
Alex Best, former wife of George Best
Calum Best, son of George Best
Lorna Hogan, former girlfriend of Calum Best
Paul Stretford, football agent
Sky Andrew, football agent
Kevin Moran, football agent
Gavin Henson, rugby player

Matt Dawson, rugby player
Samantha Wallin, racing trainer
Kieren Fallon, jockey
Chris Eubank, boxer
Karron Stephen-Martin, ex-wife of Chris Eubank
Eimer Cook, wife of golfer Colin Montgomerie
Colette Bos, unknown
Susan Kirkham, unknown
Zoe Williams, unknown
David Brooks, unknown
Lisa Higson, unknown
Edward Hynds, unknown
Mehul Shagur Mehta, unknown
Steve Bayford, unknown
Steve Bayford Jr, unknown
Jill Burchnall, unknown
Duncan Foster, unknown
Gemma Louise Abbey, unknown
Ian Richard Johnson, unknown
Jeffrey Alan Jones, unknown
Benedict Grant Oakes, unknown
Lucy Jane Taggart, unknown
Robert Ashworth, unknown
Georgina James, unknown
Barry James Patrick Culhane, unknown
HSK, friend of politician
Michelle Bayford, former girlfriend of medical trial victim
Miss X, alleged victim of rape by celebrity
Tony Iles Blackmore, uncle of woman who made false
    rape accusation
Gillian Iles Blackmore, wife of Tony Iles Blackmore
Colin Stagg, exonerated murder suspect
Robert Thompson, child murderer
Louise Woodward, nanny convicted of manslaughter
Christopher Shipman, son of murderer Harold Shipman
Alex Pereira, cousin of police shooting victim

Sheila Henry, mother of terrorist victim
Graham Foulkes, father of terrorist victim
Sean Cassidy, father of terrorist victim
Paul Dadge, survivor of terrorist attack
John Tulloch, survivor of terrorist attack
Clare Bernal, mother of murder victim
Shaun Russell, father of murder victim
Sara Payne, mother of murder victim
Sharon Chapman, mother of murder victim
Leslie Chapman, father of murder victim
Milly Dowler, missing schoolgirl

There are another 855 likely victims, yet to be named.

Appendix 2 – Arrests*

METROPOLITAN POLICE

2006

8 August – Clive Goodman, royal editor, *News of the World*, on suspicion of phone hacking offences

8 August – Glenn Mulcaire, private investigator, *News of the World*, on suspicion of phone hacking offences

2011

5 April – Ian Edmondson, news editor, *News of the World*, on suspicion of phone hacking offences

5 April – Neville Thurlbeck, chief reporter, *News of the World*, on suspicion of phone hacking offences

14 April – James Weatherup, news editor/reporter, *News of the World*, on suspicion of phone hacking offences

23 June – Taras Terenia, freelance contributor, *News of the World*, on suspicion of phone hacking offences. Cleared in July 2012

27 June – Laura Elston, royal correspondent, Press Association, on suspicion of phone hacking offences. Cleared in July 2011

8 July – Andy Coulson, editor, *News of the World*, on suspicion of phone hacking and corrupting police

---

* Some staff have left or changed jobs; their most relevant position is stated. It does not follow that those arrested will be charged.

8 July – Clive Goodman, royal editor, *News of the World*, on suspicion of corrupting public officials

8 July – Unidentified 63-year-old man, on suspicion of corruption

14 July – Neil Wallis, executive editor, *News of the World*, on suspicion of phone hacking offences

17 July – Rebekah Brooks, editor, *News of the World* and the *Sun*, on suspicion of phone hacking offences and corrupting public officials

2 August – Stuart Kuttner, managing editor, *News of the World*, on suspicion of phone hacking offences and corrupting public officials

10 August – Greg Miskiw, news editor, *News of the World*, on suspicion of phone hacking offences

18 August – James Desborough, showbusiness reporter, *News of the World*, on suspicion of phone hacking offences. Cleared in March 2012

19 August – Dan Evans, reporter, *News of the World*, on suspicion of phone hacking offences

2 September – Ross Hall, reporter, *News of the World*, on suspicion of phone hacking offences and perverting the course of justice. Cleared in March 2012.

7 September – Raoul Simmons, deputy football editor, *The Times*, on suspicion of phone hacking offences. Cleared in July 2012.

4 November – Jamie Pyatt, news editor/reporter, the *Sun*, on suspicion of corrupting public officials

24 November – 52-year-old member of the public, on suspicion of computer hacking offences

30 November – Bethany Usher, reporter, *News of the World*, on suspicion of phone hacking offences. Cleared in December 2011.

7 December – Glenn Mulcaire, private investigator, *News of the World*, on suspicion of phone hacking offences and perverting the course of justice

15 December – Lucy Panton, crime editor, *News of the World*, on suspicion of corrupting public officials

21 December – Unidentified 52-year-old female police officer, on suspicion of corruption

2012

7 January – Cheryl Carter, beauty editor, the *Sun* and Rebekah Brooks's former PA, on suspicion of attempting to pervert the course of justice

10 January – Unidentified police officer, on suspicion of making unauthorized disclosures to the press

28 January – Graham Dudman, managing editor, the *Sun*, on suspicion of corrupting public officials

28 January – Mike Sullivan, crime editor, the *Sun*, on suspicion of corrupting public officials

28 January – Chris Pharo, news editor, the *Sun*, on suspicion of corrupting public officials

28 January – Fergus Shanahan, executive editor, the *Sun*, on suspicion of corrupting public officials

28 January – Unidentified 29-year-old male officer with Metropolitan Police's Territorial Policing Command, on suspicion of corruption

11 February – Geoff Webster, deputy editor, the *Sun*, on suspicion of corrupting public officials

11 February – John Kay, chief reporter, the *Sun*, on suspicion of corrupting public officials

11 February – Nick Parker, chief foreign correspondent, the *Sun*, on suspicion of corrupting public officials

11 February – John Edwards, picture editor, the *Sun*, on suspicion of corrupting public officials

11 February – John Sturgis, deputy news editor, the *Sun*, on suspicion of corrupting public officials

11 February – Unidentified 39-year-old officer with Surrey Police, on suspicion of corruption

11 February – Unidentified 39-year-old Ministry of Defence employee, on suspicion of corruption

11 February – Unidentified 36-year-old member of the armed forces, on suspicion of corruption

24 February – Steve Hayes, owner of London Wasps and Wycombe Wanderers football club, on suspicion of computer hacking offences

24 February – Graham Freeman, a 51-year-old security consultant, on suspicion of computer hacking offences

1 March – Virginia Wheeler, defence editor, the *Sun*, on suspicion of corrupting public officials

13 March – Rebekah Brooks, Chief Executive, News International, on suspicion of conspiracy to pervert the course of justice

13 March – Charlie Brooks, husband of Rebekah Brooks, on suspicion of conspiracy to pervert the course of justice

13 March – Mark Hanna, head of security, News International, on suspicion of conspiracy to pervert the course of justice

13 March – Unidentified male employee, News International, on suspicion of conspiracy to pervert the course of justice

13 March – Unidentified man, on suspicion of conspiracy to pervert the course of justice

13 March – Unidentified man, on suspicion of conspiracy to pervert the course of justice

14 March – Neville Thurlbeck, chief reporter, *News of the World*, on suspicion of intimidating a witness

19 April – Duncan Larcombe, royal editor, the *Sun*, on suspicion of corrupting public officials

19 April – Unidentified 42-year-old male former member of the armed forces, on suspicion of corruption

19 April – Unidentified 38-year-old woman, on suspicion of aiding and abetting misconduct in a public office

3 May – Unidentified 57-year-old former member of the Met's Specialist Operations Directorate, on suspicion of corruption

15 May – Unidentified 50-year-old male employee of HM Revenue and Customs, on suspicion of corruption

15 May – Unidentified 43-year-old woman, on suspicion of aiding and abetting misconduct in a public office and money-laundering offences

25 May – Unidentified 37-year-old male journalist, News International, on suspicion of corrupting public officials

14 June – Neil Millard, reporter, the *Sun*, on suspicion of corrupting public officials

14 June – Unidentified City of London police superintendent, on suspicion of corruption

14 June – Unidentified 40-year-old former prison officer, on suspicion of corruption

14 June – Unidentified 37-year-old woman, on suspicion of aiding and abetting misconduct in a public office and money laundering

26 June – Unidentified 53-year-old man, on suspicion of computer hacking offences

28 June – Unidentified 65-year-old man, on suspicion of computer hacking offences

28 June – Unidentified 31-year-old male former National Health Service employee, on suspicion of corruption

4 July – Greig Box Turnbull, former reporter, *Daily Mirror*, on suspicion of corrupting public officials

5 July – Unidentified 46-year-old male former National Health Service worker, on suspicion of corruption

5 July – Unidentified 42-year-old female former National Health Service worker, on suspicion of corruption

5 July – Unidentified 26-year-old male employee, News International, on suspicion of conspiracy to pervert the course of justice

11 July – Justin Penrose, crime reporter, *Sunday Mirror*, on suspicion of corrupting public officials

11 July – Tom Savage, deputy news editor, *Daily Star Sunday*, on suspicion of corrupting public officials

13 July – Unidentified 55-year-old man, on suspicion of computer hacking offences

19 July – Rhodri Phillips, reporter, the *Sun*, on suspicion of handling stolen goods

30 July – Nick Parker, chief foreign correspondent, the *Sun*, on suspicion of handling stolen goods

31 July – Unidentified 37-year-old male journalist, the *Sun*, on suspicion of handling stolen goods

7 August – Unidentified 37-year-old male journalist, the *Sun*, on suspicion of corrupting public officials

7 August – Unidentified 29-year-old male police officer with Sussex Police, on suspicion of corruption

29 August – Patrick Foster, reporter, *The Times*, on suspicion of computer hacking offences and conspiracy to pervert the course of justice

30 August – Tom Crone, legal manager, *News of the World*, on suspicion of phone hacking offences

7 September – Unidentified 33-year-old journalist, on suspicion of theft, computer hacking offences and conspiracy to pervert the course of justice

11 September – Unidentified 28-year-old man, on suspicion of theft offences

11 September – Unidentified 31-year-old male prison officer, on suspicion of corruption

13 September – Unidentified 42-year-old male member of the armed forces, on suspicion of corruption

13 September – Unidentified 32-year-old woman (wife of the arrested man above), on suspicion of corruption

19 September – Unidentified 51-year-old male journalist, the *Sun*, on suspicion of corrupting public officials

19 September – Unidentified 32-year-man male journalist, the *Sun*, on suspicion of corrupting public officials

19 September – Unidentified 39-year-old male officer with Wiltshire Police, arrested on suspicion of corruption

20 September – Unidentified 31-year-old journalist, the *Sun*, on suspicion of handling stolen goods

STRATHCLYDE POLICE
Operation Rubicon

2012

30 May – Andy Coulson, editor, *News of the World*, on suspicion of perjury

16 August – Douglas Wight, news editor, *News of the World*, Scotland, on suspicion of perjury, phone hacking and conspiracy to obtain personal data

29 August – Bob Bird, editor, *News of the World*, Scotland, on suspicion of attempting to pervert the course of justice

Appendix 3 – Criminal Charges

15 May: Conspiracy to pervert the course of justice

Charge 1

Rebekah Brooks between 6 July and 19 July 2011 conspired with Charles Brooks, Cheryl Carter, Mark Hanna, Paul Edwards, Daryl Jorsling and persons unknown to conceal material from officers of the Metropolitan Police Service.

Charge 2

Rebekah Brooks and Cheryl Carter between 6 July and 9 July 2011 conspired together permanently to remove seven boxes of material from the archive of News International.

Charge 3

Rebekah Brooks, Charles Brooks, Mark Hanna, Paul Edwards and Daryl Jorsling conspired together and with persons unknown, between 15 July and 19 July 2011, to conceal documents, computers and other electronic equipment from officers of the Metropolitan Police Service.

24 July: Conspiracy to hack phones

Charge 1

Rebekah Brooks, Andrew Coulson, Stuart Kuttner, Greg Miskiw, Ian Edmondson, Neville Thurlbeck and James Weatherup, between the 3rd day of October 2000 and the 9th day of August 2006 conspired together, and with Glenn Mulcaire and Clive Goodman and persons unknown, to intercept communications in the course of their transmission, without lawful authority, namely the voicemail messages of well-known people and those associated with them, including but not limited to those whose names appear on schedule 1.

Charge 2

Rebekah Brooks, Andrew Coulson, Stuart Kuttner, Glenn Mulcaire, Greg Miskiw and Neville Thurlbeck, between the 9th day of April 2002 and the 21st day of April 2002, conspired together and with persons unknown, to intercept communications in the course of their transmission, without lawful authority, namely the voicemail messages of Amanda Dowler, also known as Milly Dowler.

Charge 3

Greg Miskiw and Neville Thurlbeck, between 13th day of May 2002 and the 29th day of June 2006, conspired together and with Glenn Mulcaire and persons unknown, to intercept communications in the course of their transmission, without lawful authority, namely the voicemail messages of Sven-Göran Eriksson and persons associated with Sven-Göran Eriksson, including Faria Alam.

Charge 4

Greg Miskiw between the 22nd day of October 2002 and the 21st day of July 2006, conspired with Glenn Mulcaire and with persons unknown, to intercept communications in the course of their transmission, without lawful authority, namely the voicemail messages of Abigail Titmuss and John Leslie and those associated with Abigail Titmuss and John Leslie, including Matthew McGuiness.

Charge 5

Rebekah Brooks, Glenn Mulcaire and Greg Miskiw, between the 3rd day of December 2002 and the 22nd day of January 2003, conspired together and with persons unknown, to intercept communications in the course of their transmission, without lawful authority, namely the voicemail messages of Andrew Gilchrist.

Charge 6

Andrew Coulson, Stuart Kuttner, Greg Miskiw, Ian Edmondson, Neville Thurlbeck and James Weatherup, between the 1st day of January 2004 and the 29th day of July 2006, conspired together and with Glenn Mulcaire and persons unknown, to intercept communications in the course of their transmission, without lawful authority, namely the voicemail messages of persons associated with The Right Honourable David Blunkett MP, including some or all of the following: Kimberley Quinn, Sally King (née Anderson), Andrew King, John Anderson and Jason Carey.

Charge 7

Glenn Mulcaire and Greg Miskiw, between the 28th day of February 2005 and the 12th day of March 2005, conspired together and with persons unknown to intercept communications in the course of their transmission, without lawful authority, namely the voicemail messages of Delia Smith and of persons associated with Delia Smith, including Michael Wynn-Jones and Ian Christmas.

Charge 8

Andrew Coulson, Glenn Mulcaire, Greg Miskiw, Ian Edmondson, Neville Thurlbeck and James Weatherup, between the 6th day of April 2005 and the 22nd day of June 2005, conspired together and with persons unknown to intercept communications in the course of their transmission, without lawful authority, namely the voicemail messages of persons associated with The Right Honourable Charles Clarke, who included either or both of the following: Hannah Pawlby and Lucy Pawlby.

Charge 9

Greg Miskiw, Ian Edmondson and James Weatherup, between the 1st day of July 2005 and the 1st day of June 2006, conspired together, and with Glenn Mulcaire and persons unknown, to intercept communications in the course of their transmission, without lawful authority, namely the voicemail messages of Jude Law and persons associated with Jude Law, Sadie Frost and Sienna Miller, who included some or all of the following: Jade Schmidt, Archie Keswick and Ben Jackson.

Charge 10

Neville Thurlbeck and James Weatherup, between the 5th day of July 2005 and the 4th day of May 2006, conspired together, and with Glenn Mulcaire and persons unknown, to intercept communications in the course of their transmission, without lawful authority, namely the voicemail messages of persons associated with Angelina Jolie and Brad Pitt, who included Eunice Huthart.

Charge 11

Ian Edmondson and Neville Thurlbeck, between the 9th day of January 2006 and the 6th day of May 2006, conspired together and with Glenn Mulcaire and persons unknown, to intercept communications in the course of their transmission, without lawful authority, namely the voicemail messages of Mark Oaten.

Charge 12

Ian Edmondson and James Weatherup, between the 17th day of January 2006 and the 1st day of August 2006, conspired together, and with Glenn Mulcaire and persons unknown, to intercept communications in the course of their transmission, without lawful authority, namely the voicemail messages of Wayne Rooney and persons associated with Wayne Rooney, who included either or both of the following: Laura Jane Rooney and Patricia Tierney.

Charge 13

Greg Miskiw, between the 17th day of January 2006, and 1st day of August 2006 conspired with Glenn Mulcaire and persons unknown, to intercept communications in the course of their transmission, without lawful authority, namely the voicemail messages of Wayne Rooney and persons associated with Wayne Rooney, who included either or both of the following: Laura Jane Rooney and Patricia Tierney.

Charge 14

Andrew Coulson and Ian Edmondson, between the 23 March 2006 and the 21st day of May 2006, conspired together and with Glenn Mulcaire and persons unknown, to intercept communications in the course of their transmission, without lawful authority, namely the voicemail messages of Calum Best.

Charge 15

Ian Edmondson and Neville Thurlbeck, between the 2nd day of March 2006 and the 26th day of July 2006, conspired with Greg Mulcaire and with persons unknown to intercept communications in the course of their transmission, without lawful authority, namely the voicemail messages of The Right Honourable Dame Tessa Jowell MP and David Mills.

Charge 16

Ian Edmondson and James Weatherup, between the 24th day of April 2006 and the 22nd day of June 2006, conspired together and with Glenn Mulcaire and persons unknown, to intercept communications in the course of their transmission, without lawful authority, namely the voicemail messages of persons associated with The Right Honourable Lord Prescott, who included some or all of the following: Tracey Temple, Joan Hammell and Alan Schofield.

Charge 17

Ian Edmondson, between the 25th day of April 2006 and the 15th day of May 2006, conspired with Glenn Mulcaire and with persons unknown, to intercept communications in the course of their transmission, without lawful authority, namely the voicemail messages of Professor John Tulloch and persons associated with Professor John Tulloch, who included some or all of the following: John Davies, Maire Messenger Davies and Janet Andrew.

Charge 18

Ian Edmondson, between the 25th day of April 2006 and the 1st day of June 2006, conspired with Glenn Mulcaire and persons unknown, to intercept communications in the course of their transmission, without lawful authority, namely the voicemail messages of Lord Fredrick Windsor.

Charge 19

Ian Edmondson and James Weatherup, between the 15th day of May 2006 and the 29th day of June 2006, conspired together and with Glenn Mulcaire and persons unknown, to intercept communications in the course of their transmission, without lawful authority, namely the voicemail messages of Sir Paul McCartney and Heather Mills, and of persons associated with Sir Paul McCartney and Heather Mills, including some or all of the following: Fiona Mills, Stuart Bell, Alan Edwards and Chris Terrill.

12 September: Conspiracy to pervert the course of justice

Lee Sandell, employed in a security role by News International, added to Charge 3 of conspiracy to pervert the course of justice announced on 15 May, so that it reads: Lee Sandell, Rebekah Brooks, Charles Brooks, Mark Hanna, Paul Edwards and Daryl Jorsling on a day between 15th July 2011 and 19th July 2011 conspired together, and with persons unknown, to do an act or series of acts which had a tendency to pervert the course of public justice, namely to conceal documents, computers and other electronic devices, from officers of the Metropolitan Police Service who were investigating allegations of phone hacking and cor- ruption of public officials in relation to the *News of the World* and the *Sun* newspapers. Contrary to Section 1(1) Criminal Law Act 1977.

24 September: Misconduct in public office

Charge 1

On 11 September 2010 April Casburn [a Detective Chief Inspector in the Specialist Operations Directorate of the Metropolitan Police], being a public officer, and acting as such, without reasonable excuse or justification, wilfully misconducted herself to such a degree as to amount to an abuse of the public's trust.

STRATHCLYDE POLICE

2012

30 May: Perjury

Andy Coulson, editor, *News of the World*, charged with perjury during the perjury trial of Tommy Sheridan.

16 August: Perjury, conspiracy to hack phones, and conspiracy to obtain personal data

Douglas Wight, news editor, *News of the World*, Scotland, charged with perjury, conspiracy to hack phones and conspiracy to obtain personal data.

29 August: Attempt to pervert the course of justice

Bob Bird, editor, *News of the World*, Scotland, charged with attempting to pervert the course of justice.

Acknowledgements

THE AUTHORS TOGETHER

Many of the central figures in this story were interviewed for or other-wise helped us with this book, including Jo Becker, Chris Bryant, Glenn Campbell, Steve Coogan, David Davies, Nick Davies (one of the great exemplars of good journalism), Paul Farrelly, Hugh Grant, Jacqui Hames, Amelia Hill, Sienna Miller, Alastair Morgan, Max Mosley, Don van Natta Jr, Peter Oborne, Alec Owens, Alan Rusbridger and 'Miss X'. Their bravery gave us confidence and hope, and we thank them.

The lawyers Tamsin Allen, Charlotte Harris, Mark Lewis, Mark Thomson and Dominic Crossley brilliantly uncovered the cover-up. Without them, this shameful business might still be concealed.

We thank our literary agent, Clare Alexander of Aitken Alexander Associates, Toby Mundy of Atlantic Books, and agent David Luxton for their help at different stages. Had Judith Attar not put us together at Hull University, we would never have reconnected in 2010.

We are grateful to all at Penguin, but especially to our editor Stuart Proffitt, whose long experience informed its writing; his efficient and ever-cheerful assistant Shan Vahidy, the editorial managers Richard Duguid and Rebecca Lee, publicity manager Thi Dinh, and Bela Cunha, our expertly thorough copy-editor.

TOM WATSON

I couldn't have survived the events this book describes without the team who have put up with the maelstrom around me: Kim Frazer,

ACKNOWLEDGEMENTS

Sophie Goodchild, Gareth Illmann-Walker, Paul Moore, Karie Murphy and Raeesa Patel. Many have shown me friendship and solidarity in tough times: Diane Abbott, Dave Anderson, Luciana Berger, Billy Bragg, Kevin Brennan, Gordon Brown, Richard Burden, Shami Chakrabarti, Darren Cooper, Paul and Karen Corby, John Cryer, Geoffrey Goodman, Simon Hackett, David Hamilton, Harriet Harman, George Hickman, Lyndsay Hoyle, Mahboob Hussain, Amy Jackson, Tessa Jowell, Fraser Kemp, Paul Kenny, Peter Kilfoyle, Tarsem King, Neil Kinnock, Ian Lavery, Ian Lucas, Kevin Maguire, Len McCluskey, Iain McNicol, Michael Meacher, Ed Miliband, Vincent Moss, Jim Mowatt, Stephanie Peacock, Tom Powdrill, Lucy Powell, Mark Pritchard, Ian Reilly, Peter Rhodes, James Robinson, Steve Rotherham, Martin Rowson, Adrian Sanders, Jim Sheridan, Tommy Sheridan, Dennis Skinner, Nicholas Soames, John Spellar, Mark and Sally Tami, Steve Torrance, Keith Vaz, Iain Wright, Peter Hooton, Pete Wylie and the extraordinary people of the city of Liverpool.

Above all, I thank my family for their love and understanding: Linda and Barry Halliwell, Meg and Will Tremayne, Dan and Jo Watson, Tony, Jan and Anna Watson, and Amy Watson. My children, Malachy and Saoirse, remain the centre of my universe and I thank them for sharing the keyboard with me.

One friend in particular helped me through some very dark times. I will always be indebted to Siôn Simon for being there when it counted.

MARTIN HICKMAN

Any journalistic career needs the help of good bosses, and I thank Paul Durrant, Nick Small and Trevor Mason.

At the *Independent*, my gratitude runs deep to Cahal Milmo, a prince among journalists; Chris Blackhurst for willingly (though – gratifyingly – not too readily) allowing me to take unpaid leave at very short notice; Evgeny Lebedev, for his support; Oliver Duff, Chris Green and the other newsdesk stalwarts; reporters Jim Cusick and Ian Burrell, who chipped away at the official version; Mike McCarthy for

Notes

1. THE WRONG HEADLINES

1. *The Man Who Owns the News*, Michael Wolff, Vintage Books, 2010
2. *Murdoch*, William Shawcross, Simon & Schuster, 1992, pp. 75–6
3. *Murdoch: The Great Escape*, Richard Belfield, Christopher Hird and Sharon Kelly, Warner Books, 1994, pp. 9–10
4. *Good Times, Bad Times*, Harold Evans, Coronet, 1983, pp. 489–90
5. *Where Power Lies*, Lance Price, Simon & Schuster, 2010, p. 333
6. *The Insider: The Private Diaries of a Scandalous Decade*, Piers Morgan, Ebury Press, 2005, p. 147
7. 'Untangling Rebekah Brooks', Suzanna Andrews, *Vanity Fair*, February 2012
8. *The Insider*, p. 382
9. Interview with Siôn Simon, November 2011

2. WAPPING'S NEWS FACTORY

1. *Murdoch*, William Shawcross, Simon & Schuster, 1992, p. 116
2. 'Tabloid's Dirty Secrets,' *Dispatches*, Channel 4, 7 February 2011
3. *Hack*, Graham Johnson, Simon & Schuster, 2012, p. 8
4. Interview with anonymous News International executive, October 2011
5. *Full Disclosure*, Andrew Neil, Macmillan, 1996, p. 160
6. Ibid., p. 172
7. *The Insider: The Private Diaries of a Scandalous Decade*, Piers Morgan, Ebury Press, 2005, p. 82
8. Ibid., p. 103
9. Ibid., p. 95
10. Paul McMullan, oral evidence, Leveson Inquiry, 29 November 2011
11. Ibid.

12. Interview with anonymous News International executive, March 2011
13. *Confessions of a Fake Sheikh*, Mazher Mahmood, HarperCollins, 2008, p. 74
14. 'Stephen Glover on the press', Stephen Glover, *Independent*, 21 March 2005
15. Interview: Andy Coulson, David Rowan, *Evening Standard*, 16 March 2005
16. 'How the Screws screwed its rivals', Tim Luckhurst, *Independent*, 19 February 2006
17. Matt Driscoll, oral evidence, Leveson Inquiry, 19 December 2011
18. Matt Driscoll, written evidence, Leveson Inquiry, 12 December 2011
19. Interview with Hugh Grant, September 2011
20. Ibid.
21. Ibid.
22. Steve Coogan, written evidence, Leveson Inquiry, 9 November 2011
23. Matt Driscoll, oral evidence, Leveson Inquiry, 19 December 2011
24. 'Former NoW sports reporter in £792k tribunal payout', Dominic Ponsford, *Press Gazette*, 24 November 2009

3 . THE DARK ARTS

1. Interview with Alec Owens, January 2012
2. Ibid.
3. Alec Owens, written evidence, Leveson Inquiry, 17 November 2011
4. Ibid.
5. Richard Thomas, written evidence, Leveson Inquiry, 6 September 2011
6. Alec Owens, oral evidence, Leveson Inquiry, 30 November 2011
7. 'Exposed after eight years: a private eye's dirty work for Fleet Street', Ian Burrell, *Independent*, 6 September 2011
8. Stephen Whittamore, BBC Radio 4 *PM* programme, 21 September 2010
9. Tom Bradby, http://blog.itv.com/news/tombradby/2011/11/phone-hacking-the-movie/, 10 November 2011

4 . FIRST HEADS ROLL

1. 'Fury After He Ogled Lapdancer's Boobs', Clive Goodman and Neville Thurlbeck, *News of the World*, 9 April 2006
2. Document written by Detective Superintendent Philip Williams, Leveson Inquiry, 29 February 2012

3. Alec Owens, written evidence, Leveson Inquiry, 17 November 2011
4. Carine Patry Hoskins, counsel to the Leveson Inquiry, during Matt Driscoll's oral evidence, Leveson Inquiry, 19 December 2011
5. 'Met failed to pursue data on tabloid phone taps', Nick Davies, *Guardian*, 5 April 2010
6. Statement by Detective Chief Inspector Keith Surtees, Judicial Review by Lord Prescott, Chris Bryant, Brian Paddick, Ben Jackson and HJK against Metropolitan Police, High Court, 30 September 2011
7. Detective Chief Inspector Keith Surtees, oral evidence, Leveson Inquiry, 29 February 2012
8. Robert Jay QC, Leveson Inquiry, 29 February 2012
9. Document, Leveson Inquiry, 29 February 2012
10. Deputy Assistant Commissioner Peter Clarke, oral evidence, Leveson Inquiry, 1 March 2012
11. Lawrence Abramson, oral evidence, Leveson Inquiry, 13 December 2011
12. Richard Thomas, written evidence, Leveson Inquiry, 6 September 2011

5. ROGUE DEFENCE

1. Interview with Mark Lewis, June 2011
2. Harbottle & Lewis, written evidence, Commons Culture, Media and Sport Select Committee, August 2011
3. Interview with George Eustice, September 2011
4. Ibid.
5. Ibid.
6. 'The World according to Rupert', Nicholas Wapshott, *Independent*, 23 July 2006
7. Interview with George Eustice, September 2011
8. 'Cameron fires up the faithful', Brian Whelan, BBC News Online, http://news.bbc.co.uk/1/hi/uk_politics/7025958.stm, 3 October 2007
9. 'Police Cameron Action', George Pascoe-Watson, *Sun*, 30 January 2008
10. Richard Thomas, written evidence, Leveson Inquiry, 6 September 2011
11. Ibid.

6. THE MANCHESTER LAWYERS

1. Interview with Charlotte Harris, August 2011
2. Email from Tom Crone to Colin Myler headed: 'Strictly private and confidential and legally privileged', 6.10 p.m., 24 May 2008, disclosed

by Farrer & Co to the House of Commons Culture, Media and Sport Committee on 31 October 2011

3. Legal Opinion by Michael Silverleaf QC to News Group Newspapers [the News International subsidiary which owned the *News of the World*], 3 June 2008, disclosed by Farrer & Co to the House of Commons Culture, Media and Sport Committee on 31 October 2011

4. Email from Colin Myler to James Murdoch, 2.31 p.m., 7 June 2008, disclosed by Linklaters to the House of Commons Culture, Media and Sport Committee on 12 December 2011

5. James Murdoch's reply at 2.34 p.m.

6. David Cameron, oral evidence, Leveson Inquiry, 14 June 2012

7. 'Bloated BBC out of touch with the viewers', David Cameron, *Sun*, 3 November 2008

8. 'Tory government "would force BBC to reveal stars' salaries"', Leigh Holmwood, Guardian online, http://www.guardian.co.uk/media/2009/jan/22/tory-government-bbc-pay, 22 January 2009

9. 'Tories would cut Ofcom powers, says David Cameron', Jason Deans, Guardian online, http://www.guardian.co.uk/media/2009/jul/06/tories-cut-ofcom-powers-david-cameron, 6 July 2009

7. ONE DETERMINED REPORTER

1. Interview with Nick Davies, February 2012

2. Ibid.

3. Ibid.

4. Interview with Alan Rusbridger, August 2011

5. 'Revealed: Murdoch's £1m bill for hiding dirty tricks', Nick Davies, *Guardian*, 9 July 2009

6. Minutes of Gold Meeting, Scotland Yard, 9 July, disclosed at Leveson Inquiry, 29 February 2012

7. Ibid.

8. Interview with Chris Bryant, June 2011

9. 'Sienna Miller: hacking's heroine', Jemima Khan, *Independent*, 23 September 2011

10. Tom Crone, oral evidence, House of Commons Culture, Media and Sport Committee, 21 July 2009

11. Phone conversation between Neville Thurlbeck and Tom Watson, October 2011

12. Alastair Campbell, draft statement to Leveson Inquiry, November 2011. This passage was included in Campbell's draft statement to the Leveson Inquiry but was omitted after he consulted 'close friends'

8. INTIMIDATING PARLIAMENT

1. Mark Lewis, oral evidence, House of Commons, Culture, Media and Sport Committee, 2 September 2009
2. Ibid.
3. James Murdoch, oral evidence, Leveson Inquiry, 24 April 2012
4. 'Email trail: How Tom Watson was stalked', *Independent*, http://www.independent.co.uk/news/media/press/email-trail-how-tom-watson-was-stalked-7771341.html, 22 May 2012
5. Ibid.
6. Robert Jay QC, Leveson Inquiry, 14 June 2012
7. 'We'd abolish BBC Trust, says Tory culture spokesman Jeremy Hunt', John Plunkett and Tara Conlan, Guardian online, http://www.guardian.co.uk/media/2009/oct/19/wed-abolish-bbc-trust-hunt, 19 October 2009
8. Generic Particulars of Claim, [anonymized] Voicemail Claimant versus News Group Newspapers and Glenn Mulcaire, High Court, December 2011
9. Matt Driscoll, written evidence, Leveson Inquiry, 12 December 2011
10. 'News of the World faces £800,000 payout in bullying case', Hugh Muir and Chris Tryhorn, *Guardian*, 23 November 2009
11. Letter from the *Guardian* to Dick Fedorcio, Guardian online, http://www.guardian.co.uk/media/interactive/2011/jul/15/letter-from-the-guardian-to-dick-fedorcio, 15 July 2011
12. 'Tabloids, Tories and Telephone Hacking', *Dispatches*, Channel 4, 4 October 2010
13. 'We must hold the powerful to account', Philip Davies, *News of the World*, 28 February 2010
14. News International Statement on Phone Hacking, *Press Gazette*, 24 February 2010

9. A MURDER

1. 'Fraudster Squad', Graeme McLagan, *Guardian*, 21 September 2002
2. Jacqui Hames, written evidence, Leveson Inquiry, 22 February 2012

3. Lord Stevens, oral evidence, Leveson Inquiry, 6 March 2012
4. Jacqui Hames, written evidence, Leveson Inquiry, 22 February 2012

10. FOLLOWING THE LAWYERS

1. Interview with Charlotte Harris, August 2011
2. Ibid.
3. Ibid.
4. Max Clifford, oral evidence, Leveson Inquiry, 9 February 2012
5. Interview with Charlotte Harris, August 2011
6. Julian Pike, written evidence, Leveson Inquiry, 14 November 2011
7. Tom Crone, oral evidence, Leveson Inquiry, 14 December 2011
8. Charlotte Harris, written evidence, Leveson Inquiry, 5 December 2011
9. Mark Lewis, written evidence, Leveson Inquiry, 21 November 2011
10. Email from Nick Davies to Martin Hickman, August 2011
11. Interview with Alan Rusbridger, August 2011
12. 'The day James and Rebekah revealed the arrogant Murdoch way of business', Guardian online, http://www.guardian.co.uk/commentisfree/2012/apr/24/james-murdoch-rebekah-brooks-simon-kelner-independent, 24 April 2012

11. OUR MAN IN DOWNING STREET

1. 'Ashdown: I warned Cameron about the huge danger of hiring Coulson', Toby Helm and Daniel Boffey, Observer, 10 July 2011
2. Ibid.
3. Rupert Murdoch, written evidence, Leveson Inquiry, 12 April 2012
4. Ibid.
5. 'Sienna Miller: hacking's heroine', Jemima Khan, Independent, 23 September 2011
6. Email from Steve Coogan to Tom Watson, October 2011
7. Generic Particulars of Claim, [anonymized] Voicemail Claimant versus News Group Newspapers and Glenn Mulcaire, High Court, December 2011
8. Email from Don van Natta Jr to Tom Watson, November 2011
9. 'Phone hacking: Andy Coulson offers to talk to police', Haroon Siddique, Andrew Sparrow, Patrick Wintour and Nick Davies, Guardian

online, http://www.guardian.co.uk/media/2010/sep/06/phone-hacking-met-now-case, 6 September 2011

10. Generic Particulars of Claim, [anonymized] Voicemail Claimant versus News Group Newspapers and Glenn Mulcaire, High Court, December 2011

11. London Assembly (Plenary) Transcript, 15 September 2010, www.london.gov.uk

12. LOSING A BATTLE

1. Interview with Max Mosley, May 2011

2. Submission from Mark Lewis to House of Commons Home Affairs Select Committee, http://www.parliament.uk/documents/commons-committees/home-affairs/Memoranda.pdf, October 2010

3. Rupert Murdoch, written evidence, Leveson Inquiry, 12 April 2012

4. 'Takeover of BSkyB must be blocked, says media analyst', James Robinson, *Guardian*, 14 September 2010

5. Rupert Murdoch, written evidence, Leveson Inquiry, 12 April 2012

6. Ibid.

7. Norman Lamb, written evidence, Leveson Inquiry, 6 June 2012

8. Norman Lamb, oral evidence, Leveson Inquiry, June 2012

9. Rupert Murdoch, written evidence, Leveson Inquiry, 12 April 2012

10. Ibid.

11. Ibid.

12. Ibid.

13. Jeremy Hunt, oral evidence, Leveson Inquiry, 31 May 2012

14. Ibid.

15. 'Exclusive: News Corp exec suspected in leak', Mark Hosenball, Reuters, http://uk.reuters.com/article/2011/07/22/uk-newscorp-lewis-idUKTRE76L30S20110722, 22 July 2011

16. Jeremy Hunt, oral evidence, Leveson Inquiry, 31 May 2012

17. Sheridan Victory Speech in Full, BBC News Online, http://news.bbc.co.uk/1/hi/scotland/glasgow_and_west/5246764.stm, 4 August 2006

18. 'Andy Coulson denies knowledge of criminal activity at News of the World', Nick Davies and Severin Carrell, Guardian online, http://www.guardian.co.uk/media/2010/dec/10/andy-coulson-tommy-sheridan-trial, 10 December 2010

19. Keir Starmer, oral evidence, House of Commons Home Affairs Committee, 5 April 2012

13. OUT OF CONTROL

1. Generic Particulars of Claim, [anonymized] Voicemail Claimant versus News Group Newspapers and Glenn Mulcaire, High Court, December 2011
2. Letter from Linklaters to House of Commons Culture, Media and Sport Committee, 25 January 2012
3. Email from Tim Montgomerie to Martin Hickman, February 2012
4. Rupert Murdoch, written evidence, Leveson Inquiry, 12 April 2012
5. 'Nick Brown says his phone was bugged', Joe Murphy, *Evening Standard*, 28 January 2011
6. 'Phone hacking: police uncover more evidence', Cahal Milmo and Martin Hickman, *Independent*, 10 February 2011
7. Interview with Charlotte Harris, August 2011
8. Ibid.
9. Rupert Murdoch, written evidence, Leveson Inquiry, 12 April 2012
10. Ibid.
11. Jeremy Hunt, oral evidence, Leveson Inquiry, 31 May 2012

14. U-TURN AT WAPPING

1. 'News International Says Sorry for Phone Hacking', Robert Peston, BBC News, http://www.bbc.co.uk/blogs/thereporters/robertpeston/2011/04/news_international_says_sorry.html, 8 April 2011
2. 'James Murdoch: no reputation crisis at News Corp', The Holmes Report, http://www.holmesreport.com/news-info/10100/James-Murdoch-No-Reputation-Crisis-At-News-Corp.aspx, 8 April 2011
3. Sue Akers, oral evidence, House of Commons Home Affairs Select Committee, 12 July 2011
4. Cressida Dick, oral evidence, Leveson Inquiry, 12 March 2012
5. 'Straw and Mandelson demand police answers', Oliver Wright and Martin Hickman, *Independent*, 10 June 2011

15. SUMMER'S LEASE

1. Rupert Murdoch, written evidence, Leveson Inquiry, 12 April 2012
2. 'Twelve face jail over hacking', David Leppard and Jon Ungoed-Thomas, *Sunday Times*, 10 July 2011

3. Lord Macdonald, oral evidence, House of Commons Home Affairs Select Committee, 19 July 2011
4. Rupert Murdoch, written evidence, Leveson Inquiry, 12 April 2012
5. 'Mandelson (dancing wildly), a "giddy" Steve Hilton, Mark Thompson of the BBC (and, of course, Robert Peston) . . . how a leather-trousered Matthew Freud hosted the decadent last hurrah of the Chipping Norton Set' , Simon Walters and Glen Owen, *Mail on Sunday*, 17 July 2011

16. A MISSING GIRL

1. John Whittingdale interview, BBC Radio 4, *Today* programme, 5 July 2011
2. 'I'm ripping up the rule book', Mehdi Hasan, *New Statesman*, 26 September 2011
3. *What the Papers Say*, BBC Radio 4, 31 December 2011
4. 'News of the World's alleged actions "indefensible" says Times' Harding', Arif Durrani, *Brand Republic*, 5 July 2011
5. 'Milly Dowler phone hacking: the reaction', Raf Sanchez, Telegraph online, http://www.telegraph.co.uk/news/uknews/crime/8617579/MillyDowler-phone-hacking-the-reaction.html, 5 July 2011
6. Interview with Hugh Grant on BBC Radio 5 Live, 5 July 2011
7. Interview with Alastair Campbell on BBC *Newsnight*, 5 July 2011
8. 'Phone hacking: reading between the lines of Murdoch's statement', Roy Greenslade, Guardian online, http://www.guardian.co.uk/media/greenslade/2011/jul/06/rupert-murdoch-phone-hacking, 6 July 2011
9. Statement from London mayor on phone hacking, http://www.london.gov.uk/media/press_releases_mayoral/statement-mayor-london-phone hacking-0, 6 July 2011
10. Interview with Hugh Grant, September 2011

17. SKY PLUS

1. http://www.alastaircampbell.org/blog/2011/07/09/steve-coogan-spot-on-in-asking-where-paul-dacre-is-in-all-this-but-his-time-is-surely-coming, 9 July 2011
2. 'Murdoch's Watergate', Carl Bernstein, *Newsweek*, 18 July 2011
3. 'Murdoch says current News Corp. management stands: embattled former editor Brooks has his "total support"', Sarah McBride, Reuters, 9 July 2011

4. 'News of the World's desperate final hours', Paul McNamara, *New York Times*, 25 July 2011

5. 'News of the World phone hacking', Guardian online, Scandal, http://www.guardian.co.uk/media/blog/2011/jul/09/phone-hacking-new softheworld, 9 July 2011

6. 'News of the World's last breath: put the handkerchiefs aside', Roy Greenslade, Guardian online, http://www.guardian.co.uk/media/2011/jul/10/news-of-the-world-last-edition, 10 July 2011

7. 'Insider reveals: "PR men would think up a Story and Rebekah's Sun and News of the World would run it, word for word. Some were complete fiction"', *Mail on Sunday*, 9 July 2011

8. 'Police chief: I failed victims of hacking', Robert Mendick, Alasdair Palmer and Patrick Hennessy, *Sunday Telegraph*, 10 July 2011

9. 'Politics live blog', Andrew Sparrow, Guardian online, http://www.guardian.co.uk/politics/blog/2011/jul/11/politics-live-blog, 11 July 2011

10. Hayman hits out at MPs after 'appalling' hacking treatment, LBC, http://www.lbc.co.uk/hayman-hits-out-at-mps-after-appalling-hacking-treatment-42292, 13 July 2011

11. 'Sunday Times reject Gordon Brown "criminal claims"', BBC News Online, 13 July 2011

12. 'Phone hacking: News International paid Neil Wallis while he was at Scotland Yard', Robert Winnett and Mark Hughes, http://www.telegraph.co.uk/news/uknews/phone-hacking/8785470/Phone-hacking-News-International-paid-Neil-Wallis-while-he-was-at-Scotland-Yard.html, 23 September 2011

18. 'WE ARE SORRY'

1. 'Rebekah Brooks's severance deal worth "about £7m"' *Guardian*, 16 October 2012

2. Full James Murdoch statement on Rebekah Brooks, *New Statesman*, 15 July 2011

3. 'Rupert Murdoch Says "Sorry" in ad campaign', Guardian online, http://www.guardian.co.uk/media/2011/jul/15/rupert-murdoch-sorry-ad-campaign, 15 July 2011

4. 'A scandal that has diminished Britain', *Daily Telegraph*, 16 July 2011

5. 'Phone hacking: John Yates "to be suspended" over Neil Wallis links', Mark Hughes, Andrew Hough and Robert Winnett, Telegraph.co.uk, 17 July 2011

6. 'NoW phone-hacking whistle-blower Sean Hoare found dead', BBC News Online, http://www.bbc.co.uk/news/uk-14194623, 19 July 2011

19. DEMOCRACY DAY

1. 'Lots of questions but very few answers', Jemima Khan, *i*, 20 July 2011
2. 'Biographer: Murdoch talks to his editors more than he admits', Oliver Wright, *Independent*, 23 July 2011

20. ASSAULT ON THE ESTABLISHMENT

1. 'Andy Coulson reportedly paid by News International when hired by Tories', James Robinson and Polly Curtis, Guardian online, http://www.guardian.co.uk/media/2011/aug/23/andy-coulson-news-international-tories, 23 August 2011

21. A MEETING IN THE SUBURBS

1. 'Rupert Murdoch urged to sell off newspapers by top News Corp shareholder', Richard Blackden, Telegraph online, http://www.telegraph.co.uk/finance/newsbysector/mediatechnologyandtelecoms/8843215/Rupert-Murdoch-urged-to-sell-off-newspapers-by-top-News-Corp-shareholder.html, 23 October 2011

22. THE PRESS ON TRIAL

1. Robert Jay, counsel to the Leveson Inquiry, opening statement, Leveson Inquiry, 14 November 2011
2. Richard Caseby, oral evidence, Parliamentary Joint Committee on Privacy Injunctions, 13 December 2011
3. Sharon Marshall, oral evidence, Leveson Inquiry, 20 December 2011

23. DARKER AND DARKER

1. *What the Papers Say*, BBC Radio 4, 31 December 2011
2. 'FBI poised to step up investigation into News Corp', James Hanning and Michael Pooler, *Independent on Sunday*, 18 March 2012

3. 'Unrest at Wapping spreads to the Sun after arrest', Ian Burrell, *Independent*, 9 November 2011

4. 'Operation Elveden: five bailed in police payments probe', BBC Online, http://www.bbc.co.uk/news/uk-16771809, 29 January 2012

5. 'Phone hacking: Met police failed to warn victims', BBC News, http://www.bbc.co.uk/news/mobile/uk-16922305, 7 February 2012

6. News Corporation Statement of UK's Parliamentary Select Committee of Culture, Media and Sport's *News of the World* report, http://www.newscorp.com/news/news_530.html, 1 May 2012

7. 'Rupert Murdoch resigns as News International Director', BBC News, http://www.bbc.co.uk/news/uk-18940016, 22 July 2012

8. 'Phone hacking: Rebekah Brooks, Andy Coulson and six others face charges – as it happened', Josh Halliday and John Plunkett, Guardian, online http://www.guardian.co.uk/media/blog/2012/jul/24/phone-hacking-cps-charges-live, 24 July 2012

CHAPTER 24. A CORRUPT BUSINESS

1. Andrew Neil interview, CNN, 16 February 2012

Index

The following abbreviations are used in the index: CPS = Crown Prosecution Service; ICO = Information Commissioner's Office; *NoW* = *News of the World*; NI = News International; *n* attached to a page number denotes a footnote.

ALLEN LANE

an imprint of

PENGUIN BOOKS

Recently Published

David Thomson, *The Big Screen: The Story of the Movies and What They Did to Us*

Halik Kochanski, *The Eagle Unbowed: Poland and the Poles in the Second World War*

Kofi Annan with Nader Mousavizadeh, *Interventions: A Life in War and Peace*

Mark Mazower, *Governing the World: The History of an Idea*

Anne Applebaum, *Iron Curtain: The Crushing of Eastern Europe 1944-56*

Steven Johnson, *Future Perfect: The Case for Progress in a Networked Age*

Christopher Clark, *The Sleepwalkers: How Europe Went to War in 1914*

Neil MacGregor, *Shakespeare's Restless World*

Nate Silver, *The Signal and the Noise: The Art and Science of Prediction*

Chinua Achebe, *There Was a Country: A Personal History of Biafra*

John Darwin, *Unfinished Empire: The Global Expansion of Britain*

Jerry Brotton, *A History of the World in Twelve Maps*

Patrick Hennessey, *KANDAK: Fighting with Afghans*

Katherine Angel, *Unmastered: A Book on Desire, Most Difficult to Tell*

David Priestland, *Merchant, Soldier, Sage: A New History of Power*

Stephen Alford, *The Watchers: A Secret History of the Reign of Elizabeth I*

Tom Feiling, *Short Walks from Bogotá: Journeys in the New Colombia*

Jonathan Haidt, *The Righteous Mind: Why Good People are Divided by Politics and Religion*

Ahmed Rashid, *Pakistan on the Brink: The Future of Pakistan, Afghanistan and the West*

Tim Weiner, *Enemies: A History of the FBI*

Mark Pagel, *Wired for Culture: The Natural History of Human Cooperation*

George Dyson, *Turing's Cathedral: The Origins of the Digital Universe*

Cullen Murphy, *God's Jury: The Inquisition and the Making of the Modern World*

Richard Sennett, *Together: The Rituals, Pleasures and Politics of Co-operation*

Faramerz Dabhoiwala, *The Origins of Sex: A History of the First Sexual Revolution*

Roy F. Baumeister and John Tierney, *Willpower: Rediscovering Our Greatest Strength*

Jesse J. Prinz, *Beyond Human Nature: How Culture and Experience Shape Our Lives*

Robert Holland, *Blue-Water Empire: The British in the Mediterranean since 1800*

Jodi Kantor, *The Obamas: A Mission, A Marriage*

Philip Coggan, *Paper Promises: Money, Debt and the New World Order*

Charles Nicholl, *Traces Remain: Essays and Explorations*

Daniel Kahneman, *Thinking, Fast and Slow*

Hunter S. Thompson, *Fear and Loathing at Rolling Stone: The Essential Writing of Hunter S. Thompson*

Duncan Campbell-Smith, *Masters of the Post: The Authorized History of the Royal Mail*

Colin McEvedy, *Cities of the Classical World: An Atlas and Gazetteer of 120 Centres of Ancient Civilization*

Heike B. Görtemaker, *Eva Braun: Life with Hitler*

Brian Cox and Jeff Forshaw, *The Quantum Universe: Everything that Can Happen Does Happen*

Nathan D. Wolfe, *The Viral Storm: The Dawn of a New Pandemic Age*

Norman Davies, *Vanished Kingdoms: The History of Half-Forgotten Europe*

Michael Lewis, *Boomerang: The Meltdown Tour*

Steven Pinker, *The Better Angels of Our Nature: The Decline of Violence in History and Its Causes*

Robert Trivers, *Deceit and Self-Deception: Fooling Yourself the Better to Fool Others*

Thomas Penn, *Winter King: The Dawn of Tudor England*

Daniel Yergin, *The Quest: Energy, Security and the Remaking of the Modern World*

Michael Moore, *Here Comes Trouble: Stories from My Life*

Ali Soufan, *The Black Banners: Inside the Hunt for Al Qaeda*

Jason Burke, *The 9/11 Wars*

Timothy D. Wilson, *Redirect: The Surprising New Science of Psychological Change*

Ian Kershaw, *The End: Hitler's Germany, 1944-45*

T M Devine, *To the Ends of the Earth: Scotland's Global Diaspora, 1750-2010*

Catherine Hakim, *Honey Money: The Power of Erotic Capital*

Douglas Edwards, *I'm Feeling Lucky: The Confessions of Google Employee Number 59*

John Bradshaw, *In Defence of Dogs*

Chris Stringer, *The Origin of Our Species*

Lila Azam Zanganeh, *The Enchanter: Nabokov and Happiness*

David Stevenson, *With Our Backs to the Wall: Victory and Defeat in 1918*

Evelyn Juers, *House of Exile: War, Love and Literature, from Berlin to Los Angeles*

Henry Kissinger, *On China*

Michio Kaku, *Physics of the Future: How Science Will Shape Human Destiny and Our Daily Lives by the Year 2100*

David Abulafia, *The Great Sea: A Human History of the Mediterranean*

John Gribbin, *The Reason Why: The Miracle of Life on Earth*

Anatol Lieven, *Pakistan: A Hard Country*

William Cohen, *Money and Power: How Goldman Sachs Came to Rule the World*

Joshua Foer, *Moonwalking with Einstein: The Art and Science of Remembering Everything*

Simon Baron-Cohen, *Zero Degrees of Empathy: A New Theory of Human Cruelty*

Manning Marable, *Malcolm X: A Life of Reinvention*

David Deutsch, *The Beginning of Infinity: Explanations that Transform the World*

David Edgerton, *Britain's War Machine: Weapons, Resources and Experts in the Second World War*

John Kasarda and Greg Lindsay, *Aerotropolis: The Way We'll Live Next*

David Gilmour, *The Pursuit of Italy: A History of a Land, Its Regions and Their Peoples*

Niall Ferguson, *Civilization: The West and the Rest*

Tim Flannery, *Here on Earth: A New Beginning*

Robert Bickers, *The Scramble for China: Foreign Devils in the Qing Empire, 1832-1914*

Mark Malloch-Brown, *The Unfinished Global Revolution: The Limits of Nations and the Pursuit of a New Politics*

King Abdullah of Jordan, *Our Last Best Chance: The Pursuit of Peace in a Time of Peril*

Eliza Griswold, *The Tenth Parallel: Dispatches from the Faultline between Christianity and Islam*

Brian Greene, *The Hidden Reality: Parallel Universes and the Deep Laws of the Cosmos*

John Gray, *The Immortalization Commission: The Strange Quest to Cheat Death*

Patrick French, *India: A Portrait*

Lizzie Collingham, *The Taste of War: World War Two and the Battle for Food*

Hooman Majd, *The Ayatollahs' Democracy: An Iranian Challenge*

Dambisa Moyo, *How The West Was Lost: Fifty Years of Economic Folly - and the Stark Choices Ahead*

Evgeny Morozov, *The Net Delusion: How Not to Liberate the World*

Ron Chernow, *Washington: A Life*

Nassim Nicholas Taleb, *The Bed of Procrustes: Philosophical and Practical Aphorisms*

Hugh Thomas, *The Golden Age: The Spanish Empire of Charles V*

Amanda Foreman, *A World on Fire: An Epic History of Two Nations Divided*

Nicholas Ostler, *The Last Lingua Franca: English until the Return of Babel*

Richard Miles, *Ancient Worlds: The Search for the Origins of Western Civilization*

Neil MacGregor, *A History of the World in 100 Objects*

Steven Johnson, *Where Good Ideas Come From: The Natural History of Innovation*

Dominic Sandbrook, *State of Emergency: The Way We Were: Britain, 1970-1974*

Jim Al-Khalili, *Pathfinders: The Golden Age of Arabic Science*

Ha-Joon Chang, *23 Things They Don't Tell You About Capitalism*

Robin Fleming, *Britain After Rome: The Fall and Rise, 400 to 1070*

Tariq Ramadan, *The Quest for Meaning: Developing a Philosophy of Pluralism*

Joyce Tyldesley, *The Penguin Book of Myths and Legends of Ancient Egypt*

Nicholas Phillipson, *Adam Smith: An Enlightened Life*

Paul Greenberg, *Four Fish: A Journey from the Ocean to Your Plate*

Clay Shirky, *Cognitive Surplus: Creativity and Generosity in a Connected Age*

Andrew Graham-Dixon, *Caravaggio: A Life Sacred and Profane*

Niall Ferguson, *High Financier: The Lives and Time of Siegmund Warburg*

Sean McMeekin, *The Berlin-Baghdad Express: The Ottoman Empire and Germany's Bid for World Power, 1898-1918*

Richard McGregor, *The Party: The Secret World of China's Communist Rulers*

Spencer Wells, *Pandora's Seed: The Unforeseen Cost of Civilization*

Francis Pryor, *The Making of the British Landscape: How We Have Transformed the Land, from Prehistory to Today*

Ruth Harris, *The Man on Devil's Island: Alfred Dreyfus and the Affair that Divided France*

Paul Collier, *The Plundered Planet: How to Reconcile Prosperity With Nature*

Norman Stone, *The Atlantic and Its Enemies: A History of the Cold War*

Simon Price and Peter Thonemann, *The Birth of Classical Europe: A History from Troy to Augustine*

Hampton Sides, *Hellhound on his Trail: The Stalking of Martin Luther King, Jr. and the International Hunt for His Assassin*

Jackie Wullschlager, *Chagall: Love and Exile*

Richard Miles, *Carthage Must Be Destroyed: The Rise and Fall of an Ancient Civilization*

Tony Judt, *Ill Fares The Land: A Treatise On Our Present Discontents*

Michael Lewis, *The Big Short: Inside the Doomsday Machine*

Oliver Bullough, *Let Our Fame Be Great: Journeys among the Defiant People of the Caucasus*

Paul Davies, *The Eerie Silence: Searching for Ourselves in the Universe*

Richard Wilkinson and Kate Pickett, *The Spirit Level: Why Equality is Better for Everyone*

Tom Bingham, *The Rule of Law*

Joseph Stiglitz, *Freefall: Free Markets and the Sinking of the Global Economy*

John Lanchester, *Whoops! Why Everyone Owes Everyone and No One Can Pay*

Chinua Achebe, *The Education of a British-Protected Child*

Jaron Lanier, *You Are Not A Gadget: A Manifesto*

John Cassidy, *How Markets Fail: The Logic of Economic Calamities*

Robert Ferguson, *The Hammer and the Cross: A New History of the Vikings*

Eugene Rogan, *The Arabs: A History*

Steven Johnson, *The Invention of Air: An experiment, a Journey, a New Country and the Amazing Force of Scientific Discovery*

Andrew Ross Sorkin, *Too Big to Fail: Inside the Battle to Save Wall Street*

Malcolm Gladwell, *What the Dog Saw and Other Adventures*

Steven D. Levitt, Stephen J. Dubner, *Superfreakonomics: Global Cooling, Patriotic Prostitutes and Why Suicide Bombers Should Buy Life Insurance*

Christopher Andrew, *The Defence of the Realm: The Authorized History of MI5*